HOUSING FINANCE AND SUBSIDIES IN BRITAIN

Housing Finance and Subsidies in Britain

Edited by

DUNCAN MACLENNAN
KENNETH GIBB
University of Glasgow

Avebury

Aldershot · Brookfield USA · Hong Kong · Singapore · Sydney

Published by
Avebury
Ashgate Publishing Limited
Gower House
Croft Road
Aldershot
Hants GU11 3HR
England

Ashgate Publishing Company
Old Post Road
Brookfield
Vermont 05036
USA

A CIP catalogue record for this book is available from the British from the British Library.

ISBN 1 85628 423 9

Printed and Bound in Great Britain by
Athenaeum Press Ltd, Newcastle upon Tyne.

Contents

List of figures and tables

List of contributors

Stuart Cameron	University of Newcastle upon Tyne
Tony Crook	University of Sheffield
Richard Eastall	University of Sheffield
Kenneth Gibb	University of Glasgow
Chris Hamnett	Open University
John Hughes	University of Sheffield
Peter Kemp	University of York
Philip Leather	University of Bristol
Sheila Mackintosh	University of Bristol
Duncan Maclennan	University of Glasgow
Peter Malpass	Bristol Polytechnic
Alex Marsh	University of Birmingham
Robin Means	University of Bristol
Alison More	University of Glasgow
Moira Munro	University of Glasgow
Peter Symon	University of Birmingham
Bruce Walker	University of Birmingham
Matthew Warburton	University of Bristol
Christine Whitehead	LSE/University of Cambridge
Roy Wilkinson	University of Sheffield
Peter Williams	University of Wales College of Cardiff
Ken Willis	University of Newcastle upon Tyne

Acknowledgements

This collection of papers from the April 1991 conference of the Housing Studies Association has been made possible by the co-operation and collaboration of numerous people to whom we are most grateful.

First, we are particularly grateful to the Joseph Rowntree Foundation, notably Richard Best, Janet Lewis and the late Roland Hirst, who all contributed so much to the development of the Housing Finance Programme, from which these papers are drawn.

Second, we would like to thank the Housing Studies Association Steering Committee for organising the meeting from which these papers are drawn. On the ground this was carried out in the main by, at York, Peter Kemp and Margaret Johnson, and in Glasgow, by Jennifer Munro. The Housing Studies Association is a voluntary body run by academics and practicioners to further knowledge about housing in Britain. The time put in by steering committee members to make the HSA work is therefore gratefully acknowledged.

Third, we acknowledge the helpful and efficient approach of our editors at Avebury, in particular, the role of Josephine Gooderham and Pat Marks. In a technical capacity the editors are very grateful to the work of Iona Young, Peter Lambie, Margaret McConnachie and John Malcolm at the Centre for Housing Research.

Finally, we would like to thank the authors of the contributions in the following chapters. They produced their chapters based on recently completed JRF research in the areas of housing finance and housing markets in good time and were patient with our efforts to produce this volume. It would not have been possible without them.

1 Introduction

Duncan Maclennan and Kenneth Gibb

Introduction

The Duke of Edinburgh's Inquiry Report of 1985 brought together a range of views about the wasteful and ill-organised pattern of housing subsidies in Britain. The report generally argued for a more tenure neutral approach to subsidy and investment, a better balance between renting and owning and diversified ownership of social rental housing. Consistent pricing allowing a reasonable return to landlords and a tenure-neutral housing allowance scheme lay at the heart of the proposals.

Since 1985 numerous aspects of the 1985 Inquiry Report appear to have influenced government. Other key recommendations, especially the reform of mortgage interest tax relief, were ignored or side-stepped by political parties. During 1987 the Joseph Rowntree Foundation, which had sponsored the 1985 Inquiry, funded a major research effort which became known as the Housing Finance Research Programme.

The Programme ran from early 1988 to mid-1991, just as the British housing market moved from prolonged boom to major bust, and spent £1.5 million. The research effort included 'think-pieces', freestanding studies (a number of them reported on herein) and six local case studies involving interviews with suppliers and more than 10,000 household interviews. The case studies were carried out in the travel-to-work areas of Bristol, Sheffield, Birmingham, Newcastle, Glasgow and Greater London.

The local case studies were designed to examine differences in housing costs and subsidies across regions, by intra-urban location and, of course, by socio-economic group. The broad findings (Maclennan et al, 1990; Maclennan et al, 1991) confirmed the growing gulf in wellbeing between social sector tenants and home-

1

owners, the chaotic pricing of rented housing and the inequity of subsidy arrangements in relation to incomes. By 1989 few British households with incomes in excess of £5,000 per annum were more subsidised in renting than owning.

The local studies were, in broad terms, only partly successful. It has been hoped that the urban settings of the research would facilitate the identification of housing supply elasticities - an elusive, largely unused number in housing policy design in Britain. However, progress on these issues has largely awaited Bramley's more recent analyses for JRF.

The work of the programme informed specific policy debates in Britain, for instance, see Hancock and Munro (1992) on approaches to measuring affordability and on equity withdrawal from housing, a major concern until 1989. The programme also reinforced Muellbauer's arguments that housing subsidy and policy arrangements in Britain were damaging national economic performance. That is (see Maclennan et al, 1991), the reform argument went well beyond the traditional equity and efficiency advocacy for change to emphasise macro-economy aspects, but in the context of housing market boom and national economic growth.

The housing subsidy measures developed and estimated, either in the local case studies or by Hill's national level research, provided important new evidence. Moreover, the British housing commentary/lobby industry now at least uses a more correct notion of subsidy. However, there were some aspects of this work which have not, yet, reached their full potential. For instance, measures of subsidy in the social sector have relied on the application of rather crude hedonic indices, which probably overstate the value of social housing, little of the research allowed for the fact that social tenants receive subsidy and dwelling in a tied bundle which they may value less than the market. If anything, the bias of technique has been probably to over-estimate the value of social sector subsidies to tenants. Technical work is continuing, at Glasgow University, to address these issues.

The programme highlighted the growing importance of Housing Benefit as the key subsidy to renters in Britain. However, time and data restricted analysis to initial incidence studies and the programme did not test its wider incentive and economic effects. Reform proposals flowing from the programme have been, in relation to Housing Benefit, marginal (changing tapers etc) rather than radical and good research is still required.

Since 1991, JRF have continued to commission relevant, related research which has examined housing repossessions, mortgage arrears and negative equity in housing. And the Foundation will undertake a programme of work on the role of housing in the national economy.

As the events of the early 1990s have unfolded much of what was said in the 1985 Inquiry and the Duke of Edinburgh's restatement of 1991, largely based on the results of the Housing Finance Research Programme, appear to form an even more convincing

2

template for housing reform in Britain. A larger private rental sector, universal benefit available to renters and owners, reform of MIRAS are all now widely recognised as valid, coherent approaches to change. The time is rapidly coming when government will recognise that the present taxation arrangements for housing not only fail to serve the national economic interest but also fail to hold the political 'middle-ground'.

The present deepening recession and southern housing market slump have become a context for crisis management rather than careful, long-term reform. Government, to their credit, have resisted short-term *ad hoc* measures to revive the housing market. But when recovery does come then, unless there is long-term subsidy reform, the tax, tenure and planning systems which have fuelled three housing booms since 1970, and not just the 1987-92 boom and bust, will still be in place. In a competitive world economy Britain cannot afford the inflationary consequences of housing-led or fuelled booms. Nor, in a civilised society, can rising homelessness and council estate squalor be widely acceptable. Housing subsidy reform offers Britain the prospect of not only faster but fairer growth.

It was a great privilege to, respectively, Direct the Housing Finance Research Programme and work on the Core research team. The policy and research outputs have been considerable.

The Joseph Rowntree Foundation housing finance programme

The Spring 1991 meeting of the Housing Studies Association afforded the opportunity to review and assess the key research of the Joseph Rowntree Foundation housing finance programme and related research funded from the same source. This collection is, therefore, a distillation of several research themes, capturing the major questions and most pressing problems that found expression in the reconvened Inquiry into British Housing chaired by the Duke of Edinburgh.

Book structure

The book is in five parts, dealing with, respectively, the regional dimensions of the housing system, the independent rented sector, local authority housing finance, and, a set of issues relating to housing-demographic, mobility and inheritance issues. There is also a short prospective chapter in part five, looking at future challenges for British housing finance. There is, of course, a lot of cross-coverage, with much of the material in chapters two and three in particular, found elsewhere, for instance, in the sections dealing with the changing financial regimes facing local authorities and housing associations.

Part one is made up of three chapters that have a regional dimension, and also make good use of the JRF housing finance household survey. It is commonplace to identify the wide regional variations in levels and cyclical patterns in house prices. However, part one also makes it clear that rental and owner subsidy have a distinctive regional pattern and that the geographical distribution of public expenditure is an important explanation of territorial variation in housing outcomes.

Chapter two (Duncan Maclennan, Kenneth Gibb and Alison More) is a synthesis of the key findings from the Housing Finance Programme's core team, which drew on all aspects of the programme's work, but is here mainly dealing with the price and subsidy evidence found among the 9,500 households surveyed in six British conurbations. The magnitude of the housing sector's contribution to the economy is analysed alongside increasing fears about its detrimental impact on inflation and economic growth. The distribution of various subsidies to owner occupiers is estimated, as is the depth of subsidy to tenants measured as a distortion from estimated market rents. The new regime for associations is evaluated and proposals for improving the private rented sector are forwarded.

Chapter three (Richard Eastall, John Hughes and Roy Wilkinson) draws on the Sheffield case study team's findings for their urban area to build wider conclusions for the reform of housing finance for Britain as a whole. The Sheffield area is a relatively low income one but tax relief remains regressively distributed, rents have risen in real terms increasingly funded by housing benefit. Housing-related poverty and homelessness have risen while the supply of affordable housing has diminished. An argument is put forward for the new supply of council housing let at economic rents along with specific proposals to reform the tax treatment of home owners, a level playing field for social sector investment in terms of capital controls, improving private renting, re-introducing property taxation, making housing benefit more generous and directly tackling homelessness.

Chapter four (Ken Willis and Stuart Cameron) builds on the work of the Newcastle case study team to define and explore the effects of different subsidy definitions and their distribution across housing tenures by modelling the impact of rent distortions on the Newcastle household data. Subsidy is here defined as the 'gap' between actual housing payments and notional payments reflecting a market return on the current capital value of the dwelling. After considering what this definition of subsidy means across tenures, economic subsidies are modelled by calculating the consumer surplus (in terms of equivalent variation) implied, since this captures the quantity-rationing elements where consumption is taken off the demand curve by households facing controls of some form. This analysis concluded that council tenants do better than other renters

4

in terms of subsidy, that the distribution of benefits is progressive, and, that there was relatively little loss in transfer efficiency (the subsidy cost in relation to its calculated benefits).

Independent rented sector

The independent rented sector, the lumping together of the non-municipal rented sectors, is the subject of part two. With the new financial regime for housing associations seeking greater management efficiency and more output per pound of public money, the role of private finance in funding the shortfall between development costs and HAG, is central to the success of the new system. The private rented sector has experienced two parallel reforms in the late 1980s: the culmination of deregulation processes in the 1988 Housing Act which generalised the assured tenancy as the basis of new tenancies throughout the sector; and, the establishment of the business expansion scheme assured tenancy rental housing company. In addition, city grant and GRO-grant (in Scotland) have provisions for the supply subsidy of private market renting. The key question is whether these interventions can reverse or even halt the shrinkage of commercial renting in Britain.

The first chapter, chapter five (by Tony Crook and Peter Kemp), asks if there is a future for the private rented sector in the light of these recent reforms and published proposals for further reform. They examine what a revival of private renting might actually mean in practice, before outlining the government's proposals and their own research findings on the business expansion scheme. Their chapter ends with a most interesting comparison and evaluation of several different reform packages for the commercial rented sector based on supply subsidies, deregulation and limited rent controls.

In chapter six (Christine Whitehead), the private component of mixed-funding of housing associations is examined. The new financial regime for associations explicitly requires the increased use of private finance to cover the gap in funding calculations. Chapter six reviews and analyses the prospects for such private funding in the voluntary housing sector - from the point of view of the private funders, asked to lend and seek profit from a financial sector of which they have had no previous experience or understanding. The development of suitable financial instruments to meet this gap is therefore crucial and this chapter describes the mechanisms in operation in the initial period after the establishment of the new regime, recognising that the funds for associations are in direct competition with owner occupation (and large scale voluntary transfers).

The chapter identifies that long term finance may not be forthcoming even at a premium because of this competition from other sources and because of the shorter term expectational impact of recession on asset value appreciation. The conclusion is that such a premium and the transfer alternatives may prevent the objective of a net expansion in social housing provision.

One of the critical areas of change in recent housing legislation has been the new arrangements for the funding of local authorities' own housing stock in England and Wales. The most important elements of this new approach are: first, the basic credit approvals system of capital borrowing consents which attempts to circumvent the previous problems with capital receipts and cascade effects; second, the ring-fencing system which creates a new subsidy, housing revenue account subsidy, bringing all local authorities back into subsidy and therefore control by the DoE; and third, the move to bring rents gradually into line with capital values assessed on Right to Buy sales.

Part three concentrates on local authority housing finance. Chapter seven (Peter Malpass and Matthew Warburton) critically assesses the new system of controlling housing revenue accounts. Taking a policy approach to the question (rather than applied economics) this chapter considers the local-level implementation of the ring-fencing regime. The authors correctly stress the importance of analysing the implementation, as well as the objectives and long term effects, of new legislative policy. The new financial regime is placed in the context of earlier developments of the local authority housing finance system before assessing the reality of the first two years of its operation, emphasising the impact of the changes on central-local governmental relations (and vice versa). The chapter concludes that the new regime attempts to reduce autonomy, was designed with implementation in mind (something evidenced by the dampening mechanism), is heavily dependent on local authority data collection, that rents were set above target guidelines in the first two years of the new regime and that some outcomes have been contrary to government expectations.

In a sense, chapter eight (Bruce Walker and Alex Marsh) further examines the logic of ring-fencing by analysing the effects of the eventual move to capital value rents on household data from the JRF survey for the case study area of Birmingham. The authors develop and model several rent-setting regimes on their data, discussing the principles that might guide a rational approach to rent-setting before presenting their results and linking their implications to the ring-fencing system. There is an understandable emphasis on average council rents in the housing literature but as important is the principles underlying the distribution of rental payments across a given housing stock. A move to capital value rents would, in most cases, lead to significant real rent increases, putting severe pressure on housing benefit and the authors argue that a more efficient outcome than large scale income transfers would be to explicitly subsidise the rent component through a reduction in the required rate of return on the capital value, following the Target Rent concept suggested by John Hills.

6

As a commodity or as a bundle of rights and obligations, or simply as stored wealth, housing plays an increasingly important part in the economic decisions of millions of households in Britain and elsewhere. In part four we tackle three different but related ways in which this is borne out. As the single largest store of personal sector wealth owner occupied housing plays a large role in macroeconomic spending (through equity withdrawal) and as a means of transferring accumulated wealth to succeeding generations (even if it represents quasi-rents on property ownership).

Chapter nine (Chris Hamnett and Peter Williams) considers the impact of the increased level of housing wealth transferred through inheritances on succeeding households.

Demographic trends and a string of developments in social policy, community care and innovative financial packages for cash poor home owners has raised a series of important policy questions grouped under the heading of housing finance for the elderly. In chapter ten (Robin Means, Philip Leather and Sheila Mackintosh), equity withdrawal through home equity plans is just one of the topics raised in a discussion of housing finance issues pertinent to older households. Beginning with an attack on ageist assumptions about housing for older people, the authors concentrate on affordability, maintenance and adaptation problems and the developing inter-relationship between housing policies and community care policies. The authors argue that much of the inequality manifested by the housing consumption of older people is a function of their housing and labour market careers rather than simply because they are old. Developments in the study of housing careers would thus have an important role in furthering our understanding of these issues.

There is a longstanding debate as to the extent to which council housing tenure is a constraint on mobility as a result of waiting lists and quantity constraints on consumption. Alternatively, it has been argued that immobility by council tenants reflects their possession of the socio-economic characteristics of the immobile and that tenure is spurious in explaining the relationship. Chapter eleven (Moira Munro and Peter Symon) inquires into the relationship between housing tenure and the probability of mobility, specifically, using the decision to move long distances. The authors consider the impact that employment-related factors have in explaining the probability of carrying through long distance moves. While their findings support the familiar correlation between tenure and mobility, they stress that labour market characteristics have been largely unmeasured in previous research, and that once they are controlled for (for instance, age, career path and socio-economic group), it becomes clear that caution should be deployed when attributing mobility patterns to the housing system.

7

The ten chapters from chapter two to eleven, reflect the output from ten different projects based on Joseph Rowntree Foundation research carried out in the late 1980s to 1990-91. The final chapter (Duncan Maclennan and Kenneth Gibb) considers the prospects for housing finance and the housing market as we look forward to the mid 1990s and beyond.

This is especially apposite since the continuing decline in the owner occupied housing market is occurring alongside increasing unemployment, a collapsing construction activity, accelerating mortgage arrears and repossessions. Although we are at the bottom of the third price cycle in twenty years, and although there are significant price variations across the country, this price collapse is the first to incorporate the effects of mortgage deregulation, nominal as well as real price falls, and the spectacular rise in mortgage default and serious arrears. This is despite the relative efficiency of the UK finance system (Diamond and Lea, 1992). Capital spending by local authorities and associations fails to keep pace with perceived notions of housing needs and the private rented sector prospects do not keep apace with government policy. The possible effects of Large Scale Voluntary Transfer and Compulsory Competitive Tendering now concentrate the minds of housing managers, while the financial implications of European integration for property markets are only now beginning to be thought through.

It is in this forward-looking context that the need for a consistent and coherent approach to housing finance and housing markets is therefore urged, one that incorporates the effects of housing on the macroeconomy and social security (housing benefit) on the housing system. And it is in this light that one must re-evaluate the Duke of Edinburgh's Inquiry and other systematic attempts to elevate the debate on housing finance reform. The papers in this volume stress the breadth of impacts that housing has on the economy and society: finance and subsidy reform must be efficient and fair, certainly, but they must also consider the growing impact of housing market volatility on the macroeconomic performance of the UK.

Part One
REGIONAL PATTERNS

2 Housing finance, subsidies and the economy: Agenda for the nineties

Duncan Maclennan, Kenneth Gibb and Alison More

Introduction

This chapter presents an overview of the second of two reports for the Joseph Rowntree Foundation Housing Finance Programme (Maclennan, Gibb and More, 1990; 1991). The JRF programme was established with Duncan Maclennan as Director to produce a comprehensive picture of the UK housing market and housing finance, thus facilitating and engaging in the debate about reform. Essentially, the programme was in three parts:

(1) six regional case studies in Bristol, Birmingham, Glasgow, London, Newcastle and Sheffield, each undertaking a large household survey.

(2) stand-alone projects by various teams and individuals on work relating to BES, private finance for housing associations, the abolition of MITR and reform to the housing finance system. Maclennan and Williams (1990a-c) represent edited collections of papers from JRF-sponsored seminars on comparative housing finance systems.

(3) the core programme team who had the benefit of using the household survey as a whole and the other findings from the research in (1) and (2).

The overview below principally derives its conclusions from the household survey of more than 9,500 cases in the conurbations of the six survey areas, but also draws on the findings of the stand-alone work. This chapter has the following structure: in the next section, we examine the important links between housing and the economy, particularly in terms of house prices, equity withdrawal and inflation. In the third section, attention turns to recent trends in public expenditure on housing. The next three sections consider the subsidy positions of owner occupiers, local authority tenants and the independent rented sector, respectively. The final section briefly concludes.

Housing markets and the economy

Housing as an economic sector remains a very significant magnitude. It represents some 4 per cent of national output; construction employs a million people and housing makes up one fifth of gross investment in fixed capital in the economy. It has long been recognised that the housing market is driven by economic change, particularly in terms of incomes, interest rates and household formation. Recent experience demonstrates that housing can reinforce negative economic change, feeding back into levels of inflation, expenditure and output. At the same time, there is a recognition that housing subsidy and policy arrangements encourage house price inflation and that rising house prices boost inflation by stoking inflationary wage demands and by encouraging higher levels of consumer expenditure. The success of any reforms to the housing finance system will depend on whether they reverse these forces and, at the same time, break the pattern of high interest rates, mortgage arrears and repossessions experienced in the last two to three years.

The boom-bust phenomenon of the UK housing market from 1986-91 has been, in many respects, typical of the last two decades. Three booms have occurred since 1969: 1971-73; 1979-80; and 1987-89. Each was followed by a 'bust', although it was only in 1989-90 that this produced a fall in nominal prices (around 3 per cent in 1990 and in Southern regions of England prices have fallen by a fifth since 1988).

Between 1969 and 1989, the money value of average house prices rose fifteen fold, that is, just over twice the level of the RPI. The doubling of the real value of dwellings and the growth in home ownership from 50 to 67 per cent meant that housing asset growth comprised two thirds of the doubling of household wealth that occurred during this period. The difference between home values and outstanding mortgage debt, the personal sector's housing asset base, reached £750 billion by 1988.

Regionally, there was tremendous variation in this expansion of property values: seventeen fold in the South East; just seven fold in Northern Ireland. Housing markets have an inevitable local dimension and there is a growing body of evidence that suggests regional house price differentials and their widening in periods of price appreciation hamper labour mobility and reinforce regional differentials in wealth (Coombes and Raybould, 1991).

Three areas in particular underlie the recent patterns of house prices: financial deregulation; the construction industry and supply elasticity; and, the effects of equity withdrawal.

Financial deregulation

Removing the corset on bank lending, the ending of the mortgage rate cartel and the Building Societies Act 1986 were the major elements of change. By 1989, borrowing had become more geared to household incomes, such that the ratio of mortgage debt to GDP rose from 32 per cent to 58 per cent between 1982 and 1989. Comparable figures in 1989 for other countries were 45 per cent in the USA, 21 per cent in France and 25 per cent in Japan (Lomax, 1991). In other countries also open to deregulation these pressures have not been so significant because they rely on larger purchase deposits. Aside from reducing collective and individual exposure to gearing, such measures increase the savings rate and boost the stock demand for rental (mainly private) housing. In the UK, however, tax systems, finance arrangements and destructive rental sector policies have guided younger households into debt-encumbered home ownership.

The housing construction industry

Housing production in the UK, reflecting lags attributable to firms as well as the planning system, commonly takes two years to respond to price signals, fuelling the boom and worsening the bust. In other words, output peaks after prices, leaving unsold stock and thereby exacerbating the downturn. In the 1980s, the housing sector has been increasing its share of the construction industry's output (39% to 42%). Within the total of new build, private sector housebuilding has steadily displaced public building of housing (whose share fell from 40% in 1980 to only 10% in 1989). At any time, the supply of vacancies on the housing market reflects not just new stock but vacancies advertised by existing owners either moving or intending to move. In 1978 the volume of second-hand properties traded (and requiring a loan) was 800,000. This rose to 1.6 million in 1988 and fell to 900,000 in 1989. The majority of moves are local in nature and can be postponed until trading conditions improve (the same applies for large developers who can hold onto their landbanks). These factors contribute to the ratchet effect on house prices which raises house prices rapidly in 'boom' periods but ensures more modest real price falls in the down-turn.

Equity withdrawal

Since the mid-80s it has been recognised that 'equity withdrawal' from the housing market can have important, sometimes adverse consequences for the economy. Rising real house prices can influence consumer spending in a number of ways:
 (1) by increasing the value of housing inheritances, the vast majority of which are sold.
 (2) through the retention of part of the net proceeds by movers when buying and selling.

13

(3) by remortgaging, extending loans etc against rising values of housing on the part of households staying put.

(4) encouraging greater spending/less saving by households who feel wealthier because they occupy more expensive houses.

The JRF programme concluded that equity withdrawal had reached £14.6 billion in 1988 (for movers only, see Lowe and Watson, 1990). In a separate study, Muellbauer (1990) reports a figure for all equity withdrawal in 1988 at £22 billion. The former figure would add 2 to 3 per cent to national spending in the economy. In the household survey, it was calculated that the average level of additional borrowing by non-movers during the period 1983-88 was £9000 in real terms and more than half of the borrowing left the housing sector.

The question remains: are we likely to see a repeat of some of these forces in the early to middle years of the 1990s? It is unlikely that demand pressures will be as great: the rate of household formation is expected to fall (Ermisch (ed), 1990); tax changes are unlikely to assist home ownership in the near future; and, real incomes are projected to grow at only 2 to 3 per cent in the next three to four years. Furthermore, the recent downturn in house prices, has increased perceptions of risk and is likely to induce greater prudence, especially for those who were over-exposed or highly geared. Finally, the constraints of ERM will, in the short to medium run, limit the flexibility of interest rate policy and supercede the needs of home owners and mortgage rate affordability. However, any real house price appreciation must be expected to accompany a further growth in equity withdrawal.

What can government do to assist stable real house prices in the long run? First, government should accelerate the removal of the favourable tax status of owner occupiers. A Capital Gains Tax is probably infeasible so attention should be directed to removing or re-structuring Mortgage Interest Tax Relief. A phased reduction over five years would lower house prices and cut interest rates by two per cent (Wilcox, 1991). Second, there is a case for a more neutral tax regime between tenures, especially until MITR is reduced. Depreciation allowances for landlords would be a worthwhile start. Finally, a purposeful approach has to be adopted for the housing construction sector which recognises the tensions between macroeconomic policy, housing output and environmental quality. Above all there should be a major review of how planning authorities plan land release and adapt to local price increases.

Public spending on housing

Overall changes in public spending were characterised by sharp reductions in housing expenditure in the early to mid 1980s. During this period (up until 1982-83) housing programmes constituted three quarters of the total cuts in public spending. The housing share of public spending fell from 5.8 per cent to 2.3 per cent. The severity of the cut-back reflected the capital-intensive nature of housing (as capital programmes can be more readily curtailed than recurrent subsidies), the government's faith in the efficacy of market solutions and the deferred nature of the consequences of housing cut-backs.

From 1976 to 1989, the housing share of public spending measured by the Planning Total in the financial statement fell from 11 per cent to 3.5 per cent of the total, and, although real spending on housing stabilised in the period since the mid- 1980s, the housing share is expected to fall to 3.3 per cent by 1993-94 (in the context of a growing public sector). These figures tell us nothing about activities funded by sales receipts, MITR or housing benefit (see Table 2.1 which indicates a long term shift away from property-related subsidies to personal or income-related subsidies). Measured in net terms, real capital spending in 1989 was only 18 per cent of its 1976 level. But for gross capital spending (including spending based on receipts) the comparable figures are 56 per cent (63% for a volume-weighted index based on the building costs index). The increasing prominence of capital receipts is made evident when it is seen that capital receipts funded 7 per cent of capital spending in 1980 and over 70 per cent in 1989.

Capital spending

From 1985 to 1988, capital spending on housing was fairly constant in real terms, before falling subsequently. The share of gross spending undertaken by the quangos fell from 1985-89 (due to higher than expected sales receipts to councils). There have, however, been significant regional variations. Over the period 1980-6, half of English local authorities experienced a real growth in spending (Scotland and Wales, 55 and 57 respectively). Within England, real capital spending on housing rose by a fifth in East Anglia, the South East and the South West but fell by a quarter in London, the North and the North West. The changes also favoured rural rather than urban areas, with spending in the conurbations falling by a fifth, and rising by 5 per cent in small towns and 10 per cent in rural areas (Kleinman, 1991). Within spending programmes there was a massive switch from new construction to renovation facilitated by the rules governing the use of capital receipts. In the period 1976 to 1989, new build by councils fell by 90 per cent while renovation almost doubled. The changing pattern for the 1980s in England also occurred in Scotland and Wales and by the end of the decade almost two thirds of local authority housing expenditure was devoted to renovation programmes.

At the end of the decade the government recognised some of the limitations of targeting capital programmes and introduced new financial regimes for housing associations (throughout Britain) and for local authorities (though not in Scotland). The importance of sales receipts was one of the factors prompting a change in England and Wales. After 1981-82, local authorities had been allowed to spend a prescribed proportion of receipts, falling from

50 to 20 per cent as receipts outstripped government willingness to allocate them to housing.

Table 2.1
Public spending on housing 1976-7 to 1989-90, £ billion at 1988-9 Prices [1]

Year	1 Current (GB)	2 Net Capital (GB)	1+2=3 Current plus net capital (UK)	4 housing benefit (UK)[2]	3+4=5 total public spending (UK)	6 MITR (UK) [3]
1976-7	3.9	8.3	12.7	2.2	14.8	3.4
1977-8	3.5	6.5	10.4	2.2	12.6	2.9
1978-9	3.8	5.7	9.9	2.1	12.0	2.7
1979-80	4.3	6.0	10.7	1.9	12.1	3.1
1980-1	4.1	4.5	9.0	2.0	11.1	3.5
1981-2	2.9	2.8	6.1	3.0	9.0	3.4
1982-3	2.2	2.6	5.1	3.5	8.7	3.3
1983-4	1.8	3.5	5.6	3.4	9.1	3.6
1984-5	1.7	3.3	5.4	3.8	9.2	4.4
1985-6	1.7	2.7	4.7	3.8	8.7	5.5
1986-7	1.7	2.4	4.4	4.1	8.6	5.3
1987-8	1.6	2.3	4.3	4.2	8.5	5.2
1988-9	1.4	1.2	3.0	4.1	7.0	5.5
1989-90	1.5	1.5	3.3	4.2	7.5	6.5

Sources: HM Treasury (1990) Tables 8.1, 8.2, 15.1, 15.2, 16.1, 16.2, 17.1, 21.2, 21.2.9, F1 and earlier equivalents; Welsh Office (1989) Table 9.1 and earlier equivalents; SDD (1990) Table 15.5 and earlier equivalents; Board of Inland revenue (1989) Table 5.1; Official Report 12 March 1990, Cols WA93-96. Table based on Hills and Mullings (1990).

1. adjusted by GDP deflator,
2. on current definitions,
3. including option mortgage subsidy until 1983-84.

Local authorities were also allowed to spend the prescribed proportion of unused sales revenues from previous years (the cascade effect). There were no such limits in Scotland (where the Secretary of State had his own measures to restrict borrowing). From 1990-91 onwards, local authorities are to have a tripartite capital budget. The Basic Credit Approval (BCA) is a borrowing permission given to each local authority, taking into account likely sales receipts (in this way government is free to allocate spending, in theory, to the 'neediest' local authorities and the Housing Corporation). The second component is sales receipts, though future debt repayments and contributions towards funding rent rebates are now deducted. The third component is Specific Credit Approvals, that is, borrowing permitted for precise forms of investment favoured by the government. The new system also extends the expenditure planning period from one to three years.

Current spending

After 1980-1, the government sharply reduced revenue subsidies to housing revenue accounts (HRAs). Previously, this subsidy had been the main instrument for reducing housing costs faced by council tenants. Compared with levels in 1979-80, by 1989-90, current spending had fallen to 19 per cent of its former level in England and Wales (15% in Scotland). In 1989, fewer than one in five local authorities in England and Wales received subsidy, compared with 95 per cent in 1981-2.

Table 2.2
Regional distribution of housing subsidy/housing support grant, 1981-1982 and 1987-1988, %

SEPR	1981-2 (%)	1987-8 (%)
Northern	4.4	2.3
Yorkshire and Humberside	4.6	0.1
East Midlands	3.6	2.1
North	4.7	2.0
London	41.3	69.6
South East	6.7	4.7
South West	2.3	0.6
West Midlands	6.2	1.9
North West	7.8	6.5
Wales	3.3	2.0
Scotland	15.1	8.1
	100.0	100.0

Sources: CIPFA Housing Revenue Account Statistics and Hansard 15 July 1988, cols 399-400.

The result of these changes was a shift in the regional impact of subsidy (see Table 2.2). Between 1981-2 and 1987-8, there was a large increase in the proportion of total grant going to the London Boroughs. Elsewhere, only the North West got close to its earlier share of the total, while Scotland's share was halved from 15 to 8 per cent. At the same time, the HRA itself was drastically restructured (Table 2.3). Faced with falling subsidies and rising costs, councils could either increase rents or increase the level of contributions made from general rate fund contributions (RFCs). Since the government wished to curb local authority expenditure, penalties and restrictions put paid to the second option, and, in consequence, rents rapidly increased. By 1989-90, almost 70 per cent of HRA income came from rental income and the overall real increase in rents in the decade to 1989 was almost 50 per cent. Restrictions on the reinvestment of receipts meant that the annual interest on those receipts covered more than ten per cent of HRA expenditure by 1989, thereby indirectly subsidising council tenants.

17

The curtailment of council investment in new build over the past decade and the reliance on receipts has resulted in the proportion of income devoted to repayments of capital and interest on loans falling from two thirds of expenditure in 1980-1 to half by 1987-88. As a result much more income has been spent on management and maintenance. John Hills (1991a) estimates that real management and maintenance spending per dwelling has grown by 4.8 per cent per annum since 1976.

Table 2.3
HRA structure in England and Wales, 1980-1 and 1987-8

	1980-1 (%)	1987-8 (%)
REVENUE		
Rents	48	68
Rate Fund Contributions	10	8
Exchequer Subsidy	32	8
Interest on unspent Capital Receipts	5	11
Other Income	5	6
	100	100
EXPENDITURE		
Loan Interest and Repayments	66	51
Repair and Maintenance	20	27
Supervision and Management	12	19
Other Expenditure	2	2
Transfer to Rate Fund	0	1
	100	100

Source: Kearns and Maclennan, 1988.

Housing benefit has been the main offset for tenants against steadily rising rents, steadily reinforcing the poverty trap. While housing subsidy (housing support grant in Scotland) totalled little over £500 million in 1989, expenditure on rent rebates was close to £3 billion. In real terms, total spending on rent rebates to council tenants has been rising. Assuming the average HB recipient reduces the average rent, then in 1989, rent rebates covered 60 per cent of the cost of providing housing services to those 3.37 million tenants in receipt of housing benefit.

Ring-fencing

Ring-fencing was introduced because government found the falling amount of subsidy and RFC meant that Whitehall could no longer control annual rent increases by withdrawing subsidy - too many councils were already 'free'. Also, the ever-increasing housing benefit bill implied that rent increases progressively manifested themselves in social security spending funded by the DSS. The main features of ring-fencing are a tighter definition of the HRA, prohibiting transfers between the HRA and other council accounts, and the introduction of a single HRA subsidy to replace the previously separate housing subsidy, rent rebates and RFCs. In constructing the new 'notional' HRA, for assessing housing subsidy, the DoE is using new allowance rates for management and maintenance spending and linking local guideline rent increases to local house price changes, but with a minimum and maximum rise to dampen rent increases. Local authorities will have to stand on their 'own feet' more under ring-fencing and rent increases will be progressively more related to capital value, giving some coherence to council rents (although see below). The greater wedge of HRAs controlled by government returns to Whitehall the ability to control rent increases.

Taxation of home ownership

There are different definitions of what actually constitutes the privileged tax treatment that home owners are presumed to enjoy. We would concur with the economistic view that it is the failure to tax the investment return to housing that constitutes the tax expenditure enjoyed by owner occupiers (O'Sullivan, 1984; Hills, 1989) but we recognise that, for practical reasons, neither the imposition of a tax on imputed rental income or a real capital gains tax on housing are likely to be successful. For this reason, following the Inquiry into British Housing (1985; 1991) we focus, for policy reasons, on the conceptually weaker definition of mortgage interest tax relief. In this section, the different measures of subsidy are presented, recognising the above caveat.

Table 2.4 summarises the average level of tax subsidy by income band and by location. MITR rises steadily with income band and is higher in house price areas such as London and Bristol compared with Sheffield and Newcastle. The subsidy associated with imputed rents is governed by length of residency and outstanding mortgage debt, therefore its pattern is less clear with respect to income, although again average values are much higher in London and Bristol than elsewhere. The absence of a capital gains tax benefits higher house price areas and does not have a particularly strong relationship with current incomes. Overall, tax subsidies fail to provide a progressive distribution of subsidy, they are inefficient and sometimes arbitrary and in no way can be said to conform to rational housing policy objectives.

Tax expenditures are not the only subsidies received by owner occupiers. Tenants exercising the right to buy received a discount of, on average, £12,000 or 46.6 per cent of their property between 1980 and 1988 in the JRF sample, varying from less than £10,000 in Birmingham and Sheffield to more than £21,500 in London. Against these trends, the government intends to reintroduce an attenuated property tax, the council tax, which will hit owner occupiers harder (gross bills for the two main tenures will be on average £361 for owners and £297 for local authority tenants with the respective net bills equalling £310 and £127, see Gibb, 1992). This helps horizontal equity policy goals but the flat distribution of price bands at the heart of council tax valuations means that higher priced properties are leniently treated by the new tax.

Table 2.4
Subsidies to home owner by income band and location

gross income band	MITR	imputed rental income tax	real capital gains tax
<2600	191	417	3455
2600-5199	126	291	2645
5200-7799	284	306	2937
7800-10399	300	291	2499
10400-12999	405	290	2888
13000-15599	440	308	3078
15600-20799	488	375	3456
20800-25999	748	605	4699
26000-31199	888	619	5545
31200>	1002	608	4330
Location			
Birmingham	469	323	2969
Bristol	566	445	3677
Glasgow	588	330	3356
London	625	610	5034
Newcastle	450	262	2465
Sheffield	392	291	2903
mean all	513	382	3403

Source: JRF Housing Finance Household Survey.

1. imputed rental income tax is the tax that would be levied on the net equity owned by the household, it is net of debt which, of course, receives MITR. The exemption from real Capital Gains Tax refers to the taxed taxable gain made after allowing for inflation, a £5000 allowance and assuming sale in 1988 and original purchase since 1982.

Local authority housing

Over the past decade, the local authority share of the national dwelling stock has fallen from 31 to 23 per cent, though there are important regional variations in tenure structure; despite rapid sales in Scotland, the council share stood at 40 per cent in September 1990. With more than 1.5m council houses transferred into owner occupation, council house renters today are predominantly poor and there are growing concerns about the further residualisation of the sector. If the problems of decay and impoverishment are to be redressed, the nature and impact of the housing finance system in achieving housing policy objectives must be reconsidered.

Within the HRA, costs and revenues are 'pooled' across the entire local authority stock. This practice is particularly effective for the 'equalisation' of loan charges, accounted for in historic cost terms, but has served to distort the relationship between rents charged and current values. Local authorities had discretion to set rents for their housing stock; studies reveal that most adopt rent schemes based on either rateable or gross annual values or on simple points criteria relating to property characteristics.

Notwithstanding local discretion, there has been a tendency for authorities to increase rents in line with standard annual increases set out by Government Departments, and this has led to some convergence in rent levels. But the variation in revenue bases across authorities, and in 'political' attitudes towards rent policies, has meant that there continue to be wide variations in absolute rent levels charged. The real rent increases of around 50 per cent alluded to above were not just a reflection of DoE guidelines, but also a consequence of the shifting composition of the HRA (noted above in Table 2.3). The gradual withdrawal of Exchequer subsidy and the increasing incidence of 'capping' created further pressures for rent increases in excess of the RPI. There were however, significant regional and local variations, for example, in the West Central Scotland conurbation, there co-existed a doubling of real rents in run-down Clydebank, alongside constant real rents in nearby well-to-do Eastwood.

These patterns raise two key considerations from a national point of view. First, the degree of local discretion rested on the ability to use (or abuse) the housing benefit system (funded almost entirely from national tax revenues) and meant that high rent policies had little impact on local authority finances. The JRF programme studies revealed a wide variety in the proportion of housing benefit meeting gross rent payments, indicating differences not in client group but in local rent-level choices. Secondly, the diversity in local rent schemes meant that often they would run counter to national housing policies, such as those seeking to promote tenure diversification, particularly into the independent rented sector. The JRF study, in examining the incidence and impact of housing subsidies, conducted detailed analyses of subsidy patterns within each of the case study areas, and developed proposals for a more coherent pricing strategy for the rented sectors.

Subsidy is generally defined as the difference between the actual rent paid and the rent which would prevail in a balanced, competitive market. To calculate subsidy, it is necessary to make a number of assumptions, both about the valuation of dwellings in the non-market sector, and what constitutes a reasonable rate of return to the landlord net of management and maintenance expenditure (and depreciation). Valuation estimates may be based on either right-to-buy sales values (before discount) or on values formed in the market sector. The latter approach uses hedonic regression techniques to impute dwelling values according to a series of attributes found to be significant in owned sector. We selected this approach (RTB valuations and re-sale values were not widely available) with one further modification. If it is assumed that the incomes and preferences of those in the council sector differ from those in the owned sector, then the weighting and absolute values of individual dwelling attributes are likely also to differ from the market as a whole. We assumed social sector choices to bear closer resemblance to property purchases in the lower half of the market, and thus these 'bottom-half' values formed the comparator for social sector properties. The shortcomings of this approach are recognised - a more appropriate comparison may be with the bottom quarter of the market - and the exercise requires to be repeated using a much larger sample.

Turning to the choice of return rates, we selected firstly a 4 per cent rate of return, as recommended by the Duke of Edinburgh's Inquiry (1985; 1991). A rate of 5.5 per cent was also tested as this represented the long run return on all (including commercial) property in Britain for the period 1969- 89. A landlord's return is made not just from net rental income, but also from real gains in property price appreciation; thus the level of rent which requires to be charged to make the full return can be offset by expected price gains. On the basis of these assumptions, a range of market rents were then estimated for each of the case study areas and measures of subsidy derived.

Subsidy measures are essentially two-fold. First, there is what we term a 'rent distortion' subsidy, that is, the difference between market rents and actual **gross** rents charged. The second is the subsidy arising through the contribution of housing benefit to defraying the gross rental charge ('housing benefit subsidy'), and this is measured as the difference between **gross** rents levied and **actual** or **net** rents paid. Total subsidy is therefore the sum of the rent distortion and housing benefit subsidies. Table 2.5 sets out a range of estimated market rents by applying the two rates of return to both 'bottom-half' and 'full-market' values. Our estimates also show separately the impact of variation in capital gain rates.

Tax expenditures are not the only subsidies received by owner occupiers. Tenants exercising the right to buy received a discount of, on average, £12,000 or 46.6 per cent of their property between 1980 and 1988 in the JRF sample, varying from less than £10,000 in Birmingham and Sheffield to more than £21,500 in London. Against these trends, the government intends to reintroduce an attenuated property tax, the council tax, which will hit owner occupiers harder (gross bills for the two main tenures will be on average £361 for owners and £297 for local authority tenants with the respective net bills equalling £310 and £127, see Gibb, 1992). This helps horizontal equity policy goals but the flat distribution of price bands at the heart of council tax valuations means that higher priced properties are leniently treated by the new tax.

Table 2.5
Actual rents and estimated market rents for council housing

	Gross Rents	No Capital Gain Full-mkt Value (5.5)[1]	No Capital Gain Bottom half Value (4.0)	Local Gain Rates Full-mkt Value (5.5)	Local Gain Rates Bottom-half Value (4.0)	Implied rent rise[2] (a)	Implied rent rise[2] (b)
Birm	1011	1933	1845	1546	1440	53	42
Brist	967	2825	2131	1529	1157	128	20
Glasg	829	2369	1964	2007	1669	122	101
Lond	1176	5194	2292	2526	1196	235	2
Newc	1045	1634	1754	1191	1250	27	20
Shef	1037	1651	1729	1068	1063	29	3

1. Figures in brackets are the rates of return applied.
2. Represents excess of market rent over gross rents.
   (a) full market value, 4%, no capital gain,
   (b) bottom-half value, 4%, local capital gains.

Were this form of capital-value pricing policy to be adopted, then it is clear that choice of both valuation and rate of return are critical. A rate of 5.5 per cent on full-market values allowing no capital gains would, for example, lead to rent increases of 200-300 per cent. On the other hand, rents based on a 4 per cent return, allowing local capital gains, on 'bottom-half' values, would produce a more feasible starting point in most regions for a consistent pricing policy. Subsidy measures derived from this more practicable combination are illustrated in Table 2.6. Table 2.6 shows that housing benefit subsidy is relatively uniform, whereas variations in rent distortion subsidy are more marked, indicating the extent to which actual rents depart from market values. (note that in some instances, such as in Glasgow, total subsidy can exceed gross rents) Subsidies, including Housing Benefit tend to be higher in the northern regions, though there are exceptions. By income band, rent subsidies within regions are less disordered than the inter-regional pattern. Housing benefit ensures that the overall distribution of subsidy is progressive up to incomes over £7,200 (in 1988), after which total subsidy falls significantly.

Further analyses by age, ethnic status and distance from city centre also revealed a number of key points. First, average total subsidies were higher amongst the youngest (16-24) and oldest (60+) age groups, considerably lower among non-whites (£467) than whites (£782), and subsidies tended to be lower closer to the city centre though this pattern was not fully consistent.

Table 2.6
Council house subsidies in 1989, by region

Case Study area	Actual gross rent	Actual net rent	EMR[1]	Rent subsidy	HB subsidy	Total subsidy as % of EMR
Birm	1011	564	1440	429	447	61
Bris	969	579	1157	188	390	50
Glas	820	495	1669	849	325	70
Lond	1176	801	1197	21	375	33
Newc	1046	522	1254	208	524	58
Shef	1037	551	1063	26	486	48

1. EMR - estimated market rent, 4% return on 'bottom-half' values and local capital gains.

Two further points should be raised. First, we have built into our preferred rent-setting criteria an assumption about future capital gains. Other research (see for example, Wilcox, 1991) suggests that capital gain rates are unlikely to return to the levels experienced in the 1980s and any move to further erode the value of mortgage interest tax relief is likely to further decrease the likelihood of significant real gains. Thus landlords might be expected to discount expected gains from the equation.

Secondly, and this adds a further dimension to possible reform routes, we have so far ignored the issue of equity with owner occupiers. Owners' payments do not reflect current property values, except for recent purchasers. If the average owner-occupier moves every seven years, then only a small proportion at any point in time are paying current prices. We calculated the average ratios of purchase price to current values for each case study area and, based on bottom-half valuations, found an average 'discount' of one third. If this average value, the 'historic weighting factor', were applied to estimated market rents for the social sector, then the second goal of achieving equity with owner occupiers could be achieved. And even in the absence of future capital gains, the required rent adjustments could be feasible in most regions, excepting London and Glasgow (see Table 2.7).

Since the survey was carried out, there have been price falls in many regions. We therefore tested the effect of a 10 per cent house price fall on estimated market rents in the council sector and the results are also shown in Table 2.7 (column 4). Only in Glasgow would rent levels require to increase significantly. Implementation of our proposal would mean an increase in the eligibility rate for housing benefit. We estimate the increase in government expenditure to be in order of 8 per cent (depending on the retention of ring-fencing if HRA surpluses contribute to housing benefit).

Table 2.7
Estimated rent levels with 'historic weighting'

Region	Gross Rent	EMR[1]	implied real rise (%)	EMR[2]	implied real rise (%)
Birmingham	1011	1254	24	911	(10)
Bristol	969	1084	12	1006	4
Glasgow	829	1355	63	1220	47
London	1176	2292	95	1306	11
Newcastle	1046	1193	14	1073	3
Sheffield	1037	1193	15	1073	4

1. EMR[1] = 4% return on 'bottom half' values, with historic weighting and no capital gain.
2. EMR[2] = as EMR[1] with 10% fall in property values.

The present local authority pricing system produces inequity across authorities and can be inefficient within them. Gross rents do not provide an adequate signal to consumers of dwelling quality or management service levels, nor do they lead to efficient use of the housing benefit system. Our proposal for a consistent pricing system would still enable authority control over service price levels on top of a basic rent related to property value. It would lead to a fairer and more efficient use of subsidy (often HRA surpluses) and encourage meaningful competition in the social sector.

The independent rented sector

One of the four main objectives of the 1988 housing legislation was to revitalise what was to become known as the 'independent rented sector'. For housing associations, it was a signal of the new world they were about to enter, free from red tape but open to new risks. For the traditional private rented sector, the new grouping provided relief from the old images of racketeering landlords. At least that was the intention. In reality, there remain at least two distinct sectors, which differ in terms of their *raison d'etre*, their profit seeking status, and their financing systems.

Traditional private renting

The current private rented sector plays at least a dual role. On the one hand, it houses low income households, often elderly, in unfurnished lets; the second and modestly growing component is in up-market usually furnished properties, appealing to young mobile and better-off households. These are generally uncontrolled lettings at or near market rents. Subsidies in the private rental sector varied widely (see Table 2.8); in London and Bristol average gross rents were already at or above market rent levels. In the other regions however 'rent distortion' subsidies in the registered sector often exceeded those in the social rented sector though were significantly lower for unregistered properties. Housing benefit ensured that total subsidies were targeted towards lower income groups but even then London tenants were on average paying net rents which exceeded gross market levels.

Table 2.8
Subsidies in the private rental Sectors[1]

region	registered rents			unregistered rents		
	rent subsidies	HB	all subsidies	rent subsidies	HB	all subsidies
Birmingham	596	186	782	413	103	516
Bristol	-22	404	382	0	124	124
Glasgow	743	276	1019	438	118	556
London	-200	124	-76	-562	115	-447
Newcastle	238	219	557	191	231	422
Sheffield	224	94	418	76	35	111

1. based on a 4 per cent return; on the lower half of capital   values, minus any local capital gain - see Maclennan, Gibb and More, 1991, p.41-45.

For any type of letting, private landlords receive no direct public assistance. Unlike home-owners, landlords are taxed on rental income and on capital gains and, in contrast with the social rented sector, they receive no recurrent subsidies nor capital grants (except improvement grants at less favourable rates); the major source of subsidy is housing benefit within the low income segment. Government recognises that the sector cannot be revived if landlords do not receive an adequate return, and our survey confirms the continued existence of 'unprofitable' lettings. If the sector is to retain its dual role - and we believe this is required - then the financing system must be   tailored to the client group served. Where landlords let to low income households, we believe they should be eligible for capital grant assistance, provided landlords agree to the type of monitoring undergone by housing associations. Where 'up-market' properties are let, landlords should be put on an even footing with other business concerns and with many of their European counterparts, through the introduction of tax concessions, in the form of a depreciation allowance.

The voluntary housing sector

Housing associations today, like councils, provide accommodation for the poorer sections of the population, although they are now encouraged to broaden their scope, as the main providers of new social housing. Housing association stock in Great Britain, at around 650,000 units, represents   3 per cent of the national total, with annual completions in the last 5 years averaging around 26,000 units. Capital expenditure has risen steadily in real terms though not sufficiently to make up for falling local authority investment, and not as rapidly as many believed. Expenditure in England and Wales has been greatly increased for the period 1991 to 1994 though Scotland's programme is barely keeping pace with inflation. Nevertheless, with the addition of private funds, the total programme in GB for 1990/91 is estimated to have reached £1.9bn.

The housing association financing system subsidises tenants differently to council tenants. Prior to the 1988 reforms, all association lettings were subject to Fair Rents set by Rent Officers; thus subsidy was not measured by Housing Association Grant (HAG) but by the extent to which fair rents differed from market rents. Actual gross rents in the survey were relatively uniform across the regions, though Glasgow rents were markedly lower. Market rents and subsidies were estimated in the same way as for the council sector. These are shown in Table 2.9.

Table 2.9
Actual and estimated market rents[1] in the HA sector

	Gross rent	Net rent	EMR[1]	Subsidy[2] (a)	Subsidy[2] (b)	Mean HB payment	Subsidies/ mkt rent (%)
Birm	1045	783	1448	403	665	262	46
Bris	1073	668	1099	36	431	405	39
Glas	828	608	1593	767	985	220	62
Lond	1160	892	1171	17	279	268	24
Newc	1078	603	1208	142	605	475	50
Sheff	1050	716	1068	24	353	329	33

1. Based on 4% return on 'bottom half' values, with local capital gains.
2. Subsidy; a=rent subsidy, b=total subsidy.

Subsidies arising from rent distortions were lower than in the council sector but varied widely across the regions and the main household socio-economic characteristics. The 'fit' between gross rents and dwelling characteristics was poor, with the latter explaining only about 25 per cent of the rent level, adding to criticisms that the fair rent system failed to adequately adjust for variety in dwelling quality, amenity etc. When housing benefit was taken into account, total subsidies ranged from a quarter of market rents in London to almost two-thirds in Glasgow. As would be expected, total subsidies were distributed more fairly according to income.

The revised funding system requires housing associations to set rents for new lettings; in consequence it might be anticipated that relative rent levels within individual associations may bear closer relationship to dwelling characteristics, given that most organisations are adopting rent schemes based on points criteria etc. However, like local authorities, absolute rent levels depend on the overall income which must be raised, and significant variation in rents across associations must be expected.

The period of adjustment to 'new HAG' has been long and drawn out and many problems remain. One of the key considerations is whether the system distributes subsidy efficiently and fairly, and enables genuine choices to be made. We would contend that it does neither, though further research is required to confirm this. The rent setting process may be better carried out by associations themselves than by a disinterested third party, but it is dogged by vague or poorly understood concepts - such as 'affordability', a term that defies unambiguous definition. The discretion given to local committees to define what their neighbours can afford is not in our view a justifiable response on the part of government which has responsibilities to ensure that taxpayers' money is fairly redistributed through tax and subsidy systems. The new HAG system is no better than its predecessor in this regard.

HAG determinations made largely on a scheme-by-scheme basis, and influenced partly by organisational targets and partly by local definitions of affordability, will continue to distort the relationship between gross rents and property values. The dual tenancy system (fair and assured rents) further exacerbates the position. A major concern now centres around the possibilities for rent-pooling. Local authorities have been criticised for this in the past but the pressures to cross-subsidise are obvious. However, government fears loss of control over associations finances and rent levels and has been unable to devise an appropriate mechanism to deal with rent surpluses. One long-term solution lies in the adopting of a rent setting strategy along the lines that we have proposed - to ensure that rent levels are consistently and fairly set and that tenants wishing to exercise choice can look to competitors financed on even footing rather than (dis)advantaged by the vagaries of their respective financing systems. Were such a proposal adopted, then housing associations, local authorities and the social arm of the private rented sector would be eligible for equal grant assistance in return for complying with a range of minimum standards. Some further reforms to the HAG regime would be required, though private finance would still be a necessary supplement to limited public expenditure.

Conclusion

In this chapter we have presented an overview of the housing finance system in the UK, pointing to its most serious weaknesses in terms of design, process and outcome. Recently several other authors have published reform packages, notably Hills (1991b) and the Inquiry into British Housing (1991). For our part, we would urge government to re-think its rent-setting and investment strategies for social renting, and put forward realistic and consistent proposals to support a commercial rented sector.

At the beginning of the chapter, attention was drawn to the relationship between the finance and subsidy system and its impact on the macroeconomy. Along with the longstanding equity arguments about owner occupied tax expenditures, it is for these reasons that we support a re-balancing of tenure- related subsidies in favour of renting, achieved by restructuring the tax regime for owner occupation. In this chapter we have omitted reference to the need to reform the public expenditure planning and control system, which many commentators feel is (at least) an important contributor to disorder in the housing finance system. Space prevents us dealing with it here in more detail but changes are urgently required to the classification of public expenditure the presentational and statistical basis of departmental reports as well as the very definition of subsidy (see Maclennan, Gibb and More, 1991, pp. 34-37).

The other critical omission is the reform of housing benefit. A way must be found to reduce the marginal tax rates faced by recipients and the zero additional cost of higher rents for recipients must be ended: Hills (1991b) proposes a dual taper scheme of housing benefit which would achieve these goals (and be relatively inexpensive).

3 Housing issues and housing policy: Some implications of the study of the Sheffield housing market

Richard Eastall, John Hughes and Roy Wilkinson

Introduction

Sheffield is a low income area and exhibits urban housing problems which are typical of those of Britain as a whole. We shall review the findings of our analysis of the Sheffield housing market and present some proposals for dealing with Sheffield's and Britain's problems. Our proposals will be set in the context of current discussion of housing policy. The principal issues on which we shall concentrate are the shortage of affordable housing of reasonable quality, the unequal distribution of financial assistance from the Government and the difficulties of low income groups in paying for housing. A comprehensive review of issues and discussion of findings is to be found in the final report on the Sheffield study.

Summary of the Sheffield findings

The supply of new housing

Private housebuilding in the Sheffield area has broadly followed recent national trends. There was a slight peak in the number of private sector completions in 1988, followed by a sharp drop in 1989-90. Housebuilders moved up-market in the 1980s to cater for existing owners trading up, rather than building starter homes. The owner-occupied sector made up 54 per cent of Sheffield dwellings in 1990, having been boosted by Right-to-Buy sales throughout the 1980s.

Building by local authorities in the Sheffield area (as in the rest of the country) was severely curtailed during the 1980s, due to declining Housing Investment Programme allocations. The majority of local authority capital spending is now taken up by renovation of existing dwellings, both council and private. The council sector has fallen from 45 per cent of the Sheffield housing stock in 1981 to 36 per cent in 1990, due to Right-to-Buy sales and demolition of dwellings with structural problems. Sheffield City Council has recently undertaken a building programme of 2000 new houses, in partnership with the United Kingdom Housing Trust. Through a deal signed in 1987, this partnership has provided a mixture of renting, shared ownership and low-cost sales, based on a financial arrangement whereby the City Council guaranteed the loans taken out by UKHT.

Building by housing associations in Sheffield increased during the latter part of the 1980s, although the sector still makes up only 2 per cent of the city's housing. The new subsidy system, introduced in 1989, has caused a change in provision away from the inner city and away from rehabilitation of older dwellings towards newly built suburban developments.

The private rented sector continues to decline and now makes up about 8 per cent of Sheffield's housing. In the unfurnished sector the only new investment came from property dealers buying tenanted property for capital gains. In the furnished sector private investment was only possible before deregulation by landlords operating on the margins of, or even outside, the legal framework. There is no evidence of an increase in supply as a result of the deregulation of private renting from the Housing Act, 1988.

Incomes of owners and tenants

There were clear differences between tenure groups in the proportion of adults in employment, as table 3.1 below shows. Eighty one per cent of households in the council sector received no income from full-time employment in 1988/89, due to the high proportions of retired and unemployed people. Amongst private tenants and outright owners there was a higher proportion of people in work, but still a majority of households had nobody in paid employment. Amongst mortgagors, by contrast, only 10 per cent of households do not receive a full-time income.

There were also differences between tenures in household type. In the rented sectors there was a high proportion of single adult households, and particularly single, widowed or divorced women. The majority of households with a mortgage include two adults, married or living as married.

Overall, either the householder or spouse was in paid employment in 53 per cent of households. Thirty four per cent of all households received a state retirement pension. Half of these also received a pension from a former employer. The other main sources of income were income support, invalidity pension, unemployment benefit and widow's pension. Child benefit was received by 26 per cent of households. Interest receipts or dividends were received by 30 per cent of households, most of whom were people in work.

Table 3.2 shows the distribution of net income, after payment of income tax and national insurance, for each tenure. This includes all income received by each housing group from earnings, benefits, pensions, rental income, interest receipts, dividends and contributions from other members of the household (a housing group is defined to be a householder and his/her spouse). Interest receipts or dividends were received by 30 per cent of households, most of whom were people in work. The mean net income for all households was £6,998, while the median was £4,940.

The mean net income of mortgagors was nearly three times that of council tenants. A majority of council tenants, private tenants and outright owners have a total income below £5,000.

For former sitting council tenants who had bought their house over the previous ten years, the mean income was £8,527 and 9 per cent had incomes below £4,000. For other recent house purchasers, the mean income was £11,664, and only 5 per cent had incomes below £4,000. By contrast, 62 per cent of council tenants had incomes below £4,000. The majority of remaining council tenants, therefore, had income levels below nearly all recent housebuyers. This confirms that for many households, especially those who are unemployed, retired or on low wages, house purchase was not an option. During 1988 and 1989, house prices in Sheffield increased sharply, making house purchase even more difficult.

Table 3.1
Household employment status, by tenure, in the Sheffield TTWA

| | owner occupier | | private tenants | council tenants | All |
	mortgagors	outright			
2 full-time employees	26	4	5	2	11
1 full-time employee	64	30	36	17	38
1 part-time employee	3	7	3	5	5
retired	3	44	18	39	26
unemployed / other not in work	4	15	37	36	21
TOTAL	100	100	100	100	100
No of cases	600	314	93	602	1609

Source: JRF Survey Data, 1989.
Note: due to rounding percentages may not sum to 100.

Housing costs and housing assistance

Housing costs are taken here to include rent, rates, water rates, service charges, mortgage payments and endowment payments, but to exclude repairs, furnishings or furniture and the other costs associated with the purchase and maintenance of housing. By housing assistance we mean all those sources of financial help to households in the purchase of their housing services.

Table 3.2
Net housing group annual income by tenure

	mortgagors	outright owners	private tenants	council tenants	all
< £3,000	4%	19%	45%	43%	26%
£3,000-£5,000	6%	32%	24%	35%	25%
£5,000-£10,000	30%	35%	18%	20%	26%
> £10,000	59%	14%	12%	3%	24%
no. of cases	374	204	73	482	1160
mean net income	£11,589%	£6,718%	£4,998%	£4,029%	£6,998

Source: JRF Survey Data, 1989.
Note: percentages may not add up to 100 due to rounding

For mortgagors the major element of housing costs was the mortgage payment, towards which nearly all households received tax relief. The average amount of tax relief was £346 a year, and it was greater for those on higher incomes. Three per cent of mortgagors received help towards their mortgage from the DHSS. All homeowners paid rates and water rates in 1988/89. Nine per cent received housing benefit towards their rates payments.

For tenants, the main elements of housing costs were rent, rates and water rates (the latter two were often included with rent payments). Sixty-eight per cent of tenants received some housing benefit, for all or part of their rent. The average amount was £1,052 a year, for those in receipt. The eligibility of a particular household for housing benefit depends on their income, capital, the age and number of persons in the household, their rent and the size of their accommodation. Housing benefit is targeted predominantly at households on low incomes, although a significant number of tenants with incomes below £5,000 did not receive any. Housing benefit does not help with water rates and since April 1988 it has covered no more than 80 per cent of domestic rates (and latterly community charge).

Table 3.3 below shows the mean amount actually paid by each tenure group towards their housing costs (after receipt of tax relief and housing benefit).

On average, council tenants and outright owners pay about the same, while mortgagors pay over three times as much. There was a considerable variation in housing costs both within and between tenures. Twenty per cent of housing groups (mainly outright owners and low-income tenants) have an annual cost of less than £252, while 20 per cent (mainly mortgagors) pay more than £2,011.

On average, net housing costs tended to rise with income, although not proportionately.

Table 3.3
Mean net annual housing costs, by tenure

	mortgagors	outright owners	private tenants	council tenants	all
cost	£2,393	£675	£1,138	£707	£1,259
no. of cases	323	182	51	454	1033

Source: JRF Survey Data, 1989.

In 1990, after the survey was completed, domestic rates were replaced by the Community Charge in England and Wales. This has increased costs for the majority of tenants and owner occupiers in Sheffield, but produced savings for most of those in the highest income groups.

Table 3.4
Direct assistance by annual gross income[1]

Housing group Gross income	Mortgagor	Outright Owner	Private Tenants	Council Tenants
<£2,400	271	34	1413	979
£2,400–£5,199	189	41	1169	813
£5,200–£7,799	104	3	1156	332
£7,800–£10,399	287	0	196	88
£10,400–£12,999	213	0	513	30
£13,000–£15,599	251	0	0	0
£15,600–£20,799	301	0	40	0
£20,800–£25,999	332	0	0	..
£26,000–£31,199	373	..	..	0
>£31,200	625	0	..	..
All	267	3	908	744
No of cases	368	245	73	500

Table 3.4 shows how direct assistance varied with income within each tenure category. In the case of owner occupiers, mortgagors received on average some £267 per annum of direct assistance and generally, the amount of assistance was related to the level of income. This reflects the fact that the assistance arose from mortgage interest tax relief and those on higher incomes buy more expensive dwellings and take out bigger mortgages. Outright owners, on the other hand, received a negligible amount of assistance; those

with incomes of £5200 per annum or less obtained housing benefit to help pay domestic rates. In the case of tenants, assistance was inversely related to income reflecting the income qualification for receiving housing benefit. The table illustrates the indiscriminate nature of direct assistance to mortgagors when compared to means-tested assistance to tenants.

Table 3.5
Indirect assistance by annual gross income[2]

Housing Group Gross Income	Owner occupier £pa	Council tenant £pa
<£2,400	313	-496
£2,400-£5,199	284	-610
£5,200-£7,799	363	-772
£7,800-£10,399	426	-795
£10,400-£12,999	537	-449
£13,000-£15599	555	-963
£15,600-£20,799	801	-757
£20,800-£25,999	984	-
£26,000-£31,199	1634	-1040
>£31,200	2321	-
All	609	-601
No of cases	503	500

As well as examining direct assistance to households, the Sheffield study also looked at indirect assistance ie the difference between what the household actually pays for its housing and the price it would have to pay in the absence of any state intervention. An accurate measure of indirect assistance needs to estimate notional price in the absence of assistance. For example, the removal of MITR might be expected to decrease the overall price level of housing especially at the cheaper end of the market, since part of the tax relief is capitalised into the market value of dwellings. The difficulties of measuring such effects mean that we have only been able to produce first order estimates of economic subsidy.

The Sheffield study found that indirect assistance tended to benefit owner occupiers more than tenants (table 3.5). The non-taxation of owner occupiers' imputed rental income and real capital gains was estimated to be worth an average of £609 per annum, and was, in fact, more significant than MIRAS. It is also positively correlated with income. In contrast, the study found that indirect assistance to tenants was negative; that is, economic rents were lower than actual rents. In general, the higher the tenant's income, the greater the difference. Hence, both direct and indirect assistance favoured owner occupiers over tenants and both were skewed towards richer owner occupiers.

Difficulties with paying for housing

Survey respondents were asked whether they had had problems finding the money to pay for their housing over the previous five years. The reply was yes for 10 per cent of mortgagors, 20 per cent of private tenants, 26 per cent of council tenants and 29 per cent of Housing Association tenants, although the question is open to different interpretations. The main reasons given for the problem, by both mortgagors and council tenants, were loss of income, increase in costs (interest rate or rent) and loss of job. Table 3.6 shows the incidence of problems by income group for the two main tenures.

Table 3.6
Payment problems, by tenure

Housing Group Income	Mortgagors			Council Tenants		
	Problem	No Problem	% with Problem	Problem	No Problem	% with Problem
£0-£2,400	2	4	33%	28	106	21
£2,400-£5,200	8	18	31%	69	182	28
£5,200-£7,800	7	30	12%	7	17	29
£7,800-£10,400	4	30	12%	7	17	29
£10,400-£13000	9	55	14%	5	11	31
£13,000-£15,600	3	56	5%	2	3	40
£15,600-£20,800	7	61	10%	2	3	40
>£20,800	1	82	1%	0	0	-

For council tenants, the likelihood of having payment difficulties was spread fairly evenly over the income bands, although the absolute number of those with problems was greatest for lower income groups. There were very few mortgagors in the lower income groups, but those mortgagors who were on low incomes were much more likely than other mortgagors to have had difficulties. The difference between the tenure groups is a reflection of the fact that assistance for tenants is targeted on the lower income groups, while for mortgagors it is not. Contrary to popular belief, those who had not bought their dwelling during the previous three years were not more likely to report payment difficulties.

Respondents who had experienced problems with paying were then asked whether they were currently in arrears with their rent or mortgage. Three per cent of all mortgagors, three per cent of private tenants, five per cent of HA tenants and 12 per cent of council tenants reported that they were. However, the latter figure appears to be an under-estimate, since statistics from Sheffield

37

City Council shows that 20 per cent of council tenants had arrears of over £100 in March 1989 (SCC, 1989). More recent local authority statistics show that the problem has got even worse since 1989. Local statistics on the level of mortgage arrears are not available, but nationally the number of mortgagors in arrears has increased since 1989 due to the high level of mortgage interest rates and increasing unemployment.

Unmet housing need

The preceding discussion, because it is based on a survey of householders, does not include those who are in the greatest housing need - that is people who share accommodation with family or friends, live in hostel or temporary accommodation or are actually roofless.

Some information about unmet housing needs is available from local authority waiting list statistics. In the City of Sheffield there were 55,260 households on the waiting lists in 1990, of whom 20,129 were existing council tenants wishing to transfer. The remaining 35,131 households included some home-owners and private tenants, as well as people who were sharing accommodation. Eighteen per cent of households on the waiting list were elderly, 41 per cent were families and 41 per cent were single. The number of lettings to people from the waiting list declined sharply through the 1980s, due to the fall in new building, the need to rehouse those displaced by demolition and an increase in the number of people accepted as homeless. Consequently, the waiting list had grown over the last few years.

Homelessness is the most extreme form of housing need. There had been a five-fold increase in the annual number of households accepted as homeless by Sheffield City Council during the 1980s, to 2095 households in 1990. These figures understate the problem of homelessness, since they do not include "non-priority" homeless people (such as many single adults and childless couples) whom the local authority does not have a statutory duty to house. A recent national study of homelessness concluded:

> 'the immediate reasons why people become homeless are many and varied, but the overriding cause is that people are unable to find or retain housing at rents or prices they can afford and with security of tenure' (Greve and Currie, 1990, p.16).

It is clear that buying a house would not be feasible for the majority of existing Sheffield tenants, as well as for many people without their own accommodation. The majority of such households are either not in work or their earnings are too low to get a mortgage. With the continued decline in the private rented sector and the lack of security for many private tenants, the social rented sector provides the only hope of decent housing for many people in Sheffield. Capital constraints on local authorities combined with cash limits and the new subsidy regime for housing associations have therefore exacerbated the problem of unmet housing need by reducing the supply of new dwellings.

Summary

Mortgage tax relief provided most help to those in the higher income groups, but assisted very few households with low incomes to purchase a house. Private housebuilders targeted output in the 1980s towards the higher income groups who received the greatest assistance towards their housing costs. Mortgagors who become unemployed faced serious problems in paying for their housing. Housing benefit was aimed predominantly at tenants in the lowest income groups, but provided only partial relief to many tenants, and no help at all to some households on low incomes. During the 1980s most rents have increased in real terms. Meanwhile, a series of changes to Housing Benefit restricted eligibility to claim and introduced modifications to the allowances available. These changes contributed to an increase in poverty in Sheffield. Supply in the social rented sector diminished and waiting lists and homelessness increased.
Overall, the current system of housing subsidies has not prevented widespread problems of unmet housing need and unaffordability.

The financial support for housing: some principles

Introduction

A variety of types of government support exist which are aimed at improving the standard and provision of housing. They vary from direct provision of dwellings to direct expenditures such as Housing Benefit and tax expenditure such as mortgagors interest tax relief. These are summarised in table 3.7.

It is to be expected that individual policies will vary in their equity, their efficiency and their effectiveness. In other words an individual policy will favour some households over others, will reallocate resources to obtain differing relative marginal benefits and will be more or less effective in achieving its objective. In order to evaluate individual policies on the basis of these criteria it is first necessary to establish the precise objectives. Why do we need a housing policy in the first place?

The need for a housing policy

In material terms the need for a housing policy and the justification for subsides or some other form of housing assistance, arises from its external effects. Government help and intervention in the housing market is required because people are unable or unwilling (thought their lack of knowledge) to spend enough on housing. Unsatisfactory or inadequate housing leads to (or is at least associated with) all kinds of negative externalities. While an improvement in housing will not on its own break the poverty cycle, it is certainly likely to be an important contributory factor. We have identified the need to increase the access of households on relatively low incomes to housing of a standard which is socially acceptable. This implies a need to reallocate both real and financial resources to help these households. The question becomes, therefore, one of identifying which policy, or set of policies, is to be preferred. In financial terms this can be formulated in terms of which measures provide the most housing, pound for pound. The theory of welfare economics teaches that welfare is maximised where individuals are given the freedom of choice in spending their incomes rather than having their spending tied to particular goods or services. This suggests a possible conflict since those measures which subsidise costs or incomes and give freedom of choice will maximise individual welfare but may not necessarily produce the greatest real increase in housing. The resolution of this potential conflict lies in the evaluation of the importance of the negative externalties to society. If society gains more from dealing with the externality, then there is a justification for pursuing policies which maximise the output of housing.

Types of housing assistance

Financial assistance for housing can be put into three broad categories: price reductions, income increases and direct expenditures to increase production.
Price reductions can be seen as resulting from either a reduction in cost which has the effect of making more housing available, or from an increase in demand, at a given schedule of prices. Whether or not the supply schedule or the demand schedule shifts, the effect is a change in market price. The increase in the quantity supplied and demanded will depend upon the relative responsiveness of supply and demand to changes in price. Irrespective of whether the subsidy is paid to suppliers or demanders the subsidy will normally be shared. Therefore the effect on the intended beneficiary households will be lessened by an amount proportional to the relative price elasticities of supply and demand. Policies to subsidise or to control rents have long been subject to criticism because of the unintended effect they have on the quality and supply of housing.

Table 3.7
Housing policy instruments

EFFECT ON

government action	demand-side	supply side
direct expenditure	cash transfers tied to housing (housing benefit)	subsidies paid to organisations to reduce costs
tax expenditure	direct tax on imputed rent and capital gains[1] mortgage interest tax relief (MITR)(-1983)[1],[2]	mortgage interest tax relief at source (MIRAS) (1983-)[1][2] zero or low rated VAT on housing goods and services. rate rebates
direct[3]		rent controls

1. Tax forgone on imputed rent etc and mortgage interest relief cannot be summed. Interest tax relief is legitimate if imputed rent is taxed, see discussion below.
2. The effects of MITR and MIRAS are identical, see discussion.
3. Note that the category of direct controls has been added for completeness. These controls on rents and land use in effect transfer resources from one private economic agent to another without the government making a direct gain or loss. It is suggested that they have a similar (but not identical) effect to an indirect tax or subsidy.

The effect on demand of a supplement to income either directly or from a tax expenditure, will depend upon the income elasticity of demand. For values of elasticity of unity, the effect will be proportional to the increase in income; for values greater than unity the effect will be more proportional and for values less than unity the effect will be less than proportional. It follows that if, as experience would suggest, the size of income elasticity is directly related to income, then income supplements will have a proportionately greater effect on housing expenditure if paid to upper rather than lower income groups. If income supplements are tied directly to housing the effect on housing expenditure will be as intended but the other items in the household's budget will be affected as the household makes substitutions at the margin to achieve a new equilibrium pattern of expenditure. In terms of welfare economics the new pattern of expenditure will give an inferior level of satisfaction to that which would obtain with complete freedom of choice because of the constraint imposed on housing expenditure. Mortgage interest tax relief can be seen in this category and can be argued to help the upper income groups relative to the lower, resulting in a less efficient as well as a less equitable allocation of housing resources while being less effective in terms of the increased amount of housing which is likely to result.

Conclusions

It appears therefore that policies which aim to maximise consumer's expenditure on housing will result in inferior welfare positions and that policies which maximise welfare will provide less housing for the lower income groups.

The possible resolution to this paradoxical situation lies in the direct provision of housing which is priced (sold or rented) at the free market level. An increase in the total supply of housing will both increase the opportunity for access and, other things being equal, lower the price level or dampen its rate of increase. Thus, capital grants to increase the supply of dwellings to the level defined by need (i.e. the estimated short-fall) should bring total demand and supply into balance. The relative prices at which the dwellings are sold or rented should then allocate them efficiently, since consumers can exercise freedom of choice and therefore choose welfare maximising expenditure patterns. Thus the policy of building more council houses and letting them at economic rents would satisfy the criterion of equity by making access easier for lower income groups, and would at the same time be more efficient and effective.

Recent proposals for reform

Four broad approaches to reform of the housing finance system have been identified (Hills, 1991). These are categorised by the extent to which they resort to the market as a means of allocating housing.

The first category, which Hills calls the 'market-orientated approach', assumes that, left to themselves, markets clear instantaneously and allocate goods and resources in the most efficient way. Hence, rents should be set at market levels and Housing Benefit reformed to eliminate 100 per cent subsidy at the margin. Other distortions such a security of tenure and, perhaps, subsidies to owner occupiers should also be phased out. These obstacles having been removed, the market can function to allocate housing and thus achieve the socially optimal result. Any extra government revenue generated by the removal of the subsidies would be used to finance general tax cuts or benefits increases but would not be tied to housing. Hills argues that such an approach would lead to many households, especially poorer ones, losing considerable sums of money each week.

The second category, according to Hills, advocates responding to 'market signals but with distributional concern'. These analysts accept the validity of the market rationale but wish to avoid the kind of losses which Hills predicts will befall households under the previous proposals. So, while advocating a gradual or controlled move towards market rents and withdrawal of owner occupier subsidies, any extra tax revenue would be used to finance a more extensive system of standardised housing allowances. Hence, subsidy or assistance would be shifted from a tenure basis to an individual basis. However, unlike the first group of reformers, some form of specifically housing related subsidy is central to these proposals. Their main deficiency can be argued to lie in their failure to recognise the entrenched sectional interests which make such 'rational economic' reforms politically infeasible.

In as much as the first two categories of reform can be said to seek 'equality of treatment' between tenures, the pragmatic approach, which Hills labels 'tenure neutrality within political constraints', is consistent with them. It differs however in that it tries to overcome the drawbacks of the modified market school by avoiding the political problems associated with 'attacks' on owner occupation. For instance, an attempt is made to modify the housing finance system so as to allow greater flexibility of movement between housing consumption and housing investment. This would help owner occupiers in difficulties while allowing tenants to invest in housing without requiring ownership rights. Other proposals include taxing owner occupiers' capital gains on final disposal of housing assets (e.g. on death) and national pooling of council rents to achieve parity with owner occupiers' historic costs. This approach could be criticised for being less theoretically robust than the simple or managed market schools (or, indeed, the non-market analysis). Its strength, of course, is in its practicality and political reality.

The fourth approach is described by Hills as 'non-market'. It views the market as an innappropriate mechanism for allocating housing, particularly to low income groups who mainly rent their housing, although it does accept that the market in owner occupied housing should continue. Concern is heavily centred on redressing a perceived unfairness in the way that state subsidy is distributed between owner occupiers and tenants. So, withdrawal of mortgage tax relief is coupled with an extension of Housing Benefit so that it covers both tenants and mortgagors and extends higher up the income scale. The drawback of this approach can be argued to lie in the adoption of criteria for judging what are fair allocations of assistance.

Hills' own proposals include gradual reform of assistance to owner occupiers (such as MITR) while in the rented sector economic rents would be introduced. However, rents would be allowed to rise only to a level which produce a 'broad equivalence' of subsidy between tenants and owner occupiers. Housing Benefit would remain 100 per cent at the margin for low income tenants and be extended to some owner occupiers in financial difficulties. Financial and other tenure distinctions would be blurred to encourage real tenure choice. Greater alignment between cash flows and underlying economic costs would increase efficiency.

Two more recent proposals for reform come from the Bristol study team in the Joseph Rowntree Foundation's housing finance research programme and from the reconvened Duke of Edinburgh's Inquiry.

The Bristol report confined itself to a few broad areas of reform which were largely pragmatic in character. While MITR would be retained, it would be redirected towards first time buyers who would benefit from greater subsidies generally (incorporating Right to Buy discounts). This reiterates proposals made during the debates stimulated by the Housing Policy Review (1977). Taking a 'rational economic' position the Bristol report supported, in theory, the taxation of both capital gains and imputed rent. However, for 'rational political' reasons the latter was dropped. In the rental sectors, private tenancies would be deregulated both for rents (to be set by market forces) and for security of tenure, but minimum standards would apply. council rents would be based on capital values while housing association rents would continue to be subsidised in the short run until pooling able to make them 'affordable'. Housing Benefit would be reformed to reduce the 'taper' and to abolish the 100 per cent marginal subsidy.

The recently completed Duke of Edinburgh's second Inquiry into British Housing advocates the phased, but total, withdrawal of mortgage interest tax relief for owner occupiers. This withdrawal would be cushioned by matching it to reductions in mortgage interest rates which are predicted to occur in the 1990s (it is not clear what would happen if interest rates fell insufficiently or not at all, or if the Government 'missed the boat'). The resultant savings to the Treasury would then be used to finance a broader means-tested housing allowance which would help tenants and owners alike to meet their housing costs. In addition, there would be tax breaks to private landlords to improve their returns while local authority housing departments would become more financially independent and would be able to reinvest more capital and revenue resources into housing. A form of national rent pooling would shift surplus resources from high capital value authorities to lower ones. While the Inquiry report stresses its wish to continue local authorities' provider role, it advocates a pluralistic regime where tenants get a better deal because of the competitive pressure on landlords. The Inquiry's proposals, therefore, attempt to remove the distortion of indiscriminate MITR subsidies to 'successful' owner occupiers and 'failed' tenants but without taxation of imputed rent and/or capital gains, and with much higher rents in the social rented sector it appears unlikely that renting will appear more attractive to those who have the economic ability to exercise genuine choice.

A criticism of most of the foregoing reform proposals, including Hills', is that they concentrate on housing demand at the neglect of supply.

The creation of a level playing field in housing finance, so that tenure neutrality is enhanced, provides only part of the answer to current housing problems. It is also important that any reforms produce an increase in housing supply which can alleviate problems of homelessness and poor housing. Supply-side subsidies will be necessary to achieve this result.

Proposals for reform

Introduction

In this section we outline some proposals for reform in order to achieve a greater supply of affordable rented housing, greater equity between tenants and owners, greater efficiency in housing and tax expenditures and assistance for those in all tenures who have difficulty in paying for their housing.

We are not suggesting a radical overhaul of the current system of housing finance and most of our proposals are not particularly new or innovative. We have tried to suggest incremental reforms which could be implemented in the short term and which go some way towards alleviating the inequities and inefficiencies of the current system.

Owner occupation

The current system of financial support for owner occupation gives most assistance to those in higher income groups, who need it least. It has also failed to prevent widespread problems of mortgage arrears and repossession, especially for mortgagors who lose their jobs or suffer a loss in income.

We would propose that mortgage tax relief should be restricted, in order to tackle the inequity and inefficiency of the current system. There is now widespread agreement, apparently even within the Government, that MITR should be restricted to the basic rate of tax and that the £30,000 limit should be retained indefinitely. We would suggest further reform of MITR, to reduce tax expenditures to higher income groups while retaining it for first time buyers. What form this might take is beyond our present scope but the proposal is in line with those from many commentators.

It is logical that capital gains tax should be extended to housing. This would work in a similar way to taxation of gains on other assets, so there would be a tax-free allowance of £5,000, (£11,000 for married couples) above which real capital gains would be taxed at the owner's marginal income tax rate (25% or 40% currently). There would be roll-over relief, so that proceeds which were invested back into housing would not be taxed. This proposal would act as a disincentive to equity leakage.

In order to assist mortgagors on low incomes housing benefit could be extended to mortgagors. This could perhaps be introduced along similar lines to the current system of DSS assistance for mortgagors on income support, which has safeguards to prevent payment of 'excessive' housing costs. The introduction of shared equity schemes would also allow mortgagors with payment difficulties but not eligible for income support to stay on in their homes, as tenants of a local authority or housing association, to avoid the need for repossessions.

Local authorities and housing associations

It is clear from the Sheffield Study that there is a shortage of rented housing and that a large proportion of the Sheffield population are not able to purchase a house. There is therefore an obvious need for more housebuilding by both local authorities and housing associations in the Sheffield area. The capital controls which currently constrain local authorities would need to be relaxed in order to allow this building to take place. This could be partly achieved by allowing councils to increase their spending of capital receipts. In areas of particular housing need, where capital receipts tend to be lower (such as the City of Sheffield), there would also need to be an increase in credit approvals. As we pointed out above, efforts to increase the supply of housing are likely to be most effective in improving the economic welfare of those households most in need.

There is currently an inconsistency between the subsidy systems for local authorities and housing associations. The former receive subsidy on loan charges, while the latter receive capital grants. There are also very different assumptions about rents and management and maintenance in the two sectors. We have not devised our own proposals for how the subsidy systems might be reformed, but it would seem reasonable to move towards a 'level playing field' within the social rented sector. A possible system has been suggested by Hills (1988b, 1991b).

There have been suggestions that one way of achieving a level playing filed would be for Council rents to move towards market levels. There is disagreement about exactly how market rents should be defined, but there is a widespread belief that they would be higher than the rents currently charged by most local authorities. It is clear that the majority of Sheffield tenants, in both the council and housing association sector, could not afford to pay higher rents. About two thirds are already in receipt of housing benefit and many of the rest are not far above the poverty line. If rents were increased further, the result would be an increase in the cost of housing benefit, an increase in the level of rent arrears and an increase in the number of tenants in the poverty trap. When the actual rental values were taken into account in Sheffield, it can be seen, in table 3.5, that tenants were in fact paying more than the market value and might benefit from a move toward economic rents. However, much depends on the way in which economic or market rents are calculated.

Further increases in actual rents would result in a further and costly deterioration in the position of council tenants in Sheffield. In cases where economic rents may exceed actual rents, a move to economic rents would have the same results. The situation cannot be resolved simply by manipulating rents. The supply of rental housing needs to be increased.

Private landlords

Deregulation on its own has not created a healthy private rented sector, with habitable and affordable rented housing. Whilst the subsidy provided by the Business Expansion Scheme has created net new investment, it is unlikely to have led to more than a temporary increase in supply. Whilst the housing finance field is still tilted against private renting a more appropriate subsidy would be required to attract an enduring flow of investment (Crook et al, 1991)

Property taxation

There have been proposals that the taxation of imputed rental income should be re-introduced. This proposal has little political support in any party, because of widespread unfamiliarity with the concept of an imputed rent. This is somewhat surprising in view of the fact that the domestic rate was in fact a tax on imputed rent which people appeared to have no difficulty in understanding.

It is more realistic to argue for a local property tax as a replacement for the community charge. While the Labour party has advocated a tax on capital values, with rebates for those on low incomes. The Government seems to have now accepted the need for some form of local property tax and is introducing, from April 1993, the Council Tax which is partly based on banded capital values of dwellings.

A property tax accords more closely with the principles of equity and efficiency. A local property tax, under which payments are proportional to the capital value of the property, is to be preferred to the Council Tax, which will result in a much narrower range of payments and lead to inequity of treatment between high and low incomes.

Housing benefit

There have been a number of changes to the housing benefit system during the 1980s, which have removed entitlement from many people altogether, and increased the poverty trap for others. Claimants on family credit now face a 96 per cent marginal tax rate, and the rate is 87 per cent for others. The current system, whereby Housing Benefit claims are referred to the Rent Officer for the determination of a market rent, has created difficulties for many tenants whose benefit is consequently restricted.

We would advocate a reduction in the housing benefit taper, so that it reaches further up the income scale and reduces the marginal tax rate. Housing benefit should also cover mortgage interest payments and 'rates' (the new property tax). We would also support the re-introduction of housing benefit for students. Rent Officers should determine an appropriate market rent level for Housing Benefit purposes before a property is let, so that tenants are aware that Housing Benefit will be restricted before they take on the tenancy.

These proposals would go some way towards tackling the widespread problems of poverty and unaffordability faced by low income tenants and homeowners in Sheffield.

Homelessness

The building of more council houses, the improvement of the housing benefit system and the avoidance of mortgage repossessions would, in due course, reduce the numbers of people made homeless. We would advocate also the widening of the scope of homelessness legislation to include "non-priority" homeless people (mainly single adults). This would give local authorities a duty to assist the increasing number of young, single people sleeping rough in Britain's cities. Housing associations could also be given a duty to accept a certain number of homeless people, especially in areas of housing stress. This, however, is simply a way of coping with the existing problem. In the longer term, more affordable housing and a more stable housing market is required.

Summary

We have described the main findings from our study of housing finance in Sheffield, in particular identifying some inequities and inefficiencies in the current system and have presented our proposals for reform.

Our proposals generally fall within the mainstream of recent reform recommendations. However, the particular housing problems in Sheffield, many of which are prevalent also in northern cities, have given our proposals a distinct emphasis in two respects. First, we have suggested that there should not be a general increase in the level of rents in Sheffield, because of the low income of most tenants. Second, we have concluded that the reform of housing subsidies would not be sufficient to solve the long term problems of housing shortage and urban decay in Sheffield or the rest of Britain. In order to achieve fundamental improvements there is a need for increased capital investment assisted by public supply subsidies, to promote urban renewal and a greater supply of social rented housing.

Notes

1. Direct assistance takes the form of housing benefit for tenants and mortgage interest tax relief (MITR) and housing benefit (for rates) for owner occupiers.

2. Indirect assistance for owner occupiers is the sum of the estimated value of exemption from taxation of both real capital gains and imputed rental income. For tenants it is the estimated value of the difference between economics rents and actual rents.

4 Costs and benefits of housing subsidies in the Newcastle area: A comparison of alternative subsidy definitions across tenure sectors and income distributions

K.G. Willis and S.J. Cameron

Introduction

Subsidies form a major element in housing, perhaps more so than any other sector of the economy, with the exception of agriculture, which takes up a comparable proportion of household expenditure. Subsidies are directed to houses in all tenures with the exception of the uncontrolled private rented market, but even here households may be eligible for a subsidy. Most subsidies are borne by government; although rent control in the private rented sector imposes a cost on landlords who in effect subsidise tenants by being legally able only to charge a proportion of the market rent for the property.

Subsidies were instituted at various points in time, in different tenure sectors. However, many housing subsidies do not accord closely with any notion of efficiency nor equity (Ricketts, 1981). Renovation grants, subsidies towards GIAs and HAAs in the 1970s, can be seen as correcting for market failure in terms of neighbourhood or spillover effects created by prisoner's dilemma situations (Willis, 1980). In such cases subsidies are efficient because they restore market efficiency and produce benefits greater than the costs of the subsidy (Case, 1968). Rent control imposed in 1915 dealt with a particular equity issue: rent increase due to housing shortage as a result of the 1914-18 war, an 'economic rent' (in the true Ricardian sense) transfer from tenant to landlord with no reciprocal housing quality gains. However, many subsidies are not concerned with efficiency nor equity. For example, mortgage interest tax relief disproportionately benefits upper income households; while private rented sector housing, containing a large number of poor people, attracted no housing allowance payments until long after these had been introduced into the local authority sector.

Concepts of subsidy vary, but can be broadly segregated into financial subsidies and economic subsidies. Financial subsidies are largely concerned with public exchequer payments to, or the absence of tax on, housing. Financial subsidies themselves can be sub-divided into two types. First, those which incur a direct payment from the exchequer (e.g. payments to building societies to compensate for loss of interest through building societies giving mortgage interest tax relief at source (MIRAS)). Such direct tax flows are monetary amounts which a household would be normally expected to pay. Second, indirect financial subsidies are those which do not involve exchequer payments to housing actors and agencies, but result in a loss of exchequer revenue because tax principles applied to other consumption and investment goods (e.g. stocks and shares, company cars, etc.) or another tenure sector in housing (e.g. private uncontrolled rented sector, where rent from the property is taxed as well as any capital gains on the value of the premises), are not applied.

Economic subsidies are not concerned with cash flows from government to households nor tax losses as such, but with the more general concept of whether any difference exists between the market value of a house (its economic value or opportunity cost) and the amount actually paid or cost incurred by the household in its occupation of the property.

Because such housing subsidies can distort, along with non-price methods of allocation such as waiting lists using time or non-transferable points, the choices of households together with the amount of housing they consume, economists are also concerned with trying to estimate the benefits that subsidies confer on occupants. If a subsidy to a household is £1000 per year, does the household derive £1000 worth of housing benefits from this subsidy? or fewer benefits? and if less how much less? In other words, if instead of a £1000 subsidy, the household was given a £1000, would it still spend it all on housing? These questions can be explored through the concepts of consumer surplus and equivalent variation.

This chapter seeks to explore some of these financial and economic subsidy issues across different tenures, taking the Newcastle housing market area as an example, and using data from the Newcastle Case Study of the Joseph Rowntree Foundation Housing Finance Research Programme.

Newcastle housing market area

The Newcastle housing market area exhibits similarities to other conurbations in Britain, but there are also notable differences. The Newcastle area has an unusually high level of rented housing compared with the rest of England and Wales: council housing makes up 35 per cent of the total, compared to 23 per cent elsewhere; owner occupation stands at 51 per cent compared to 65 per cent of households elsewhere.

The area covers a wide range of types of housing and location; inner city and suburban private and public housing within the urban 'core' along the Tyne, with a small number of high-class housing areas in the city; mining villages on the North-East Durham and South-East Northumberland coalfields; commuter villages beyond the Green Belt in the rural areas to the north and west. The whole area is characterised by low house prices and rents compared to most other conurbations in the UK.

The region has suffered severe economic decline, especially in shipbuilding and engineering, and through the closure of steel making at Consett. But the area has seen massive programmes in housing renewal, including slum clearance and redevelopment and improvements of older housing, which have produced comparatively good housing standards.

The Newcastle study (Cameron, Nicholson and Willis, 1991) revealed huge differences in the social and economic circumstances between owners and renters. Owners were much more likely to have at least one member of the household in paid employment, and most of those with middle to high incomes were in owner occupied housing.

Renters, especially tenants of local authorities and housing associations, had a very high proportion of households with no- one in employment, through unemployment, old-age or chronic ill-health, and entirely dependent upon state benefits. Local authority and housing association tenants in particular were heavily concentrated in the lowest income groups.

Financial subsidies

The main intention of this paper is to look at economic subsidy and the issues of equity and efficiency in it's distribution. As explained above economic subsidies can be seen as the 'gap' between actual housing payments and notional payments reflecting a market return on the current capital value of the dwelling. Before examining economic subsidies, therefore, it is useful to consider what, in each tenure category, actually produces this gap. Usually discussion of housing subsidies distinguishes the two concepts of subsidy - financial and economic. Financial subsidies as defined above, whether direct or indirect, do not in themselves account by any means for all the difference between actual housing costs and those based on current capital values. There is, in effect, an intermediate element between financial and economic subsidies in each tenure sector. This involves the mechanisms, other than financial subsidy, which reduce the actual cost of housing consumption below it's 'economic' price. These are essentially pricing mechanisms such as housing payment and accounting systems and rent controls. The discussion looks in diagrammatic form at financial subsidies in each tenure, and also at the overall pattern of financial subsidies across

TENURE

Owner Occupation	Local Authority	Private Rented	Housing Association
Mortgage Tax Relief at Source (MIRAS)	Housing Revenue Account Subsidy	Housing Benefit	Housing Association Grant
Non-taxation of Imputed Rent and Capital Gains	Housing Benefit	Improvement Grants to Landlords	Housing benefit
Improvement Grants		Business Expansion Scheme Tax Benefits	
Council House			
Sales Discounts			

Figure 4.1   Main forms of financial subsidy by tenure

tenures. It then examines how, in each tenure, other mechanisms operate to reduce housing costs below market levels and discusses the distribution of these effects and their interaction with financial subsidies in each tenure.

The range of commonly-recognised financial subsidies by tenure sector is shown in Diagram 4.1. Although there is a wide range of financial subsidies in the housing system, the overall pattern which had developed by the early 1990s can be described in quite simple terms. It is dominated by two elements - MIRAS to owner-occupiers and Housing Benefit to renters. Moreover, the key component of change from the recent past is also simple - the decline and virtual elimination during the 1980s of general subsidy to the local authority Housing Revenue Account (HRA) from the Exchequer and from the Community Charge (formally Rates) Fund.

The results, in terms of the distribution of the main financial subsidies across tenures by income groups, is shown for the Newcastle area in Diagram 4.2. It demonstrates a pattern, familiar also from other studies, of what has been called a U-shaped distribution of subsidies (Brownhill et al 1990). Means-tested Housing Benefit is strongly progressive, going mostly to renters in the lowest income groups. MIRAS is strongly regressive, giving the most benefits to those in the highest income groups (This effect will have been reduced but by no means eliminated by the ending of MIRAS on higher band taxation in the 1991 Finance Act). In between, the lower to average income bands have average benefits from financial subsidies which are substantially lower than those at the upper and lower extremes on the income groups.

Housing pricing mechanisms

Owner Occupation

Although the notion of a gap between actual housing payments and notional payments based on current capital value is usually discussed only in relation to the rented sector, the same concept can be applied in owner-occupation. This is because actual housing payments are based on historic costs of purchase rather than current market values. In the Newcastle Case Study, for example, actual average mortgage payments by owner-occupiers were only 50 per cent of payments based on current capital values. Of course, this effect is very unevenly distributed between owner-occupiers, essentially on the basis of length of ownership. Recent market entrants have payments much closer to current value payment levels. Moreover, the difference between recent entrants and long-term owners is greater than implied by housing payments alone in that long-term owners tend to 'climb the housing ladder' to occupy better quality housing. One illustration of this from the Newcastle area is that the average housing payments of owners in detached houses was only 10.7 per cent higher than of owners in terrace

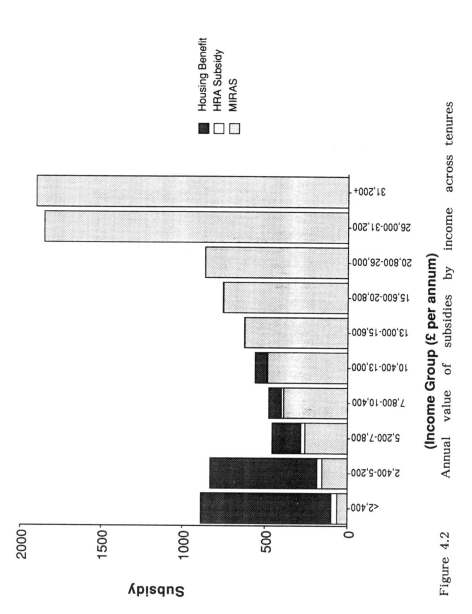

Figure 4.2 Annual value of subsidies by income across tenures

houses, while the market value of detached houses was 115 per cent higher than that of terrace houses.

Mention was made above of the inclusion of non-taxation of imputed rent income and capital gains in the definition of subsidies to owner-occupation. This is sometimes seen as an alternative to MIRAS, treating housing as an investment rather than a consumption good. Alternatively, it is sometimes seen as an additional subsidy. In the context of the foregoing discussion the removal of these two forms of indirect subsidy can be viewed as means by which the value of low historic cost to established owner-occupiers could be reduced and hence their actual housing costs moved nearer to payments based on current capital values.

One element of owner-occupation in which historic cost accounting is not the major source of the gap between actual and current value payments is in the case of dwellings bought by sitting tenants from local authorities, primarily under the 'Right-to-Buy' provisions of the 1980 Housing Act. In this case it is the direct financial subsidy in the form of discounts on the sale of the dwelling - averaging about £8,000 in the Newcastle area. Interestingly, even with these substantial discounts, actual mortgage payments of Right-to-Buy purchasers are closer to market value payments - at 63 per cent - than for other owner-occupiers. This is, of course, because Right-to-Buy owners are, on average, more recent entrants to the market; this difference will diminish over time as the value of low historic costs builds up for Right-to-Buy owners.

Overall, the effects of these subsidies and pricing mechanisms in owner-occupation are cross-cutting in distributive terms. MIRAS is strongly regressive, benefiting those with highest incomes most. The effects of low historic cost relate mainly to length of time in the market. However, neither element is progressive in the sense of benefiting those with lower incomes most.

Local authority

In the case of local authority housing, the difference between actual housing payments and payments based on current market values is attributable to three elements. Two of these are direct subsidies - Housing Benefit and general subsidy to the Housing Revenue Account (the study pre-dated the changes to HRA subsidies in the 1989 Local Government and Housing Act, but in effect these changes simply reinforced the trends discussed below). As has been said, of these two kinds of financial subsidy Housing Benefit has become by far the most important. The third element - as with owner-occupation - is the fact that the housing payments in the local authority sector are determined on a historic cost basis. That is, they reflect the historic debt costs of the housing stock rather than its' current market value. While in the owner-occupied sector this value of historic cost pricing accrues to the individual owner over time, in the case of the local authority

57

sector it is distributed between tenants in each housing authority through rent pooling in the Housing Revenue Account. Thus the value of historic cost pricing is distributed evenly to tenants within each local housing authority. This does not, though, take account of the pricing of individual dwellings. It is clear that in council housing rent relativities do not match the pattern of notional market values. Typically, local authority rent setting systems do take some account of the housing services provided by a dwelling - numbers of bedrooms etc. They do not, though, usually take account of other factors - such as dwelling type and the social status of the neighbourhood - which would create substantial variations in actual market values between dwellings.

In practice, local authorities are not free to utilise the value of low historic cost in rent setting, they are constrained by influences from central government. There is a complex recent history of attempts by central government to influence local authority rent setting (Malpass 1990) culminating most recently in the 1989 Local Government and Housing Act. By the time of our study in 1988 this pressure had reduced to relatively low levels the effects on rents, not only of subsidy to the HRA but also of historic cost pricing through rent pooling. This means that at the time of the study, in the Newcastle area, the gap between actual rents and market value rents in council housing was attributable mainly to Housing Benefit. On the basis of the assumptions used in the Newcastle Case Study, Housing Benefit accounted for about 90 per cent of the gap between actual and market value rents. In terms of distribution this is, of course, heavily concentrated among those council tenants with lower incomes.

Private renting

The Newcastle Case Study took place before the implementation of the 1988 Housing Act, and the analysis of data from tenants in the private rented sector distinguished between a controlled section with registered rents at Fair Rent levels, and an uncontrolled section with rents simply agreed between landlord and tenant.

In the uncontrolled sector rents are, therefore, at 'market levels and the only element of subsidy is Housing Benefit. This does not necessarily mean that market rents determined by agreement between landlord and tenant are the same as notional market rents based on a market return on the capital value of the dwelling. In particular, allowance may be made for the possible additional returns to landlords from real house price increases, and the importance of potential capital gains to landlords was reflected in the small survey of landlords in the Newcastle Case Study, as it has been in other studies (Crook & Martin, 1986). Nevertheless, in the case of the Newcastle area in the late 1980s average actual rents in the uncontrolled market sector were very close to the estimated capital value rents, although there were wide variations in individual rent levels.

58

In the case of the controlled sector, rent control constitutes a subsidy from landlords to tenants which can reduce the actual cost of renting below market value levels. However, the analysis of data on this sector in the Newcastle Case Study suggested that the gap between actual rent levels and notional market values was actually less than the average value of Housing Benefit to tenants. This implies that, using our estimation of market values, subsidies from landlords were negative; that is actual gross rents exceeded notional market rents.

The conclusion to be drawn from this in the private rented sector, as in the local authority sector, is that the gap between actual rent payments and market value rents is attributable to Housing benefit, and hence was concentrated among those tenants with low incomes.

Housing association

The housing association sector provides an interesting contrast to the other rented sectors in retaining a significant element of financial subsidy to dwellings in addition to Housing Benefit - that is Housing Association Grant (HAG). Placing this within the context of the foregoing discussion, the necessity for HAG to continue to play an important role can perhaps be seen as a result of the recent creation (post 1974) of much of the housing association sector. As a result, in comparison with other sectors and especially with council housing, the ability to utilise low historic cost has been limited. In a sense the availability of HAG has filled the role of rent pooling (although recently the reduced levels of HAG available under the 1988 Housing Act have led some housing associations to consider the introduction of rent pooling).

In the analysis of the Newcastle Case Study it did not prove possible to identify the value of HAG to housing association tenants in the survey. Nevertheless, it seems clear from the results that, for the housing association sector too, it is Housing Benefit which constitutes the most significant element of economic subsidy.

Economic subsidies

Market value and actual payment

One definition of subsidy is the difference between actual payments per period for occupancy per housing unit and the opportunity cost (or market value) of that unit. In tenures such as controlled private rented, local authority and housing association, property is let at below market price either through force of law or voluntary choice.

$$\text{Subsidy} = P_m Q_m - P_m Q_c$$

where PcQc = controlled price (Pc) of the quantity of housing consumed (Qc). PmQc = market price (Pm) of the controlled unit (Qc).

Owner occupiers fit uncomfortably into this framework. As has been illustrated, owner occupiers' mortgage repayments are typically less than the annuitised market value of their property, as a result of inflation over time (arguably, so too are local authority tenants' rents, also as a result of inflation and historic cost accounting). However, owner occupiers themselves bear the opportunity cost of the difference between market value and mortgage loan, since they are both tenant and landlord.

Consumer surplus measure of subsidy benefit

Although the difference between market value and actual payment is intuitively simple and represents the cost of the subsidy to the landlord, it is not an adequate measure of the benefit of the subsidy to the tenant. Some form of control implies elements of non-price rationing, e.g. waiting time, points or eligibility criteria, or difficulty in moving between housing units. Because of this, households may consume 'off their demand' curve. Thus it is important to estimate the demand for or willingness-to-pay (WTP) by households in the absence of controls. Households may not be willing to pay the market price the property would rent for in the absence of subsidies/controls i.e. the benefit they derive may be less than the reduction in rent.

The methodology for this evaluation follows the work of Olsen (1972), Neary and Roberts (1980), Schwab (1985) and Malpezzi et al (1990). All of these authors present a basically similar methodology for calculating the benefits of price control or in-kind programmes such as public housing, which restrict the consumption of goods such as housing to specified levels at subsidised prices determined by government. It can be shown that if the price elasticity is constant, the benefit of a housing programme can be written as;

$$\text{benefit} = (1/Q_m)^{1/b} (b/b+1)[Q_c^{(b+1)/b} - Q_m^{(b+1)/b}] + P_mQ_m - P_cQ_c$$

where

benefit = cash equivalent value, a measure of change in consumer's surplus
PcQc = rent currently paid for the current controlled unit
PmQc = rent that the current unit would rent for in the absence of controls
PmQm = rent that a household would pay if they were at their equilibrium demand at market prices
b = price elasticity of demand for housing, where b not equal to -1.

60

The estimation of this model requires data on the above four pieces of information. Actual payments (PcQc) by each household for their subsidised dwelling unit can be derived from the JRF random sample survey in Newcastle. More difficult to specify is the without control situation. There is no truly uncontrolled housing sector in Britain which could be taken as a reference point against which to estimate subsidies in other sectors or tenure groups. The uncontrolled private rented sector probably comes closest to this counter- factual position. But even this sector is subject to taxation. Moreover, the small number of these observations in the JRF sample did not permit its use as a comparative base. Thus, this paper adopts the owner occupier sector as the base against which to measure subsidies in other housing sectors, namely local authority (LA) housing, controlled private rented (PR), and housing association (HA) properties. Thus, while it does not document the absolute size of subsidies across tenures, it does document relative subsidy changes between tenures, and hence throws light on the concept of and extent to which tenure neutrality is present in subsidy provision.

Since the JRF study did not ascertain the market value of owner occupied property in the sample, this was derived by a hedonic price method based on 3648 mortgage applications to the Halifax Building Society in the Newcastle area in 1988. The precise hedonic model can be found in Nicholson and Willis (1991a). This model simulated market house prices in the Halifax data set quite accurately, and with the similarity of housing structure between the Halifax and JRF samples, including controlled sectors within the JRF sample, suggested that the estimate of rents in the absence of controls (PmQc) was relatively robust. Table 4.1 summarises the results by income quartile.

The hedonic price index produced above was used to estimate the market value of the dwellings in the owner-occupier sector of the JRF data. The estimates of market value were then used as the dependent variable in a housing demand model, to assess demand in the uncontrolled sector of the market in the JRF sample. The coefficients from this demand model were then used to estimate the demand for housing in the controlled sectors in the absence of controls (PmQm). Table 4.1 again shows these estimates by sector and income quartile.

Work by Rosenthal (1989) and other indicate a price elasticity of demand between -0.5 and -0.6. Results under these two headings in Table 4.1 show the benefits of housing subsidies and rent control to tenants.

Table 4.1
Costs and benefits of rent control

1988 prices	(£)GG	PcQc	PmQc	PmQm	Cost	ben1	ben2	ben3
					(PmQc-PcQc)	b=-1	b=-.5	b=-.6
L.A.	Q1	168	1216	1641	1048	981	899	929
	median	550	1377	1759	827	778	721	741
	Q3	1350	1602	2144	252	169	69	104
	mean	751	1411	1858	660	596	518	546
H.A.	Q1	384	994	1647	610	431	181	274
	median	1040	1207	1733	167	66	-62	-16
	Q3	1425	1423	2111	-2	-147	-335	-266
	mean	989	1216	1854	227	83	-108	-38
PR(cont)	Q1	746	1040	1575	294	175	19	76
	median	988	1184	1700	196	97	-29	17
	Q3	1220	1436	2169	216	54	-158	-81
	mean	1065	1398	1847	333	268	189	217

Estimates of costs and benefits were produced using both means and medians. Median results provide the most representative picture, and imply a benefit to tenants of between £721 and £741 for LA tenants, and -£29 to £17 for PR's. HA tenants suffered a cost of between £16 and £62 p.a.. There was a cost to the landlords as a result of rent control of a median of £827 p.a. for LA's; £196 p.a. for PR's; and £167 p.a. for HA landlords. Thus, LA tenants receive by far the greatest benefit from rent control and LA landlords the highest cost.

A number of conclusions can be drawn from table 4.1. First, (median) tenants pay between 40 per cent (LA) and 86 per cent (HA) of the market rent for the unit. Second, the cost to the landlord of the median renter as a result of rent control is £827 for LA, £167 for HA and £196 for controlled PR per annum. Third, the transfer efficiency for the median renter is the ratio of benefit to cost. The efficiency level is high for LA median tenants at 87 per cent, but much less for other sectors. Fourth, tenants in the upper quartiles lose from controls and a 'take it or leave it' allocation policy: there is strong evidence of a fall in the benefits accruing as tenant income rises.

Equivalent variation

The Hicksian equivalent variation is an unrestricted cash grant that would be as satisfactory to the recipient as its in-kind transfer. This definition of subsidy is the amount of money a household requires if the in-kind transfer did not happen to make the household as well off as if it did. This is a much more difficult concept to work with, since it requires utility to be held constant while income varies. (Such problems do not affect the notion of Marshallian consumer surplus, which simply traces out a quantity price relationship).

The Hicksian equivalent variation has been modelled by DeSalvo (1971, 1975), Olsen and Barton (1983) and DeBorger (1985) amongst others, using either a Cobb-Douglas or a Stone-Geary utility function. Using a Stone-Geary utility function, Nicholson and Willis (1991b) found equivalent variation measure of the benefits of controlled rents on and subsidies to LA, HA and controlled PR tenants to be much smaller than the Marshallian consumer surplus estimates.

This partly reflects the high proportion of income spent on housing (on average HA tenants spent 22 per cent of their net income on rent; LA tenants 15 per cent; and controlled PR tenants 18 per cent), and the income elasticity of demand for housing in the Newcastle area. But it also probably partly reflects the functional forms employed in the models, where there is no guidance in theory as to what the functional form should be nor at what values the coefficients in the models should be set, and where choice on grounds of statistical significance may not be entirely appropriate.

Conclusions

This paper has taken as it's starting point the conventional distinction made in housing between financial and economic subsidy. However, the discussion does not go on to suggest that these two concepts of subsidy are necessarily opposed and irreconcilable. Instead they are used together to examine the distributive effects of subsidy in a particular situation, the Newcastle area in the late 1980s. This involves an examination of how in each sector financial subsides and pricing mechanisms combine to produce the gap between actual payments and those based on current market values which constitute our definition of economic subsidy. It also involves an analysis of the distributive efficiency of economic subsidies in renting.

The analysis of the distribution of economic subsidies to renters revealed three main features: Council tenants gained more than other renters. The distribution of benefits in all tenures was progressive; low income tenants gained most, and in the case of housing association and private tenants there were negative subsidies for higher earners. There was relatively little loss in transfer efficiency, even in the council sector the cost of subsidies was little higher than the benefits to recipients.

The analysis of the combined effects of financial subsidies and pricing mechanisms in each tenure throws light on the reasons for these findings on the distributive efficiency of economic subsidies to renters. The relative advantage of council tenants is perhaps attributable mainly to the residual benefits of historic cost accounting through rent pooling. However, the main feature in all rented sectors is that the most important element of the gap between actual and notional market rents was Housing Benefit - strongly targeted to lower income groups and therefore highly efficient in distributive terms.

Our study immediately preceding the implementation of the Acts of 1988 and 1989, which fundamentally reorganised the rent systems in all tenures. These Acts were predicated on the assumption that existing renting systems were highly inefficient and wasteful, and needed to be reorganised on a market basis. In the Newcastle case this assumption is not borne out by this study. Already the main element of economic subsidy to renters was highly-targeted Housing Benefit. This stands in sharp contrast to the regressive and inefficient pattern of subsidy and pricing in owner-occupation.

Finally, it could be claimed that these conclusions are based on the use of a particular set of derived capital values - using building society sales data - and that different derived values would produce different results. This is true, but then any application of the concept of market value rents to the rented sector will involve deriving and using artificial notional market values.

Part Two
THE INDEPENDENT RENTED SECTOR

5 Reviving the private rented sector?

Tony Crook and Peter Kemp

Introduction

The privately rented sector is now firmly on the housing policy agenda. After years of relative neglect, concern about what to do with the sector and how it might be revived has become an important policy issue.

The Conservative Government, for example, passed a number of measures in 1988, aimed at creating a revival of investment in private housing to let. But while it might have been expected that the Conservative Government should seek to revive private renting, the Labour Party is also developing proposals with this objective. Again, the *Second Report of the Inquiry into British Housing* (IBH, 1991), like the earlier *Report* (IBH, 1985) put forward a package of proposals aimed at creating a more efficient and effective system of housing finance and provision, including instruments aimed at encouraging new investment in private housing to let.

In this paper we draw on Rowntree funded research by Crook, Kemp, Anderson and Bowman (Crook et al, 1991) into the first two years (1988/89 and 1989/90) of the Business Expansion Scheme [BES] to shed light on what is required to revive the privately rented sector in Britain. In successive sections of the paper we discuss what a revival of private renting might mean, outline the Government's approach, summarise briefly the findings of the BES research, and examine a number of proposals that were put forward during 1991 to revive the privately rented sector.

What revival might mean

The privately rented sector [PRS] has been undergoing net disinvestment for much of this century. Most of this decline has been concentrated in the unfurnished subsector, reflecting an important shift in the range of household types which rent their home from a private landlord. Instead of being the main housing tenure, accommodating most household types, the PRS has become increasingly specialised. By 1989 a quarter of private renters were living in accommodation that was tied to their job or business, a quarter were living in furnished accommodation and only one half were renting their accommodation on an unfurnished basis. The ratio of furnished to unfurnished lettings changed from 1:4 in 1971 to 1:2 in 1989. Increasingly, the PRS is becoming less geared towards providing long term accommodation and more towards short term lettings and immediate access housing (Kemp, 1988a).

The reasons for this long decline of the PRS are complex and their relative importance is much debated (cf Nevitt, 1966; Minford et al, 1987; Hamnett & Randolph, 1988). There is considerable agreement, however, that the housing finance system has had an important negative effect of the sector, shifting both supply and demand away from private renting (Nevitt, 1966; HCEC, 1982; Hills, 1991).

This decline has brought with it an array of problems, including low rates of return, insecurity of tenure, poor stock condition, and problems of access in a context of excess demand. The ownership of privately rented housing is for the most part fragmented, small scale and in the hands of individuals rather than property companies, while much of it is owned by organisations letting to their employees. It is in the PRS that many of the worst housing problems are concentrated (DoE, 1977; HCEC, 1982; Whitehead & Kleinman, 1986; Kemp, 1988a).

Although there is a concern about how to improve conditions in the existing sector and manage the process of decline (see Kemp, 1988a), much of the recent debate has been focused on how to bring 'new model landlords' and new stock into private residential letting. In a sense this is an acknowledgement of the intractable nature of the problems of the existing PRS and reflects a belief that it is more effective to target resources on new supply and new investors and thereby to create a more modern form of private renting than largely exists at present.

While there is a growing concern to breath new life into the PRS, there seems to be little belief that the sector can or should be revived to anything like its former size or even to a scale comparable to that which exists in many other countries (on which, see Harloe, 1985; Maclennan, 1988). Instead, much of the debate has assumed that home ownership will remain as the tenure of the majority of the population and that a sizeable minority will wish or need to rent from social housing landlords such as local authorities and housing associations. The aim has rather been about halting the decline of the PRS and, at best, achieving a marginal increase in its size and enabling it to more adequately meet the needs of certain groups of household, such as job movers, young adults and others in need of immediate access or short term accommodation (for example, Maclennan, 1982; Boviard et al, 1985; DoE, 1987; Kemp, 1988a).

In order to achieve even this rather limited revival of private renting, many commentators have accepted that some kind of financial assistance to private landlords is necessary (for example, HCEC, 1982; Kemp, 1988). Much of the debate has been about what form this subsidy might take and what, if any, conditions should be attached to its receipt.

Although subsidy in the form of the Business Expansion Scheme has been introduced, it is only intended as a short term expedient.

The question remains as to whether, like the BES, such subsidy should in fact be time limited and aimed at giving new investment in the PRS a 'kickstart'; or instead be part of the more permanent array of policy instruments in the housing system and aimed at closing the gap between what landlords require in rental income and what private tenants can afford to pay. As we shall see, the Conservative Government takes the former rather than the latter view.

The Conservative approach

The Housing Act 1980 introduced a range of measures aimed at encouraging private letting but these had relatively little effect (see Crook, 1986; Kemp, 1988a). Indeed, during the 1980s the PRS declined in size by one third.

Following its re-election for a third term of office in 1987, the Conservative Government set about creating a more market oriented and pluralist system of rented housing provision (see Kemp, 1990). It's approach to reviving the PRS has been as follows. First, the Housing Act 1988 deregulated new private lettings. Existing lettings - those entered into before 2 January 1989 in Scotland and 15 January 1989 in England and Wales - remained largely unaffected. With some exceptions (such as holiday lets) all new lettings were to be either assured tenancies or assured shorthold tenancies (short assured tenancies in Scotland), with the rents set by the market.

Second, the Business Expansion Scheme was extended by the Finance Act 1988 to include assured tenancies as a qualifying trade. This scheme - which we describe in more detail in the next section - provides investors in BES companies with substantial tax relief. The aim of extending the scheme in this way was to give a 'kickstart' to new investment in the PRS. It was hoped that the generous tax relief provided by the BES would overcome investor concern about the risks of investing in housing to let and thereby demonstrate that attractive returns were once again possible in this sector of the market economy. The scheme will cease to apply to assured tenancies at the end of 1993, by which time the Government hopes that the demonstration project will have worked and investment will thereafter flow into the sector without the benefit of tax relief (Crook, et al, 1991).

It is important to note that the Government's approach is underpinned by a belief that, in the long run, deregulation will be sufficient to revive the PRS; but that in the short run the fiscal equivalent of a blood transfusion is necessary only to get the patient back on its feet. This follows from their faith in the market and the belief that restrictive legislation is central to the continuing decline of private renting; and that by 'setting the market' free, the market can, and in fact will, work without the need for a permanent life support subsidy within the existing housing finance framework.

The business expansion scheme

Instead of devising an incentive scheme specifically designed to attract investment into the newly deregulated sector, the government amended the rules of the BES in 1988 to make assured tenancies a qualifying activity. Originally, rented property was excluded from the BES.

The scheme was set up in 1983 to assist new businesses seeking to raise capital. Individual investors get income tax relief in the year they buy shares on the money invested in companies raising funds under the BES. If a shareholder retains the shares for at least five years, no capital gains tax is paid on chargeable gains realised by any subsequent sale of the shares. The Government thought that this generous tax relief was justified because of the significant risk of company failure amongst new businesses (Mason et al, 1988).

Crook et al estimated that, during the first two years, £544m was raised either by public share issues or by private placings and that almost 10,000 properties would be acquired from these funds. These properties will have been provided at significant cost to the Government. They estimated the net tax expenditure involved over the first five years of BES assured tenancy companies by calculating both the tax foregone by the Government and the taxes it receives as a result of the companies coming into existence.

The detailed assumptions used in calculating the net expenditure (for example, about shareholders' income tax rates) are set out in their book (Crook et al, 1991). The best estimate of the net tax cost of each property acquired was £31,000. This assumes that the company keeps trading at the end of four years. If it is wound up after first selling the properties, the cost is less (£25,000) because of the corporation taxes paid on chargeable capital gains. These estimates were arrived at by calculating the total net tax expenditures arising from funds raised in the second year of BES assured tenancies (1989/90) and averaging this amongst the total properties to be acquired from these funds. The second year provides a more accurate measure than the first because of the exceptional level of tax relief available in the latter.

It is important to stress that the *total* net tax expenditure is independent of the cost of the properties provided. Although the *average* per property does depend on property prices (since cheaper property enables companies to acquire more for a given sum subscribed in shares), the total depends mainly on shareholders' tax rates. It is also important to stress that part of the tax expenditure is 'lost' to housing since some of the funds raised are used to pay for the issue costs involved in selling shares. These costs are significant (6 per cent of funds raised were used to pay for issue costs) and arise from the expenses incurred when a large number of companies attempt to raise funds from a large number of individuals for a complex tax shelter.

In its first two years, the BES stimulated a supply of new and higher standard rented housing in locations where private renting was not usually found and which had been let to a wide range of highly satisfied tenants including, distinctively, professional and managerial job movers. Just over one half of BES tenants said they found it easy or very easy to afford the rent (Crook et al, 1991).

The evidence suggests that this new supply would not have happened without the subsidy provided by BES. In other words, the BES has resulted in an additional supply of private rented housing that would not otherwise have been created. Company directors said that they could not have raised money for private renting without this or some other subsidy. Whilst deregulation had been a necessary condition, it was not, of itself, sufficient (Crook et al, 1991).

This evidence on the short run impact is, however, necessarily partial. We do not know for certain if BES displaced investment that shareholders would have put into the non subsidised private rented sector nor if BES diverted tenant demand from the non subsidised sector. It is possible that the BES may have crowded out the unsubsidised sector, for BES landlords can, with the benefit of their subsidies, undercut the rents that other landlords need to charge. Moreover, as Whitehead (1991) has pointed out, whilst BES may have raised additional finance for private renting, it has not necessarily created net new investment in the housing stock, but may merely have kept some builders in business. Interviews with BES company directors suggested that the scheme has bought additional finance into private rented housing and that it is still difficult to raise non subsidised investment in the deregulated market (Crook et al, 1991).

It is premature to make a definitive assessment of the long term impact of BES. This cannot be done until the companies have been running for five years, when the initial shareholders will want to sell their shares. Much of the initial commentary on BES assured tenancies assumed that there would not be a long term future; that like other new landlords who have come into private renting in the recent past (see Crook & Martin, 1988), BES landlords would soon get out taking their capital gains with them. It was thought, therefore, that companies would invest to maximise capital gains and would select tenants whose mobility would 'guarantee' vacant possession after five years when the properties would be sold into owner occupation, the company wound up and the net of corporation tax proceeds distributed to shareholders.

While companies have generally invested so as to maximise capital appreciation, they have not tended to let to very short stay tenants. In fact, many companies were anxious to have tenants who did not move out too soon, since this increased voids and other management costs associated with rapid turnover. Nonetheless, most companies did not want very long term tenants either since this would make it difficult to wind up the company if it proved impossible to make competitive returns from renting rather than from capital gains. Companies assumed, in making this judgement, that the value of sitting tenant property would be a lot less than its value with vacant possession, even in a deregulated market. Thus sales of tenanted property to another landlord would not be as financially attractive as sales of vacant property (Crook et al, 1991).

The preliminary evidence is that the long term impact is likely to be negligible. Most companies did not think they had a long term future. Although many would like to stay in business providing houses to let - albeit recognising the difficulty they would have in organising a market for their shares to allow initial shareholders to exit - a lot thought that, ultimately, they would sell their properties into owner occupation and wind up the company. Moreover, few of them thought they could raise funds without subsidy under the current housing finance system because rents did not give a competitive return (Crook et al, 1991). This point is illustrated by the figures in Tables 5.1 and 5.2.

Table 5.1
Prices paid for properties and weekly rents (respondent and partners) by country and region

	average price paid by BES company	weekly rent fully furnished	unfurnished	all (inc partly furnished)
Scotland	£34,000	£69	£73	£65
North & Midlands England	£37,000	£55	£47	£50
London	£95,000	£99	£104	£99
Rest of Southern England	£65,000	£81	£73	£77
Britain	£53,000	£77	£56	£67

Source: Crook et al (1991)

Table 5.2 shows that gross returns were nearly 8 per cent in Britain as a whole but that net returns were under 5 per cent.

Although gross returns from fully furnished lettings were greater at 10 per cent, compared with 6 per cent for unfurnished lettings, the net returns were more similar because of the higher costs involved in furnished lettings (it is possible that the prices paid for properties let furnished and unfurnished are different but we do not have the information to confirm or deny this).

Table 5.2 also shows some significant regional variations with higher gross returns being earned in Scotland (especially) and in Northern England than elsewhere, a reflection of the lower property prices as much as of the rents obtainable. Although rents were at their highest in London the high property prices there resulted in returns which were lower than in much of the rest of Britain. Moreover, the returns noted in Table 5.2 are probably too high since they do not allow for the 'discounts' achieved on the prices of the properties acquired.

Table 5.2
Estimated rates of return (1), excluding capital gain, from BES assured tenancies by country and region in 1990

	unfurnished		furnished		all lettings (inc partly furnished)	
	gross(2)	net(3)	gross	net	gross	net
Scotland	12.2	9.5	11.6	5.6	11.0	6.7
North & Midlands England	6.8	4.1	9.3	3.6	7.7	4.0
London	5.7	4.1	8.3	5.2	7.8	5.5
Rest of Southern & SW England	5.8	4.2	7.4	3.9	6.8	4.2
Britain	5.7	3.7	9.7	5.3	7.7	4.6

1. Returns calculated as annual rents as per cent of acquisition price (average rents per region as per cent of average acquisition price per region).

2. Gross rents are calculated as the total rent paid by the whole household and allow for rents paid by all households in multi-household properties.

3. Net rents are the gross rents with deductions for: voids (4% unfurnished, 10% furnished); management and maintenance costs (Housing Association allowances, allowing for regional variations and differences in maintenance between new build and rehabilitation); building depreciation, allowing 8 per cent pa for new build and 1 per cent for rehabilitation on 80 per cent of acquisition price, the latter to allow for the value of land); and an annual allowance for the depreciation of furniture (based on prospectus data and writing its cost down to 1/3 over five years).

These returns from rents were, according to company directors, insufficient to attract long term finance In their view tax breaks or some other subsidy were needed to make such returns attractive. In the next section we examine whether such subsidy is appropriate and the form it might take.

Appropriate subsidies for the private rented sector

The BES has had an important impact, albeit at a considerable cost in tax foregone. It has produced the first significant wave of new investment in the PRS since the second world war (Crook, et al, 1991). In doing so it has introduced investors and the venture capital industry to residential property as an investment. And it has helped to put the question of appropriate subsidy for the PRS onto the policy agenda.

Yet the evidence suggests that the BES is unlikely to provide a 'kickstart' to an enduring flow of unsubsidised investment in the PRS. That is to say, strictly as a demonstration project, the BES is likely to fail. This is because the PRS requires not a temporary subsidy to act as a demonstration project but rather a long term subsidy to close the gap between what private tenants can afford to pay and the rate of return that landlords require in order to let accommodation rather than invest their money elsewhere. A more permanent subsidy arrangement is required rather than a 'kickstart'' if the PRS is to be revived.

This is particularly necessary because of the lack of a 'level playing field' between renting and owner occupation. A number of studies (Milner Holland, 1964; Nevitt, 1966; HCEC; 1982; Whitehead & Kleinman, 1988; Hills, 1991) have shown that the housing finance system in Britain disfavours the provision of private housing to let. The extensive tax reliefs given to owner occupiers shift demand from private renting to home ownership. They help to create the gap between sitting tenant and vacant possession house prices and give landlords an incentive to sell their property to owner occupiers rather than relet it to tenants.

Thus in the absence of a wider reform of housing finance, a subsidy is required if the PRS is to be able to provide habitable, secure and affordable housing on a commercially viable basis (Crook, et al, 1991). But even so, the BES as presently structured is not necessarily the best vehicle for achieving that objective. This is because the tax relief provided by the BES gives investors an incentive to disinvest after 5 years rather than keep their money in the company. Investors are exempt from paying tax on the money they have invested in the scheme and on capital gains but not on the dividends they may receive. This gives them an incentive to view the BES as a short term tax shelter for achieving capital gains rather than a long term scheme which is attractive for the rental income it provides (Crook et al, 1991).

During 1991 a number of reports were published which made recommendations for providing more suitable subsidies for the PRS than the BES. In the remainder of this section we review proposals by (1) the Inquiry into British Housing, (2) John Hills, (3)

Maclennan, Gibb and More, and (4) Crook, Kemp, Anderson and Bowman. We review these proposals in relation to what we see as the four main issues confronting the design of an appropriate subsidy regime for the PRS. These are:

- what roles is the PRS best placed to perform, ie, who would be most appropriately housed in the PRS in the future?
- what rate of return is required to provide housing for such groups?
- what level of subsidy is required to ensure that rate of return and what form should the subsidy take?
- what conditions, if any, should be attached to the receipt of such subsidy?

We discuss each of these four issues in turn. Table 5.3 attempts to summarise the main approach of each of these authors to these four issues.

It is important to note that while Crook et al's proposals were aimed at developing a more appropriate policy instrument than the BES for the private rented sector, the three other sets of proposals considered here had a much broader remit; they were concerned with housing finance more generally. As a result, they did not necessarily address in detail the four issues which we have identified for discussion here.

Tenants

Generally speaking, much of the recent discussion about creating an acceptable subsidy regime as part of a new policy towards the PRS has been addressed to new lettings. It has largely been accepted that existing tenants - many of them elderly, long term, low income tenants in unfurnished accommodation - should not have their tenancy (rent and security of tenure) regime substantially modified. Rather than introduce a package of deregulation and subsidy for existing lettings, it is felt that it would be better to aim for a 'managed decline', which might include a housing association rehabilitation 'buy out' strategy in inner city areas (Maclennan, 1988).

Discussion about reforming the PRS has therefore largely centred on the types of tenant for whom a new model PRS is best able to cater. *The Second Report of the Inquiry into British Housing* (hereafter IBH) put forward proposals for rent regulation and subsidies which were to be restricted to new lettings (including re-lettings of unfurnished accommodation below a certain capital value). The tax subsidies proposed in the Report were intended to help give investors an economic return in a context of rent regulation in the form of capital value rents of 4 per cent.

Table 5.3

Summary of alternative policy proposals

proposal	target market	returns required	subsidy	conditions of subsidy			exclusion from subsidy/controls		
				rent control	tenancy	landlord approved	existing lets	top of market	other
IBH	young and mobile	7%–8% net of expenses	either harmonise with owner occupiers (a) tax relief on net income and on real capital gains to individuals & companies or (b) 100% capital allowance in year 1	yes, 4% net of expenses on capital value	yes, assured and assured shorthold	yes	yes	yes	furnished lettings
Hills	those needing immediate access/ making short moves	5% net of expenses	depreciation allowances to create equivalence with other business	yes, limit to 5% on capital values	-	yes	-	yes	-

Table 5.3 (continued)
Summary of alternative policy proposals contd...

proposal	target market	returns required	subsidy	conditions of subsidy			exclusion from subsidy/ controls		
				rent control	tenancy	landlord approved	existing lets	top of market	other
Maclennan et al	mobility needs of younger households & others at or greater than average incomes	not discussed accept that 4% net is inadequate (see text)	(a) harmonize with owner occupiers: depreciation allowances and relief from capital gains tax. (b) first step: a depreciation allowance of £750 per annum.	-	-		yes	-	-
	Lower income groups	-	Tender for grants in competition with housing associations	Same as for Housing Associations					
Crook & Kemp	mobile households, easy access, those unable to buy/ get into LA/HA	not discussed accept market rents inadequate	(a) income tax relief for individual investors on share purchase & dividends (b) 75% capital allowances for companies	no	assured	yes	yes	yes	no

The 'top end' of the PRS market would be excluded from both regulation of rents and tax incentives because it is assumed that tenants will be sufficiently well off and able to make their own judgements, hence market forces can be allowed to determine rents.

The furnished sector would also be excluded because the IBH recognised the 'acute need' that exists for easy access housing for job movers, owners moving house, students and those experiencing relationship breakdown. Capital value rents would prevent the market from clearing, thereby inhibiting the easy access role of the PRS.

Maclennan, Gibb and More (1991) argue that one universal reform would not meet the diverse needs and circumstances of the PRS. Instead, a two-tier approach is proposed. First, they propose 'limited tax concessions' that would, they argue, allow the PRS to meet the 'mobility needs' of younger and other households with average or above average incomes for who, home ownership is the long term aim. Second, they propose that private landlords should be allowed to tender for capital grants from Scottish Homes and the Housing Corporation, to provide low income housing in competition with housing associations. They accept that, unless private landlords are significantly more efficient than housing associations, rents would be higher with their lettings.

Hills (1991) agrees that there is an important, albeit limited, role for a PRS providing immediate access accommodation both for those unable to become home owners but who fail to qualify for social housing and for those making relatively short-term moves.

Crook et al (1991) argue that a PRS is essential because it performs a range of important roles, in particular facilitating mobility for job movers and owner occupiers moving house, providing easy access housing for young and newly formed households, and accommodating those who do not want to or cannot buy but who are unable or do not want to rent from a social landlord.

Rates of return

The rates of return that would be required to ensure a commercially viable PRS have not been very extensively discussed. There is agreement, though, that liquidity, risk (including political risk) and the reputation of the PRS are all important factors.

In the early 1980s the British Property Federation (BPF) argued that a return of 9 per cent gross (equivalent to 6 per cent net) was the required rate of return, net of capital gain. The Small Landlord Association (SLA) suggested 12 per cent gross (10 per cent net) but, if security of tenure were to be reduced, thus making it possible to realise capital gains, a lower return than 12 per cent would be sufficient to attract new investment into the PRS (HCEC, 1982). It seems that these minimum gross rates of return referred to unfurnished lettings: higher returns would presumably be required on furnished lettings.

In its first report, the IBH (1985) advocated net returns of 4 per cent real by linking rents to capital values to generate such a return. They argued that 4 per cent was equivalent to the yield on index linked gilts. However, Whitehead and Kleinman (1988) pointed out that setting rents at this long run equilibrium level would not allow the market to clear (hence short run queues would not be eliminated where excess demand existed). Moreover, a uniform return of 4 per cent did not take account of the very different costs that exist in different subsectors of the PRS.

The 1991 IBH Report also advocated 4 per cent capital value rents but recognises that higher returns are needed to ensure a competitive return. The Report implicitly accepts the higher cost of capital and the greater risk for private landlords than for social housing landlords. The IBH's subsidy proposals are therefore aimed at enhancing the 4 per cent returns from rental income, to 7 to 8 per cent net.

John Hills (1991) argues that landlords need a long term return on new investment which is competitive with that on other businesses. He suggests that this return might be 5 per cent in real terms; in some parts of the market (see below) rents would be linked to capital values to generate this return.

Maclennan et al (1991) make no specific recommendation about the required rates of return. However, in contrast to Hills who suggests the need for returns to be competitive with other business investments, Maclennan et al argue that there is a need to harmonise the PRS and owner occupied regimes if the present regime for the latter is maintained and if private renting is to expand (they have since suggested that 5.5 per cent might be required to attract investment - personal communication with the authors).

Crook et al (1991) also do not make any specific recommendation about rates of return. Instead they simply argue that returns need to be competitive with other investments and that existing rates of return are insufficient.

Subsidy framework

The IBH (1991) propose two alternative subsidy regimes, between which investors would be able to choose. The first of these alternatives would involve remission of all income and capital gains tax for individual landlords and of corporation tax on profits and capital gains for companies. Making certain assumptions about tax rates, the Report calculated that this remission of tax would make a 4 per cent capital value rent equivalent to 7 to 8 per cent net. The alternative to this would be 100 per cent capital allowances which would write off capital costs in the first year of a project. The Report prefers capital allowances on the grounds of effectiveness (the benefit is front-loaded and also minimises interest costs) but notes that remission of tax (the first option) would be more appropriate in creating neutrality with the tax position of owner occupiers. Both options would be better than BES, however, the Report argues.

Hills advocates taxing private landlords in a way equivalent to other businesses. This would involve scrapping the BES and instead allowing (like other businesses) depreciation as a tax deduction. Depreciation allowances are common in many advanced industrial nations (see Harloe, 1985).

Maclennan et al argue in respect of average or above average income tenants in the mobile sector that, if owner occupier subsidies are not changed, and if rental housing is to expand, then two tax incentives are required to broadly harmonise private renting with home ownership. These are, first, allowing depreciation against tax on rental income and, second, a capital grant or tax exemption to equate with owner's fiscal privileges in respect of capital gains. Because in their view the Treasury would not support the costs that this would involve, they advocate as a first step, allowing depreciation allowances equivalent to the average, first year level of MIRAS (£750). For the low income sector, as we have seen, they suggested that private landlords should be allowed to tender for capital grant for new projects.

Crook et al suggest two subsidies. First, a rental housing tax incentive scheme for individuals investing in companies. This would give tax relief on dividends (unlike the BES, which gives relief on capital gains) and on share purchase (as with the BES, but possibly at a lower rate). This would be phased over a period of years (whereas in the BES the relief is allowed in the year of purchase).

Second, capital allowances for companies to be re-introduced, at the same rate as allowed for old-style assured tenancies in 1982-84 (see Kemp, 1988b). These capital allowances would not be available to companies raising funds under the rental housing tax incentive scheme.

Crook et al put forward their subsidy proposals on the assumption that the rest of the housing finance system was not altered. In contrast, the other authors' proposals for the PRS were part of a wider package of housing finance reform.

Conditions attached to rents and subsidies

The IBH's proposals related, as we have seen, only to unfurnished accommodation below the 'top end' of the market. For the regulated sector, rents would be limited to 4 per cent of capital value plus allowances for management and maintenance. In return, landlords would get tax reliefs, as described above. But only approved landlords would get tax exemptions. Local authorities would certify that the property was above the fitness standard, while the landlord would only be approved if they had not been a bankrupt or convicted of harassment. The letting would have to be either an assured or an assured shorthold tenancy. If the property in respect of which a capital allowance had been awarded were sold within ten years of receipt of the allowances, the subsidy would be claimed back on a sliding scale. The purpose of these conditions is to create the political consensus needed within the PRS.

John Hills would exempt lettings above a given value (such as the median owner occupied price) from controls. For other lettings, controls would be used to rule out 'excessive returns on capital values' but this would not be a 'binding constraint'. Landlords would be approved so as to eliminate the disreputable.

Maclennan et al suggest no explicit conditions to the receipt of their proposed tax reliefs in the mobile, better off PRS. But for low income projects, in order for private landlords to tender for capital grants, they would be required to conform to the same controls and conditions as housing associations.

Finally, Crook et al's scheme would (i) retain the BES value limits - currently £125,000 in London, £85,000 elsewhere - in real terms (ie, they would be uplifted annually in line with house price inflation); (2) require properties to conform to the fitness standard; and (3) apply only to assured tenancies. Although not explicitly discussed in their report (but see Kemp, 1988a) they would also introduce a default landlord approval scheme: tax exemption would be removed if the company breached the three conditions or was convicted of fraud, harassment or other malpractice. A right of appeal would exist against disqualification from tax relief.

Evaluation

In this final section we evaluate each of these four sets of proposals for reviving the PRS. We do so by comparing the rates of return that each would generate and the cost of the subsidy in terms of tax foregone. These are then compared with the returns and cost produced by the BES and with the returns produced by letting without these subsidies.

The results are shown in Table 5.4 on a per dwelling basis using for illustrative purposes the average market value (£53,000) with vacant possession of dwellings purchased by BES companies (see Crook et al, 1991). The assumptions used to calculate the rates of return and tax revenue foregone are set out in the appendix to the chapter.

Table 5.4 shows that the rates of return resulting from these alternative subsidies vary significantly. Only the BES, the Inquiry in British Housing and the Crook et al subsidy regimes raise rates of return to above the 6 per cent net minimum specified by the British Property Federation in 1982 (which is not necessarily what the minimum would be today).

Table 5.4(a)
Rents and pre-tax relief rates of return

PROPOSAL	gross rent	net rent	pre-tax return on net rent	pre-tax return with capital gain	year 1 post tax return with capital gain
	£pa	£pa	%	%	%
Status quo	4072	2419	4.6	6.1	4.1
BES	4072	2419	4.6	6.1	4.1
Inquiry					
- tax relief	3055	1998	3.8	5.3	3.6
- capital allowance	3055	1988	3.8	5.3	3.6
Hills	4018	2369	4.5	6.0	4.0
Maclennan et al					
- tax relief	4283	2616	4.9	6.4	4.3
- 'First step'	4283	2616	4.9	6.4	4.3
Crook/Kemp					
- tax incentive	4072	2419	4.6	6.1	4.1
- capital allowance	4072	2419	4.6	6.1	4.1

The tax revenue foregone as a result of these different subsidy regimes also varies considerably. The two schemes providing relief against the initial purchase of shares (BES and Crook et al tax incentive) are very much more costly than the others, though one of them (Crook et al) provides the highest returns to investors. Both of the two remaining schemes which provide returns above the BPF minimum are based on capital allowances. Looking at the five and ten year costs, there is little to choose between the IBH and the Crook et al capital allowance schemes, but the latter provides significantly higher rates of return to investors.

Both the Hills and the two Maclennan et al schemes are considerably cheaper than the others considered here but have commensurately little impact on rates of return compared with non-subsided lettings.

Table 5.4(b)
Post tax relief rates of return and discounted net tax expenditure

PROPOSAL	year 1 post tax return with capital gain %	year 1 post tax return after subsidy %	discounted net tax expenditure over:	
			5 years £	10 years £
Status quo	4.1	-	-	-
BES	4.1	(6.9)	25,700	21,600
Inquiry				
- tax relief	3.6	6.9	5,000	10,600
- capital allowance	3.6	6.9	4,500	9,200
Hills	4.0	4.6	700	1,400
Maclennan et al				
- tax relief	4.3	4.9	1,300	2,800
- 'First step'	4.3	4.9	1,400	2,700
Crook/Kemp				
- tax incentive	4.1	10.3	17,100	22,200
- capital allowance	4.1	8.0	5,200	10,800

Conclusion

The experience of the first two years of the BES suggests that a long term subsidy of some sort is required to provide a commercially viable, affordable and habitable PRS. It also suggests, however, that the BES is not the most appropriate form of subsidy with which to achieve that objective. In this paper, we have therefore examined a range of alternatives to the BES, put forward from a non-party political perspective, which are aimed at providing a more coherent financial regime for private renting than exist at present.

Among the proposals we examined, there was broad agreement that there is an important, albeit limited, role for the PRS, relating to particular market niches which are often less adequately catered for by other tenure forms. These include young and newly formed households as well as job movers and other, non-priority need households. There is a consensus, too, that some form of landlord approval or registration system is required to eliminate the disreputable landlords as well as a quid pro quo for the subsidies that they would receive - though, inevitably, the precise details vary between the individual schemes.

Where the proposals differ is over the form of the subsidy and the rent regime. Both affect the rate of return that can be obtained from rented housing.

The tentative conclusion to be drawn from our preliminary analysis of the different tax incentives is that capital allowances would appear to provide the more cost effective means of providing subsidies to the PRS. Capital allowances are probably also a much more suitable way of attracting the larger corporate firms into private letting than schemes like the BES which are focused on small scale investors. Both approaches are probably required, one aimed at the small investor and the second at institutions and other firms.

The difference between the Inquiry and Crook et al results is partly due to the different form of capital allowance but even more to the different rent regime put forward by each of them. The Inquiry suggests a form of regulated rent (as do Hills and Maclennan et al) while the Crook et al team propose a market rent regime as with the BES. Essentially, the difference between them is that the Inquiry aims at providing landlords with the long run equilibrium rent whereas Crook et al believe that it is important to allow the market to clear in the short run.

Whitehead and Kleinman (1988) have provided an incisive critique of capital value rents in both social and private housing, while Kemp (1988a) put forward arguments against their application to the PRS only. Leaving the technical arguments aside, creating a commercially viable climate for rented housing will probably require not merely that the returns are sufficient but also that investors have sufficient confidence in the market for rented housing. Re-introducing rent regulation - even if on a less inflexible basis than previous forms of control - seems unlikely to achieve that aim.

Appendix: Assumptions used to calculate the figures in Tables 5.4(a) and 5.4(b)

1. *Gross rent*: is the market or regulated rent, as appropriate to the proposal.   Where it is a regulated rent we have added, to the net rent required to generate the real return specified, allowances for management and maintenance (M & M), building depreciation and depreciation of furnishings (as appropriate).

2. *Net Rent*: is the gross rent less the allowances in note 1 plus a deduction for voids and arrears of 7 per cent. Half of the lettings are assumed to be furnished except in the IBH case which specifically excludes furnished lets from regulation and here voids/arrears of 4 per cent are deducted.

3. *Rates of return*: are based on vacant possession market value of £53,000 (see Crook et al, 1991).

4. *Capital gains*: a real gain of 1.5 per cent pa has been assumed.

5.	*Post-tax returns*:	are calculated as in the relevant proposals. An average tax rate of 37 per cent has been assumed.

6.	*Tax expenditures*:	the net cost of the flow of tax expenditure and the tax revenue have been calculated using a 5 per cent discount rate.	In all calculations it has been assumed that rents increase annually in line with house prices (by the index suggested in each proposal) except in the case of the BES and Crook/Kemp where it has been assumed that rents increase by 6 per cent p.a.	In all cases it has been assumed that costs increase at 5 per cent, house prices by 6.5 per cent and RPI by 5 per cent.	The assumptions behind the calculation of net tax expenditure in the Crook et al proposal follow the method used in our earlier work (Crook et al, 1991) and include an estimate of tax foregone by the diversion of investment.	We have assumed that capital gains are realized after 5 and 10 years and relief granted according to the relevant proposal.

7.	*Capital allowances*:	we have followed Lumby (1984) in treating capital allowances as a form of depreciation allowance, i.e. it is used to offset tax liabilities in later years where the allowance exceeds first year liabilities.	In the case of the IBH proposal the allowance would eliminate tax liabilities after 12 years; with the Crook/Kemp scheme it would do so after 10 years; after which the government 'recoups' the allowance from the tax revenue generated.	An alternative would be to deduct the capitalised value of the tax saved by the allowances from the initial investment and to compute the post tax return on the basis of the lower effective cost of the original investment.

8.	Maclennan et al propose the granting of relief on capital gains tax as well as allowances for depreciation and maintenance - the latter are already allowed by the Inland Revenue and are therefore not included in our calculation of the returns after subsidy.

6 Private finance for housing associations

Christine M.E. Whitehead

Objectives of the research[1]

The introduction of private finance into the provision of social housing necessarily requires the development of suitable financial instruments to meet the specific demands of both social landlords and private financiers. The immediate objective of our research was simply to present a detailed description of what has been going on in the market and thus to provide a baseline from which to assess how the system develops and its effectiveness in ensuring that adequate finance is available at an acceptable price. More basically private finance for social housing is in direct competition with demand from owner-occupation so financial institutions must assess their relative risks and returns on a comparable basis. As a result, at least in principle, the finance system could become an important engine integrating the overall housing market in a way which has not been possible in the past because of the very different financing systems used by the different tenures.

This paper provides a summary of some of our findings about the private finance market for social housing up to mid-1991, concentrating on the way in which provision has evolved, the problems that have been encountered and the attitudes of different actors[2].

The baseline in 1988

Historically social housing has been funded entirely through government. In particular, housing associations received capital grants from central government such that first year costs were fully covered given fair rents, although that grant could be clawed back once the association went into surplus. Associations could build using wholly private finance but such developments had to be treated entirely separately from their publicly funded stock. This separation was in part an outcome of the rules relating to the Public Sector Borrowing Requirement (PSBR) which normally treats all funds involving any element of public sector finance as part of public expenditure.

This situation started to change in the mid-1980s when government introduced challenge funding initiatives by which associations were offered additional funds if they initiated projects involving an element of private funding such that the need for public sector grant was reduced - initially to 30per cent. Most of the proposals coming forward involved additional elements of subsidy, for example through land provided by local authorities at below the market price. However, only the central government grant was included in the PSBR.

These demonstration projects suggested that private finance could be raised for social housing but that, if the system were to work for social housing overall, grant rates would have to be significantly higher. In particular they suggested that asset rich associations might find it relatively easy to raise funds on the private market - because the outcome of past grant mechanisms meant that associations were unencumbered by the types of debt that equivalent private sector organisations would normally have incurred. Thus past capital gains could in principle be used to finance current investment.

At the same time government had clarified, in the Housing and Planning Act 1986, the mechanisms by which local authorities might sell their stock through large-scale voluntary transfers to the independent rented sector. This again provided the potential for capital restructuring through the introduction of one hundred percent private finance at current values.

However, it was the 1988 Housing Act which laid the financial framework by which private finance was introduced into all new housing association developments and it became feasible to finance the transfers of existing stock on the private market. The Act included three main elements relevant to the introduction of private finance:

(i) Fair rents were replaced by assured tenancies at up to market levels for all new tenancies in the independent sector. This meant, on the one hand, that associations could set rents in relation to actual costs and, on the other, that private financiers could see that rents could be raised, up to market levels, to offset unexpected changes in costs and therefore to maintain their cash flows - a freedom which had not existed in any part of the regulated rented sector since 1915;

(ii) The new financial framework included the requirement that associations should fund the difference between the grant rate (set at an average of 75per cent of costs in the first year of the new system) and the cost of production. This grant rate is set to produce acceptable rent levels taking account of imputed costs including the interest rate associations can be expected to have to pay and assuming the use of low-start finance.

(iii) Tenants choice, by which occupiers of local authority property may initiate transfer to another landlord or vote to accept such a takeover rather than simply validate a local authority initiative.

This approach clearly reflected the general objectives of the government's privatisation programme: reducing public expenditure, introducing market incentives and constraints so that organisations both produce more efficiently and face the true costs of supply including the costs of the risk incurred, and enabling consumers to make their voice more effective.

Of most immediate importance was the capacity to control public expenditure. The reduction in grant rates allow a given level of public expenditure to fund a larger development programme - as long as it is accepted that the PSBR can be defined to exclude the private finance element. This entails ensuring that the government is in no way guaranteeing that finance, so that private institutions are bearing market risks. This has been the main force determining the form and price of the private finance that has been made available.

The second element was the emphasis on liberalisation in both the housing and the finance markets. In the housing market this involved rent deregulation within a clearly defined contractual framework which in principle both allows investors to evaluate expected revenues on the basis of market evidence and consumers freedom of choice, given relative prices. Because this regulatory contractual framework was introduced for the whole independent rented sector, associations were in principle to be regarded as in direct competition with private commercial landlords. The whole sector was thus put on the same playing field - although that playing field was by no means flat because of the differential grant and tax rates faced by different landlords. With respect to the finance market more general deregulation had already provided the framework within which wholesale finance could be introduced into housing thus opening up a far larger supply of potential finance - at rates which reflected relative costs and returns against all other financial investments. What the 1988 Act did was define the subsidy framework in which that finance would be forthcoming and therefore the price that associations would have to pay. Both of these factors opened housing associations up to the discipline of the marketplace - in the housing market itself by limiting the extent to which rents and therefore costs could be increased and in the finance market by requiring associations to offer a competitive risk/return package. Thus, in principle at least, associations had the incentive to provide as efficiently as other suppliers and had to pay for the risk involved in providing social housing. Of course, in practice, the extent of this market pressure was limited by the lack of choice available to most consumers, the limited range of alternative suppliers and the extent to which grant cushioned associations from the true costs of production.

In addition the Act introduced the implicit use of low start finance, which reduces first year payments and thus the grant rate necessary to obtain a particular rent level as well as matching cash flows more effectively over time. This not only reduced public expenditure but also specified a suitable form of private financial instrument, but did not, of course, ensure that the market would be prepared to provide funds on these terms.

Finally, tenants were given greater choice over the landlord who would own and manage their property - so again in principle allowing potential competition to increase efficiency and responsiveness to demand. In the longer term tenants were also expected to gain greater control over the allocation of property as rents came better to reflect costs and opportunities and tenant involvement in management was increased.

The difference between the principles that lay behind the framework put in place by the 1988 Act and what would be achieved on the ground were clearly going to be very great. New markets had to be built up and the process would be both costly and lengthy. There were also far more fundamental limitations, including the differential impact of the financial framework on different tenures and therefore the lack of a flat playing field in which competition could evolve and relative efficiency be measured; the lack of genuine choice for many consumers, especially those on low incomes; and particularly the extent to which the whole system continued to depend on government though grant levels, grant rates and the provision of housing benefit. It was in this context that the private finance market for social housing started to evolve.

The form and extent of finance required

The introduction of private finance into social housing involved two entirely different forms of finance:

(i) Mixed funding by which existing associations were initially required to raise an average of 25 per cent of their finance for new investment from the private market. This proportion has been increased to about 30 per cent and can be expected to increase further. Because the majority of the funds still come from government through the Housing Corporation the form of investment is heavily regulated. Projects or programmes are therefore agreed in detail before subsidy is made available and the operation of associations is monitored regularly. Security is provided either by the attachment of specific assets or through a general charge over the association's assets. Reserves may be used to subsidise rents. Thus the risk faced by the private sector is extremely circumscribed, especially where associations have significant unencumbered assets.

(ii) 100 per cent financing of large scale voluntary transfers which involve no direct government funding but where the value of the assets being transferred is determined in relation to expected net cash flows (Gardiner et al 1991). All the early sales involved voluntary transfers by local authorities under the 1986 Act rather than tenants' choice under the 1988 Act. Most could be regarded as debt financed management buy-outs, by which housing departments were re-organised and transferred into the independent rented sector, almost always in the form of housing associations[3]. The process clearly involved revaluation of the capital assets and therefore the right-off of past mistakes. The price which reflects future cash flows including Right to Buy sales suitably discounted is thus determined by the form of contractual arrangements - including in particular investment, allocation and rent determination commitments. Most agreements specify how rents will rise over the next few years but give freedom to increase rents thereafter in response to cost variations - thus protecting private financiers from the risk associated with unexpected cost increases up to market rent levels. Agreements with financiers include regular monitoring of outcomes against the association's business plan and involvement in management decisions whenever significant divergencies occur. The extent of risk clearly depends on the accuracy of the initial capital valuation and thus the accuracy of predicted cash flows and interest rates as well as on the effectiveness of management. The individual financial packages are very large in comparison to the sums involved in mixed funding and normally entail a significant element of low-start finance.

In addition to these two main uses, private finance has also to be raised for shared ownership projects and for 'pure' private schemes[4]. Shared ownership attracts central government subsidy and is therefore subject to Housing Corporation monitoring. It involves three types of private finance - development finance for the association, finance to fund the rental element net of grant and mortgage finance for the element purchased by the shared owner. It has proved to be the most risky element of private financing because of the effect of the recession both on capital values in relation to costs and on the capacity of potential owners to fund their mortgages. Also many of the shared ownership schemes are operated by association subsidiaries with few reserves. 'Pure' private schemes involving no central government grant normally involve some other form of subsidy such as the provision of land by local authorities at below market prices or cross-subsidy from earlier purely private schemes. They have always formed an important element in certain associations' programmes and are evaluated by the private market on purely commercial terms.

The amount of funding required for mixed funding for rent and shared ownership depends entirely on the level of HAG provided, together with the grant rate. Over the period from 1989-1993 the Housing Corporation estimates that some £1500m of private finance will be required and that so far some £800m has actually been raised. The projected requirements for private schemes are expected to be of a similar order, although this figure is far less well founded because it involves no direct subsidy and therefore no automatic monitoring. Moreover, the level of such investment is heavily influenced by local authority initiatives and market viability.

The extent of finance required for transfers depends not only on the desires of authorities and tenants but on the terms and conditions under which private finance is made available in relation to the valuations agreed by the Department of Environment. The first sixteen transfers up to April 1991 required some £1050m and involved fewer than 100,000 units. There are large numbers of potential transfers in the pipeline not only under the 1986 Act but also under tenants' choice. Under certain circumstances it is clear that this transfer demand could come to dominate the market and would required a quite different level of access to the finance market than that which has so far been achieved[5].

The number of institutions that have been involved in provision have been relatively limited. The vast majority of the finance has come from banks, notably the National Westminster and, especially for transfers, Banque Paribas and a small number of Building Societies, notably the Halifax. The Housing Finance Corporation (THFC) has been set up as a basically uncapitalised intermediary and has tapped the wholesale market with a range of different instruments. However institutions such as insurance companies and pension funds which could provide longer term funding have not been prepared to be involved to any significant extent either through the THFC or more directly (European Capital Co Ltd, 1991, Pryke and Whitehead, 1991a).

The instruments used have also been relatively limited and traditional. The majority of those used for mixed funding have been at variable rates and for variable terms. Others have had an element of fixed rate funding. The initial emphasis on low start finance has, in the main, been shown to be misplaced, in part because of a lack of understanding of the nature of the risks involved (including the way such loans are treated for accounting purposes, see Bromwich et al 1991) and in part because of lack of demand for such instruments from the institutions. Limited quantities of index linked funds have been available. Low start finance however forms a significant part of transfer funding although even here the majority is only available on a short to medium term basis. The majority of funds so far raised will have to be refinanced within the next seven years.

The main problems

The most obvious problem about the introduction of private finance into social housing has been the fact that it was an entirely new market. Prior to 1988 institutions had not seen it as a possible use for their funds, their organisational structure took no account of it and they had little or no information about the nature of the risks involved.

In many ways this lack of understanding related as much to the nature of residential investment as a whole as to social housing in particular. The private rented sector had been financed either through the, declining, involvement of large landlords, who had made their decisions long in the past, or through small individual investors. There was thus no flourishing finance market for commercially let rented housing, the information from which could be transferred to the evolving social rented market. Even the owner-occupied sector still depended in the main on the retail market, although during the 1980s larger societies, banks and new lenders were developing an expertise in tapping wholesale finance (Whitehead and Pryke 1991b). This problem was made worse by the timing of the expansion of demand which occurred initially at the height of the boom in the housing market but which soon turned into one of the worst housing market recessions ever encountered, and the first with large scale falls in money prices.

The second source of misunderstanding relates to the nature of housing associations. They are hybrid organisations technically within the independent rented sector but at the same time acting as social landlords, dependent on government funds, limited in their capacities to build surpluses and subject to extensive regulation by the Housing Corporation. Understanding the powers and constraints of such organisations is not straightforward, especially as a major aim of the 1988 Act was to transform them into quite different entities. The fact that associations are also extremely heterogeneous, varying from large asset rich national organisations with many decades of experience in rented housing provision for the full range of lower income households, to newly set up, small, local, specialist associations with few unencumbered assets. Although these last are not expected to raise private finance, but continue to borrow through the Housing Corporation at a higher rate of interest to offset the risk they transfer, the range of those seeking private funds remains very large. Moreover, the only relatively easy way of assessing risk without detailed examination of the operation of each association remains the information provided through Housing Corporation monitoring and especially through registration with the Corporation.

This situation inherently means that the actions of the Housing Corporation are a major determinant of the terms and conditions in which private funds can be raised. The Corporation plays two quite distinct roles: that of funder and that of monitor. With respect to the first, the main element that private funders are looking for is certainty in terms of the extent and timing of funding, so that their matching funds can be effectively provided. During the first three years of the new regime, and particularly in 1989/90, the Corporation failed to provide this certainty, resulting in higher transaction costs for associations and particular difficulties for the THFC. On the other hand the Corporation, through its own monitoring role, reduces the costs faced by individual lenders in assessing loans. This places a considerable burden on the Corporation in that if one loan fails, the viability of others will be adversely affected. The outcome of this has undoubtedly been a very cautious approach by the Corporation, both in terms of allocations and their response to problems faced by individual associations.

A particularly important question for the private finance market has been the status of HAG as a loan rather than a grant. HAG is technically a loan repayable if an association sells the property involved other than to another association or if the association goes out of business. Under earlier financial regimes surpluses have also been repayable to central government as net incomes has risen with inflation. Many private institutions were initially unclear about the formal status of HAG and, in particular, whether repayments would take precedence over their own loans. More generally they were worried by the lack of surpluses generated by associations and by their limited cushion against sudden changes in cash flow. With respect to the first question the Housing Corporation has clarified that HAG is a subordinated loan, only repayable after other debt under specified circumstances. Moreover, the financial framework has also been specified in such a way that, after well defined commitments have been met, especially to the sinking fund required for future capital maintenance, associations may be building surpluses on post 1989 lettings to use as a cushion or as a way of subsidising the rents on new developments in their early years. In the longer term therefore the potential for internal pooling exists. However, it will take many years before most associations will reach a stable position, especially given the growing development programme and the relatively low rate of inflation expected over the next few years.

The most obvious and basic question remains however the nature and viability of **social** housing and its effect on both cash flows and capital values. Three distinct aspects can be distinguished: the types of tenant to be housed; the types of property involved; and the conditions under which the capital values can be realised when necessary. With respect to tenants the majority of associations provide accommodation to households nominated by local authorities. Many will be homeless and almost all will be on relatively low incomes. Others house those with special needs, many of whom will have no income other than that provided by the state. This raises two quite separate issues - the level of rent that those with incomes just above benefit levels can be expected actually to pay without jeopardising the rental income through arrears and vacancy (a question which is distinct from what tenants should be expected to afford which has been the subject of continuing debate notably by the NFHA - see eg National Federation of Housing Associations, 1989) and the level of benefit which central government is prepared to pay for those unable to afford their own rent. Under the 1988 Act housing benefit is available up to market levels, subject to certain constraints on occupation and on rent levels in relation to the highest rented properties in a given area. This 'guarantees' the rental stream from the majority of tenants who are eligible for benefit.

94

However if costs or rents rose in a way that government regarded is unreasonable they can be expected to attempt to restrain rent rises. Changing political imperatives could also modify the basis on which benefit is available. Thus the expected rent stream is very obviously subject to political risk.

The ultimate security against which the private sector lends is the capital value of the association's assets, made up mainly of their stock of dwellings. While a proportion of association property is exactly like that available in the private market, and may even have been bought in that market, the majority of their stock has been developed or improved by the associations themselves. Much of it in the form of small purpose built flats in urban areas - more saleable than much local authority stock but certainly not easily valued. Some is built specifically for special needs and therefore cannot be sold at anything like the cost of production. As importantly tenants usually have a range of rights including security of tenure, which limit the owners' own property rights and reduce the resale value. In the main therefore private financiers have assumed that only units falling vacant will be available for sale, and then on a restricted market. What looks like a very large capital base can in this way start to look like a relatively risky investment.

Given all these circumstances it is not surprising that the private market has been quite slow to response to the new opportunities. Money has been forthcoming, but at a price which reflects the market view that investing in housing associations is risky. The initial funds, for instance those raised by North Housing on the basis of their own very large and unencumbered equity base were raised at an interest rate less than 1per cent above the 'riskless' rate of interest. By mid-1991 the cost of funds for mixed funding was often $2\frac{1}{2}$per cent plus above that riskless rate. Moreover, there was some evidence that the market was becoming saturated, with few new entrants and some existing lenders reaching the limit of the amount of this type of debt which they wished to hold in their portfolios. An important question is therefore what types of financial instrument long-term large scale lenders actually required.

What do lenders want?

Not surprisingly what lenders require are simple, easily evaluated, instruments which will help to reduce the risks that they face within their overall portfolios. What they do not want are special types of investment which involve them in looking through the instruments to the details of the management, organisation and investment behaviour of particular associations. At the present time however that is exactly what they have.

The three main attributes stressed by long term lenders were simplicity, size and liquidity. They were not interested in new types of instruments which were difficult to evaluate. In particular they saw no benefits in deferred interest instruments because these have many of the same attributes as equities, which already form the majority of their investments, but give no comparable possibility of an above normal return. They did see some role for index linked debt as this removed their inflation risk. However most institutions only wish to hold a small proportion of such debt and would rather obtain it from organisations that are better understood than housing associations.

Most long term lenders do not want to deal in small amounts, nor indeed in one-off deals. Transaction costs can be significantly reduced through size and repetition. To some extent this makes transfer funding more desirable than mixed funding. More generally it points to the value of an effective intermediary such as a capitalised THFC which can, in principle, raise regular large scale funds and repackage them into acceptable loans to individual associations (see European Capital, 1991, for a detailed discussion of this option). However large scale funding of this type would be far more acceptable if there were a well-developed secondary market which would allow investors to on-sell their debt and so maintain liquidity (see Pryke and Whitehead, 1991b, for more detailed discussion of this approach). Indeed liquidity was often seen as the most important attribute required if large scale, long term finance were to be made available.

The development of such instruments is seen as requiring a far more commercial approach on the part of associations. Internally they will be expected to build up their capacity to develop business plans, effectively to monitor and control actual outcomes, to generate surpluses and to develop their treasury management skills. This could mean that meeting the requirements of private financiers may well take precedence over meeting housing objectives, especially as tenants bear the ultimate risk arising from variations in cost. This will be particularly true for transfer associations which are wholly dependent on private finance and for any association that runs into financial difficulties (a situation which has already arisen where associations have made poor decisions with respect to shared ownership). An important medium term consequence of private financing is undoubtedly going to be a two (or multi) tier system where large, well run, highly capitalised associations will have quite different access to the market than the majority of smaller or newer associations and particularly those who are seen to have made mistakes.

The development of the market is also seen as depending on an effective role for the Housing Corporation in terms of the provision of information about associations, of stabilising the flow of HAG finance, and, on the one hand, of alleviating problems when they arise and, on the other, of allowing adequate flexibility so that associations can respond to changing demands. What is clear however is that the Housing Corporation cannot guarantee private funds so, at the limit, they must either let an association that gets into trouble go bankrupt or, more likely in practice, transfer the ownership and management of such associations to other, more effective, organisations. An important question is the extent to which private insurance and credit enhancement are efficient mechanisms for transferring and reducing the costs of risk. Another equally important question is the way that the private market views the Housing Corporations' role in ensuring that liabilities are transferred to other associations rather than ultimately borne by the market.

Lenders clearly want, and are prepared to press for, some form of guarantee at the end of the line. They argue that such a mechanism has been developed with respect to export credits, in such a way that the government bears ultimate responsibility but the cost of mistakes are still borne through the insurance system. They also argue that many of the risks faced by private lenders to social housing are political rather than market risks and so are properly borne by government. Finally they suggest that no other country, however market oriented, expects to fund social housing without a guarantee of some sort and that in many countries, especially in continental Europe where social housing is provided by a range of suppliers, these guarantees are up front and clearly recognised by all those involved as the only basis on which low cost finance can be provided (Whitehead, 1991).

Conclusions

The difficulties of such a 'guaranteed' approach to private funding within the current government's ethos are obvious. The very fact that the market sees a guarantee as so valuable can be regarded as evidence that its provision would significantly reduce and at its limit remove the market's incentive effectively to assess risks and allocate funds in relation to those risks. A guarantee however limited would therefore offset many of the perceived benefits of private financing.

On the other hand without such a guarantee there are fears that long term finance will not be forthcoming, even at interest rates significantly above those currently on offer. This fear relates to three main elements:

(i) The expected rapid growth in the total quantity of funds required over the next few years as a result of the expansion of the mixed funding programme, of other opportunities arising from local authority enabling powers and from the build up in demand for finance for large scale transfers of local authority stock.

(ii) The lack of any evidence that the market is prepared to provide long term, as opposed to development and short to medium term, funds and the extent to which this is already building up a growing demand for refinancing over the next few years.

(iii) Changing attitudes to housing as an asset and its potential for long term capital growth as a result both of the current recession and of a more realistic understanding of longer term trends.

All of the factors suggest that even if funds are made available the price relative to the riskfree rate of interest would be relatively high. They also suggest that most of the effort made to introduce private funding will be dissipated into transfers and higher costs of finance rather than into significant expansion in provision. If the objective were to house more lower income households for a given level of government involvement it is unlikely to be achieved.

On the other hand the market for private finance for social housing is a very young one. The actors are only just starting up the learning curve and the necessary instruments are only beginning to be developed. In a few years time it may be possible to observe a situation where associations are able effectively to tap the world finance market through instruments which provide both liquidity and a suitable mix of risk and return to the institutions involved. But there is a long way to go before such instruments will be generally acceptable and in the process associations may well change their nature more to satisfy financiers than tenants.

As in all markets there is a price at which funds can be made available. What is not clear is how high this price will turn out to be and whether given that price, private financing, as currently envisaged, is the most effective way of achieving social housing objectives.

Notes

1. Christine Whitehead is Senior Lecturer in the Department of Economics, London School of Economics and Director of the Property Research Unit, Department of Land Economy, University of Cambridge. The research discussed here was funded by the Joseph Rowntree Foundation as part of a project examining the development of financial instruments for housing in both the owner-occupied and social rented sectors. The main researcher on the project was Dr Michael Pryke.

2. The main findings of the research were published by the Joseph Rowntree Foundation in Findings No. 24 and a forthcoming Discussion Paper No. Two publications from the Department of Land Economy describe the work in more detail: Pryke and Whitehead (1991a) and Pryke and Whitehead (1991b). A third publication, available in late 1992, will provide an update of the situation in the social rented sector (Pryke and Whitehead, forthcoming).

3. Among the first sixteen transfers fifteen were organised as housing associations and one as an industrial and provident society.

4. Since this paper was presented an additional source of private finance has come from BES schemes where associations raise funds from private investors giving a guaranteed return of around 16per cent but obtaining the funds for about 11per cent.

5. The extent to which these transfers will actually come to the market will depend upon new government proposals on transfers to be published as a consultative document in July 1992.

Part Three
LOCAL AUTHORITY RENT REGIMES

7 Implementing change in housing policy: The introduction of the new financial regime for local authority housing

Peter Malpass and Matthew Warburton

Introduction

The new financial regime for local authority housing finance in England and Wales introduced by Part VI of the Local Government and Housing Act 1989 has been in operation since 1 April 1990. In that time, local authority rents in England have risen by an average of 30 per cent, while in London rent increases of 50 per cent have been common, and in Ealing rents have more than doubled (Department of the Environment, 1991; Association of District Councils, 1991; Association of Metropolitan Councils, 1991). These have been the most obvious and dramatic effects of "ring-fenced" housing revenue accounts and the new subsidy system, but our research suggests that the new regime has had other less obvious but no less significant repercussions for local authority housing and for central-local relations.

Most work on housing finance, exemplified by the core studies in the Rowntree programme, falls within the boundaries of applied economics. But our research adopts a different perspective, a policy approach to housing finance, which seems more appropriate to a study of the local implementation of central government legislation.

The study of implementation and its vicissitudes is an essential supplement to the usual run of work on housing finance and its reform. Much has been written about the level of rents which, in the view of those proposing reform, ought to be charged by local authorities, but much less about how local authorities are to be persuaded or coerced to set rents at these levels. The history of local authority housing finance strongly suggests that this is neither an insignificant problem nor an easy one to solve.

Background to the new financial regime

A feature of the history of council housing in Britain is the high level of real autonomy enjoyed by local authorities in relation to patterns of investment, rents, allocations policies, management structures and accounting practices. This freedom was never, of course, completely unbounded, and central government always sought to influence (rather than direct) local policies, and in particular to limit the Treasury's financial liability. But over the last twenty years successive governments have adopted measures designed to restrict local autonomy, although it would be a mistake to see this as a simple, unproblematic and wholly successful exercise for the centre. (Malpass & Murie (1990), Malpass (1990), Forrest & Murie (1990), Houlihan (1988)).

For the last twenty years successive governments have sought an effective and politically acceptable form of deficit subsidy system. A key problem thrown up by the preference for deficit subsidy is that it creates new tensions in the central-local relationship. The old system of fixed annual payments combined three important features which enabled it to endure for so long. First, it meant that the Treasury's financial liability was quite highly predictable from year-to-year, the only element of uncertainty being the level of local authority house building. Second, it gave local authorities considerable freedom over rents, whilst also giving them an incentive to control costs (since any increased costs would not be reflected in higher subsidy). It should be remembered here that authorities could draw on their own local tax base to enhance central subsidy, although the use of such rate fund contributions was generally confined to high cost areas, especially in London. Third, the old system enabled central government to influence local authority rent levels by means of financial leverage, without breaching the convention that authorities had full responsibility in this area. A shift to deficit subsidy inevitably raised the questions of what were appropriate levels of income and expenditure, and who was to decide. This move also raised the issue of rent setting. Under the old system the total rental income was set by reference to the cost of providing the housing service, but deficit subsidy implied setting rents independently from costs. Thus the shift from investment to deficit subsidy systems can be seen as embracing a parallel move from historic cost pricing to current value pricing.

The first legislative attempt to introduce a deficit subsidy system to British local authority housing was in 1972 when a Conservative Government introduced a system based on 'fair rents', deficit subsidy and mandatory rent rebate scheme. This can now be seen as a false start which foundered on local opposition and inadequate legal draughtsmanship. A key problem was the complete removal of local autonomy in relation to rent setting, and reliance on administrative and judicial means of enforcing rent increases. The combination of exogenously imposed rents with deficit subsidy meant that, in effect, local authorities lost control of spending levels, too.

The Housing Act, 1980, represented a new approach to the same basic policy problem. This time the problem was implicitly formulated in terms of the desire to secure rents which more closely reflected current values, while ensuring an equitable distribution of subsidy, without completely eroding local autonomy. In an era of disinvestment, accompanied by inflation and large scale council house sales, which the Act inaugurated, this implied that the system would have to address the issue of Housing Revenue Account surpluses, as well as deficits.

The 1980 Act also marked a return to financial leverage as the means of exerting central government pressure on local rents. The important breakthrough represented by the 1980 subsidy system was the introduction of notional housing revenue accounts as the basis for subsidy calculation. The advantage of this approach was that it preserved both limits to central government's financial liability and an element of local autonomy.

Under the 1980 Act system, subsidy was paid according to the centre's assumptions of year on year changes in income and expenditure, while local authorities remained free to set their own rents and expenditure on management and maintenance. Local authorities remained free to draw on the rates to supplement rent income, and were permitted to budget for a surplus on the Housing Revenue Account, which could be transferred out of the account to support rate fund spending. In terms of central-local relations the adoption of a notional Housing Revenue Account gave the centre considerable power whilst providing local authorities with no opportunity for public defiance of the exercise of that power. It was, therefore, a highly potent and successful device for reducing subsidy and raising rents: in the first year of operation, 1981/82, council rents rose by 48 per cent on average, and in three years the real value of general subsidy fell by over 80 per cent.

However, the 1980 Act system soon began to lose its potency, because leverage on rents was dependent upon there being some subsidy which could be withdrawn. It very quickly became clear that a majority of authorities were 'going out of subsidy', and the Government in the early 1980s lacked the political will to utilise other powers which it possessed to put further financial leverage on rents, by reducing the rate support grant of those authorities whose notional Housing Revenue Accounts were in surplus. In the face of opposition from Conservative-controlled councils the Government gave way and conceded both that a majority of councils would be released from direct central government pressure to raise rents, and, where authorities chose to raise rents to levels which produced Housing Revenue Account surpluses then those surpluses would be available to enhance local expenditure on non-housing services, with no reduction in rate support grant. This concession was good for local authorities but it fatally undermined the coherence of the revenue side of council housing finance, which meant that eventually the government would move to reform it.

The new financial regime

After their third consecutive election victory in 1987, the Conservatives embarked on a new round of housing legislation, in the form of the Housing Act, 1988, and then the Local Government and Housing Act, 1989. Part VI of the Act introduced new accounting arrangements and a new subsidy system for local authority housing, and Part IV introduced a new system for the control of borrowing and capital expenditure which also has important repercussions for rents and revenue spending, particularly on maintenance.

Five basic characteristics of the new regime can be highlighted:

(i) The Housing Revenue Account is now ring-fenced, which means that authorities have lost their historical freedom to use their local tax income to support housing, and, except under special circumstances, their more recently acquired freedom to use Housing Revenue Account surpluses to support expenditure which would otherwise be financed by local taxation.

(ii) Authorities have also lost much of their freedom to transfer spending between capital and revenue accounts, and the Housing Revenue Account is deprived of the benefit of the interest on invested capital receipts.

(iii) Housing subsidy and rent rebate subsidy, which were formerly separate, are now amalgamated into a single Housing Revenue Account subsidy. This subsidy may be less than total expenditure on rent rebates, so that part of local expenditure on rent rebates is met from rent income. Housing Revenue Account subsidy is effectively the sum of the two elements, rent rebate subsidy and housing subsidy, the second of which may now be negative.

(iv) The method of calculating the "housing subsidy" element of Housing Revenue Account subsidy has been changed:

(a)   subsidy is no longer calculated incrementally by reference to year-on-year changes in notional income and expenditure, but directly from first principles - comparing notional income with notional expenditure - each year;

(b)   guideline rents are no longer the previous year's amounts increased for all authorities by the same amount and allowances for management and maintenance are no longer constant in real terms; in the new system guideline rent increases and management and maintenance allowances vary from authority to authority;

(c)   changes in charges for capital are normally matched pound for pound by changes in subsidy - this works mostly to the government's benefit since the revenue benefits of compulsory debt redemption accrue to the government as reduced subsidy, but the quid pro quo for local authorities is

106

that debt charges on new borrowing for capital purposes are also fully covered by subsidy.

(v)   But, subsidy is still based on a notional Housing Revenue Account, so that local authorities remain free to set their own rents and expenditure levels.

In the 1987 Housing White Paper (Department of the Environment, 1987), subsequent consultation papers and in parliamentary debate, the government claimed that its two main objectives in reforming the local authority housing financial regime were:

(i)   to "target" subsidy to the authorities and tenants which needed it, ending indiscriminate subsidisation and bringing rents closer to "what the property is worth".

(ii) to create a "landlord account" which, by preventing transfers to and from the Housing Revenue Account, would establish a closer relationship between the rents paid by tenants and the cost of the service provided.

The first of these declared objectives is by no means new. It has been a continuing theme of government policy since the late 1960s that local authorities should be persuaded or compelled to charge rents closer to market levels, while remaining in some sense affordable. The objective is both to reap the claimed efficiency advantages of market pricing, and assist the revival of an (unsubsidised) private rented sector, while at the same time economising on Exchequer support in the form of subsidy.

The second is a newer theme, in that it reflects the more recent view that, left to themselves, local authorities cannot be trusted to manage their housing either effectively or efficiently. The new regime, it was argued, would impose new disciplines on local authorities:

(i)   by relating rents more closely to costs, a landlord account would discipline authorities to improve efficiency, or else tenants would use their Tenants' Choice powers to seek better value for money from other landlords;

(ii) authorities would no longer be able to set rents so low that tenants accepted a poor standard of service in return; there would no longer be any short-term political advantage in choosing to minimise rents rather than adequately repairing and maintaining the housing stock.

The first two years of the new financial regime

The first point to be made about the introduction of the new financial regime, and it is an important point in the context of a focus on implementation, is that local authorities did not idly wait for the new system to take effect on 1 April 1990. They engaged in a variety of anticipatory action, the most significant form of which was to increase capital expenditure. Authorities had accumulated capital receipts to a greater or lesser extent during the 1980s and the consultation paper of July 1988 revealed that they would lose their ability to spend up to 100 per cent of their receipts. As a result, 1989/90 saw a 25 per cent increase in local authority capital spending.

The second point concerns the government's determination to press ahead with the new financial regime in 1990/91 even though certain key aspects of the system had not been finalised. Thus, the 1990/91 management and maintenance allowances were based directly on actual spending levels from 1986/87 to 1988/89, and in 1991/92, "targeted" allowances were introduced for maintenance, but not for management. Detailed specification of the "ring-fence" - what items of expenditure should be included within the Housing Revenue Account - will not be complete before 1993/94.

At the aggregate level, capital spending fell sharply in 1990/91 (Department of the Environment, 1991, p.95) and is likely to do so again in 1991/92 (Association of District Councils, 1991; Association of Metropolitan Councils, 1991). The compulsory setting aside of 75 per cent of accumulated capital receipts resulted in an estimated £3,200 million reduction in local authority housing debt in 1990/91 and this in turn helped to produce subsidy savings for central government.

Guideline rent increases have been subject to damping in both years, to limit the maximum increase and prevent any decreases implied by the capital value-related distribution principle. Guideline increases varied between 95p and £4.50 per week for 1990/91 and between £1.38 and £2.50 for 1991/92. In 1990/91 43 per cent of authorities had the minimum guideline increase of 95p, but in the three northern regions 88 per cent of authorities were in this position. Eighteen per cent of authorities were given a £4.50 guideline, and all but two of these were in London, the South East or East. In 1991/92 the polarisation of authorities to one end or other of the range was even more pronounced: 275 authorities were at the top or bottom of the range, compared with 229 in 1990/91. Ninety per cent of northern authorities were given minimum guidelines, while 82 per cent of authorities in London, the South East and East were at the maximum guideline increase.

In practice, most authorities, both in 1990/91 and 1991/92, raised their rents by more than their guideline. Seven authorities made no increase at all in 1990/91, but the highest increase was £15.68 per week, in Redbridge. Sixty five per cent of authorities raised their rents by more than the guideline, and only 10 per cent by less. The same pattern recurred in 1991/92, with the highest increase of over £28 in Ealing. There is a clear regional pattern to rents: all the authorities in the list of the top 20 rent increases in 1990 are in the south of England, and 19 of the top 20 for 1991.

As might be expected, there is a close relationship between rents above guidelines and management and maintenance spending above allowances. In 1991/92, aggregate spending on management and maintenance is likely to be 30 per cent higher than the government's aggregate allowances.

The management and maintenance allowances for each authority in 1990/91 were based on the average of real actual spending on management and maintenance by the authority in 1986/87, 1987/88 and 1988/89. For 1991/92, an element of redistribution was introduced into the allowances for maintenance spending. Targets, based on stock characteristics, were calculated for each authority. The 44 authorities whose allowance for 1990/91 was more than 60 per cent above their target for 1991/92 received the same allowance in 1991/92 as in the previous year. The resources so released were redistributed to the 34 authorities whose allowances would otherwise have been furthest below them. Eighteen of the gainers were in London and the remainder were evenly spread through the regions. Of the losers, 27 were in the South and 9 in the North.

This dramatic deviation of actual rents and spending decisions made by local authorities from the guidelines set by government is the most striking feature of the new regime to date. But is it an indication that the regime is failing to deliver the outcomes government wants?

The policy approach

'Policy' is a difficult term to use unambiguously because of the multiplicity of meanings attached to it in everyday speech and in the academic literature, and because the distinction between policy and implementation is notoriously difficult to draw. A distinction can be made between policy objectives - the ends of policy - and policy instruments - the means by which it is intended that these ends should be realised. The new financial regime has been described as a new policy instrument intended by government to secure broadly the same objectives as previous subsidy systems since 1972, in a situation where the old system had ceased to be able to deliver these objectives. However, it is important to avoid a naive view of the relationship between the system as it has emerged from legislation, and the objectives claimed by government.

It would be a mistake to take the government's claimed objectives at face value. Arguably, the White Paper and other government statements from which the above objectives are distilled cannot be assumed to be part of a rational structure wherein objectives and policies are logically related. They have at least in part a polemical purpose, concerned with securing and confirming support for legislative change. In this connection objectives may be included and benefits claimed for reform on the pork barrel principle that it is necessary to show that the legislation offers some positive outcome for every interest whose support is needed to secure its passage. Particularly where local government will be responsible for implementation, central government can adopt policies and claim benefits for them, secure in the knowledge that it will not be held responsible when outcomes fail to match up to claims except where the causal chain leads undeniably back to the centre.

Consequently, stated objectives may conflict, may vary in priority, and some may be purely symbolic; other objectives may be unstated but crucial. This has implications for the evaluation of the implementation process. Whether, from the Government's point of view, the system is a "success" or "failure", can only be judged against the objectives they actually regard as important. What these are cannot be read off from policy statements, which are only one source of evidence about objectives and may be supported or contradicted by other sources.

It is also important to recognise that the government is not the only policy maker in the field. In our example the legislation primarily provides a framework within which various actors - most importantly the Secretary of State for the Environment and local housing authorities - both make policy and seek to implement it. In one sense the Secretary of State is an agent through which the government seeks to implement the policy objectives which motivated the legislation, in another he is a key policy-maker since the legislation gives him sufficient power to dilute or amend those objectives. The local authorities, too, are policy-making agencies pursuing their own objectives, which will often not coincide with those of the central government. The success or failure of the new regime, for the government, hangs on whether it is successful in so constraining the policy-making activities of the local authorities that their many and various local decisions deliver outcomes consistent with central government's objectives. For the authorities themselves the success or failure of the system depends upon how far they can continue to pursue their own locally determined objectives within or despite it.

Nor can the relationship between the government's policy objectives and the new regime, as it has emerged from legislation and been operated in practice, be taken for granted. Legislation does not begin from an otherwise blank piece of paper at the top of which are written the desired objectives; it amends and adapts a pre-existing framework of legislation in ways that are governed as much by practicability as by the objectives in mind. Like other policy-making processes, it is a process of negotiation. As Barrett and Fudge (1981) have argued, "policy is not a 'fix' but a series of intentions around which bargaining takes place and which can be modified as each set of actors attempts to negotiate to maximise its own interest and priorities."

To this it should be added that the initial negotiating stance of a set of actors may already incorporate concessions to other parties, recognising what can realistically be achieved in the negotiating process, bearing in mind the power of other actors and what is practicable. A considerable number of amendments were made to the proposed structure and operation of the new regime as the Local Government and Housing Bill passed through Parliament, some in response to local government representations. But there are also clear signs that the initial proposals, before any amendment, fell short of a system which could guarantee delivery of the objectives claimed by government.

Accordingly, our approach to the analysis of the new regime has been to look first at its structural characteristics - what it is capable of delivering, and what it cannot - and how it has been operated by the Secretary of State and civil servants in the Department of the Environment to date. This analysis provides some clues as to the objectives which underlay the introduction of the system, and their relative importance for the government, then and as the political priorities of the government have changed over time.

The impact on central-local relations

It was argued above that the turn in the early 1970s from an investment to a deficit subsidy system had important implications for central-local relations. From then on the government found it necessary to take a closer interest in what local authorities spent on managing and maintaining their stock and on the rents they charged. On one view, the new regime can be seen as the culmination of this process, with the government specifying for individual authorities the guideline rents they "ought" to charge, and the amounts they "ought" to spend on management and maintenance, and, through ring-fencing, severely restricting authorities' freedom to deviate from these guidelines. On this view, the new regime is a response by government to the fact that local authorities were using their freedom under the old system to follow rent and spending policies which failed to correspond to government objectives. Government, in retaliation, has tightened control from the centre in order to ensure that its objectives are met.

What is missing from this account is any explanation of why it is only now that government has moved to ring fence the Housing Revenue Account, and why the new regime leaves an important degree of freedom available to local authorities - freedom to set rents and spending levels which deviate from government guidelines. The short answer is that increased central control has costs as well as benefits for the government.

Local democracy and the autonomy of local government are rightly regarded as important principles in their own right. We would stress here, however, the case for local autonomy which derives from efficiency arguments. A government which has little regard for the importance of local democracy may nonetheless be persuaded that central control is more costly and less efficient that local autonomy in relation to specific services.

The concept of implementation almost by definition involves flexibility in the application of general policy principles to specific situations. The centre never has complete information and therefore cannot anticipate the circumstances in which its policies will be implemented. When outcomes fail to match expectations, it may be difficult to decide, even in principle, whether it is the policy or its implementation which has failed.

These observations suggest that the appropriate response to implementation problems is not necessarily to tighten control from the top. If the top cannot anticipate the full range of situations in which its policy will be implemented, tighter control from the top does not prevent policy failures but merely denies the implementers the flexibility needed to respond to the unanticipated. Further, the top finds it much more difficult to blame failure on those responsible for implementation. The Poll Tax is a good example of this problem. Central government was able in the first half of the 1980s successfully to blame local authorities for excessive rate increases, even though the withdrawal of rate support grant was a major cause. With the introduction of the Community Charge and unified business rate, however, coupled with widespread capping of local authorities, the restriction of local discretion became such that the widespread perception was that central rather than local government was primarily responsible for the level of the tax.

In the housing context, the Housing Finance Act, 1972, still stands as a warning of the problems which arise for government from central control. Where rent-setting powers are removed from local authorities, the government is seen as responsible for any increase, and local authorities lose any incentive to constrain spending, since it will not affect rents. Central government then faces the unpalatable choice between an open- ended commitment to subsidise spending and central control of spending as well as rents.

Central control of spending would be a nightmare for central government because of the multiplicity of local factors influencing the "need to spend", which cannot be reflected in a simple formula applicable to all authorities. Fine-tuning the formula to fit each local situation would be a time-consuming and costly process, while ignoring local variation in costs would leave the government open to the charge of underfunding the service to tenants.

Linking subsidy to a notional Housing Revenue Account, while leaving authorities to determine actual rents and spending levels, mitigates these problems, but does not avoid them altogether. Now that all authorities are brought back within the scope of the subsidy system, and given the ring-fencing of the Housing Revenue Account, the annual subsidy determination is a much more significant element in a local authority's annual budgeting process. Authorities are much more vulnerable to an unfavourable subsidy determination than when they could use a rate fund contribution to compensate. Consequently they are much more motivated to renegotiate the determination if they can. Conversely, civil servants at the Department of Environment and Welsh Office have a greater interest in avoiding determinations which can be represented in public as arbitrary in their effects, and are motivated from their side to negotiate. Moreover, the method of calculating subsidy leaves plenty of scope, at least in the early years, for negotiation, since it is based on data supplied by the local authority which the authority can, to some extent, influence.

Examples of this include authorities, such as Sandwell, which reopened its accounts for 1988/89 in order to decapitalise £15 million in repairs spending with the effect that the subsidy allowance for maintenance in 1990/91 and 1991/92 was significantly increased.

However, the use of a notional Housing Revenue Account is not without its disadvantages. It means that, in effect, the government has a single policy instrument with which to influence local authority behaviour - the amount of subsidy provided. Although the subsidy determination is based on a guideline rent and management and maintenance allowance, the amount of subsidy is related to the difference between the two. The same amount of subsidy is therefore equally consistent with the combination of a high guideline rent with a high management and maintenance allowance or low rent and management and maintenance allowances.

The notional Housing Revenue Account approach offers the local authority a trade-off between rent levels and management and maintenance spending, the terms of which can be varied by central government giving or withholding subsidy. But its basic limitation is that one policy instrument cannot deliver more than one policy objective. The government can use withdrawal of subsidy to force up rents, provided local authorities wish to maintain the same real level of spending on management and maintenance. Alternatively, the provision of additional subsidy may encourage higher spending on management and maintenance, on the assumption that authorities are not likely to prefer to reduce rents, although there is no guarantee that authorities would use the extra resources efficiently. But the government cannot use the subsidy system to induce authorities to raise rents in order to finance higher spending and a better standard of service.

This analysis suggests, and the history of the first few years of the 1980 Act system bears out, that this type of system works best as a means of forcing up rents, perhaps providing incentives to cost-efficiency as a side effect, as authorities strive to preserve services while minimising the rent increase.

A further consequence of the notional HRA approach is that government is not constrained to ensure that management and maintenance allowances really reflect the "need to spend" in individual authorities, or that actual rents correspond to guidelines.

Like its predecessor, the new regime is PESC-driven. Thus, a senior civil servant responsible for the administration of the system took pains in a SAUS seminar in 1990 to deny that guideline rents are based on capital values, even though they are proportional to capital values. He meant that capital values and their movements are not the starting point for the annual determination of guideline rents. A PESC-generated amount for aggregated guideline rents is the starting point, and capital values are used only as the means of distributing the aggregate between local authorities.

The same applies to management and maintenance allowances; these are not derived from an estimate of an authority's need to spend. The aggregate allowance for management and maintenance is determined once aggregate subsidy and rents are known (together with aggregate capital spend and receipts estimates), and targeting of management and maintenance is only a means of distributing this total.

In the PESC process, the government, too, is faced with a trade-off between rents and spending levels. A given total amount of subsidy can be distributed to local authorities by specifying relatively low rent guidelines and management and maintenance allowances or higher rent guidelines matched by higher management and maintenance allowances.

It was claimed in the 1987 White Paper that some local authorities tend to spend too little on repairing their housing stock, because they are politically biased towards low rents regardless of the consequences for repairs spending. This suggests that, in order to address this problem, the government ought to adopt relatively high management and maintenance allowances, and rent guidelines to match.

However, this choice has political and economic consequences. Although Conservative governments have not shown themselves unwilling to seek rent increases from local authorities, there is an upper limit to the increases that the government wishes to be seen to be recommending, particularly in a system where rent guidelines vary with capital values and the highest capital values are in Conservative-controlled authorities in the South. Equally, projected local authority rent increases are fed into economic forecasting models, so that it may be necessary for the government to limit rent increases in order to make plausible a projected fall in inflation. Thirdly, the terms of the subsidy trade-off for government are such that an increase in rent guidelines does not permit a pound for pound increase in management and maintenance allowances, since higher rents also mean that provision must be made for additional rent rebate subsidy.

These considerations, we argue, have tended to bias annual subsidy determinations towards a relatively low rent-low management and maintenance pairing, particularly within the context of a substantial reduction in overall subsidy, despite the claimed long-term objective of higher repairs spending.

The effects of this bias are apparent in the experience of the first two years of the new regime - the majority of authorities are spending well above their allowances for management and maintenance, and financing this spending with rents substantially above government guidelines. Paradoxically, therefore, the new regime has achieved the government objective of higher spending financed by higher rents, despite the limitations of the notional Housing Revenue Account approach.

Conclusions

In summary form, the following provisional conclusions can be drawn:

1) The new financial regime attempts to impose a significant reduction in local autonomy, to secure centrally-imposed objectives from local authorities which are perceived by the centre to be indifferent or hostile to them. However, an important by-product of the tightening of central control is increased scope and incentives for negotiation between the centre and local authorities.

2) The structural features of the system indicate that it was designed with implementation problems in mind. In particular, the composition of the Housing Revenue Account subsidy reflects the importance attached to recouping surpluses at the local level and the history of difficulties in implementing this objective.

3) Despite the stated objective of greater simplicity, the new regime is highly complicated, in part because it relies on local authorities to collect large amounts of data from which the rent guidelines and management and maintenance allowances are calculated.

4) The government has two stated objectives relating to rents and management and maintenance, and it seeks to deliver these by giving or withholding subsidy. This single instrument is incapable in principle of delivering both objectives, and is more powerful in relation to rents than management and maintenance.

5) The evidence from 1990/91 and 1991/92 shows that in practice authorities tended to set rents above guidelines and that they did so in order to spend above management and maintenance allowances.

6) Thus, although, the structure of the new regime makes it impossible for the government to impose both higher rents and higher management and maintenance spending, this appears to have been the most common outcome of the system in its first two years of operation.

8 Alternative rent setting regimes in the public sector: Some implications

Bruce Walker and Alex Marsh

Introduction

This chapter is concerned with the nature of rent-setting in the local authority sector and the implications of alternative rent-setting regimes. Central to our work here is a comparison of the rents actually set by local authorities, particularly at the time of our research (1988/89), and those that might be set under alternative regimes. Some distributional implications are also highlighted. The analysis presented here is a summary and extension of part of the results of our research into the housing finance and subsidy system in the Birmingham Travel to Work Area (TTWA) which are discussed more fully elsewhere (Walker *et al*, 1991).

We proceed as follows; the next section briefly discusses the principles which might guide the choice of rent-setting regime while the third section examines the rent-setting methods operating at the time of our study. We then consider some alternative regimes and present the methods by which rents could be calculated under each. Having established these principles, we present the results of our analysis for 1988-89 and discuss the developments following form the 1989 Local Government and Housing Act. The relevance of our analysis to questions of principle are considered in the concluding section.

Rent-setting in the public sector - questions of principle

Bramley (1991) has provided an illuminating discussion of the principles which might govern the setting of rents in the public sector. Three such principles are particularly pertinent to the subject matter of this chapter.

The first concerns the need to ensure that tenants are able to afford the rents set. As Hancock (1991) has shown, affordability is open to a number of interpretations, but it is clear that, if a primary objective in the provision of public housing is to allow tenants to consume more housing services than they could in the private market, then in order for at least some of the eligible households to be encouraged to enter the sector rent payments for such housing must bear some relationship to tenants' perceptions of their ability to pay. Broadly, there are at least two methods of keeping rents affordable. On the one hand, the housing operations of local authorities can be in receipt of a general subsidy enabling rents to be set at a level below that required to cover all housing-related costs and, on the other, a system of tenant-specific income-related assistance can operate. Both systems currently operate in the public sector, with tenant specific subsidy provided by the Housing Benefit (HB) system.

The second principle concerns the role of rents in promoting efficiency in the provision, use and maintenance of the public housing stock - that is, the extent to which rents in the public sector should act as price signals to suppliers and consumers in the manner ascribed to prices in traditional market analysis. To the extent that they should, then this suggests that rents should reflect the costs of providing rental housing. We discuss below which costs are relevant to rent-setting, but note here that rents set according to historic costs are likely to differ substantially from those reflecting the current value of housing services. However, it is the current value of housing services which, in terms of allocative efficiency, are pertinent to the determination of rents. A related efficiency consideration is that provided by the principle of second best which suggests that, given the existence of non-market pricing in other sectors of the housing market, setting rents related to current values in the public sector could be sub-optimal. Moreover, such rents are likely to be inequitable as between similar households in different sectors. To the extent that distortions in other sectors are being removed - through, for example, the de-regulation of the private rented sector - the force of the second best argument is weakened.

The final consideration is that of positive externalities in the consumption of public housing. To the extent that the rest of society benefits in a material or psychological sense from such consumption by tenants, then the rents set should reflect this external benefit. A problem here is that at present such benefits are largely unmeasured and thus afford little practical guidance in this context.

Limiting our attention to affordability and efficiency, it is clear that the two principles can conflict. A rent-setting regime which solely pursues efficiency on the basis of some market criterion is likely to impose intolerable costs on some households and, in practice, is likely to place heavy burdens on national taxpayers through the income support system. Alternatively a rent-setting mechanism designed solely in the light of some affordability criterion may lead to rents which bear little relationship to the true resource costs of housing. Consequently, an acceptable rent-setting mechanism is likely to reflect a trade-off between these two principles.

Rent-setting in the public sector

With the notable exception of the period 1972-75, local authorities have long had autonomy in their decisions as to both the rent-setting method employed and the rent levels set. Thus, it might be expected that generalisations as to the nature of the public sector rent regimes would be fraught with difficulty. In practice, however, all the local authorities in the Birmingham TTWA - in common with around half such authorities nationally (Maclennan, 1986) - have traditionally employed the gross value method (GVM) for determining rents. The key parameter under the GVM is the ratio of the aggregate sum to be raised from rents to the gross value. The gross value is the rateable value of the stock plus an allowance for repairs and maintenance. The rent for an individual dwelling is determined by applying this ratio to its gross value. The rent may subsequently be subject to adjustments according to, for example, the desirability or environmental quality of the area in which the dwelling is located.

Given this, at least three important issues require consideration. Firstly, the aggregate sum to be raised in rents; secondly, the relationship between the rents set using the GVM and historic costs and, finally, the relationship between those rents and current values.

Consider first the aggregate sum to be raised in rents. This is a product of both past and current local policy decisions and, in addition, is subject to central government influence. The required gross rental income is partly determined by total expenditure on the Housing Revenue Account (HRA) and the other non-rent sources of income on which an authority can draw, as well as local policy as to whether the HRA should balance or generate a surplus. It is also influenced by national government determinations as to the level of Exchequer subsidy entitlement and the ability of, or effective cost to, local authorities of drawing on alternative sources of income.

To clarify, consider Table 8.1 which shows the combined HRA for England and Wales in 1988/89, the year of our study. Approximately one third of all income to the HRA accrued from sources other than gross rents. The most important single source was interest receipts from (primarily) the sale of council dwellings. General Exchequer subsidy and contributions from the rate fund (RFCs) can be seen as transfers from national and local taxpayers respectively which lower the average rent which an authority needs to set in order to meet its financial objectives of either balancing or making a surplus on the HRA. While Central Government

119

influences on the amount which local authorities needed to raise from their stock during the 1980s have been documented elsewhere (e.g. Hills, 1991a; Malpass, 1990) we note here that over the 1980s Exchequer subsidy fell from 31 per cent of income to the HRA in 1980/81 to the 5 per cent shown in Table 1. In addition, during the 1980s transfers to the HRA from the rate fund in excess of those assessed under the notional HRA deficit (E7) component of the Rate Support Grant became increasingly costly for those authorities - the majority - facing negative marginal rates of grant (see Hills, 1987). Over the same period the tenant-specific rent rebate element of HB rose from 8.1 per cent to the 33 per cent shown in Table 1. This can be interpreted as a conscious attempt by Central Government to redirect assistance away from rents in general and towards those tenants likely to face affordability difficulties, as defined by the HB regulations.

Table 8.1
Combined housing revenue account: England and Wales,
1988/89

expenditure (%)			income (%)
loan charges	43	31	net rents
management	18	33	rebates (HB)
repair and maintenance	24	2	other charges
transfers to rate fund	3	5	exchequer subsidy
other expenditure	2	2	other rents
balances	9	3	miscellaneous
		12	interest receipts
		5	RFCs
		8	balances
total (%)	100	100	
Total (£bill)	6.8	6.8	

Source: CIPFA, HRA Actuals, 1988/89

The complexity and variation of these influences on rent levels nationally is mirrored locally in the Birmingham TTWA, even though, as already noted, all the constituent authorities employed versions of the GVM. Birmingham, Bromsgrove and Lichfield, for example, in 1988/89 received no Exchequer subsidy, whereas 12.5 per cent and 31.1 per cent of income to the HRA in Tamworth and Redditch respectively came from this source. No authorities were assessed as being in E7 deficit and only Birmingham City made any significant use of RFCs, although these amounted to less than 5 per cent of income. Some 8 per cent of the expenditure in Bromsgrove consisted of transfers to the rate fund while Redditch made small transfers of less than 1 per cent. Approximately two thirds of tenants in the TTWA were in receipt of HB in 1988/89, broadly the same proportion as public tenants nationally.

120

Table 8.2 shows the results of these influences on gross rent levels and rent rises in six of the TTWA authorities.

Table 8.2
Average gross rents in 1988/89 (£ p.w.) and gross rent rises 1982/83–1988/89

district	average gross rents 1988/89	% rise in average rents 1982/83 - 1988/89
Birmingham	18.77	41.2
Solihull	19.48	45.8
Bromsgrove	14.64	8.6
Redditch	19.01	28.5
Tamworth	19.93	34.8
Lichfield	17.03	35.9

Source: CIPFA, Housing Rents Statistics

The range of average gross rents was relatively narrow at £5 per week, but the experience of tenants in respect of rent rises varied enormously across authorities. There is clearly no simple relationship between Exchequer subsidy, E7 and the net use of RFCs, on the one hand, and rent levels and rent rises on the other. Indeed during the 1980s Central Government was less concerned with the rent levels set in individual authorities and with the method used to set those rents, than with the desire to see rents in general rise and public expenditure reduced. Because explicit specification of a required or desirable rent level - as opposed to rent increase - for individual housing authorities was not a feature of the 1980s housing finance system, local authorities could continue to generate the required gross rental income using the GVM.

This leads us to our second issue. Since the GVM is used to distribute the required rental income across the stock, there is no necessary relation between the costs - historic and current - attributable to an individual dwelling and the rent set for that dwelling. To the extent that gross values do not reflect such costs, rents are likely to fall below loan charges and maintenance expenditure on high cost property and exceed those costs on low cost property. Seen in this historic cost accounting framework, local authority tenants are cross- subsidizing each other. Indeed, this can be seen as a desirable feature of the GVM. Given that tenants may have had little choice regarding the particular dwelling which they occupy, a rent-setting method that spreads rents across the stock such that a tenant does not face the actual costs of occupying their property can be argued to be more equitable. A study of the effects of such rent pooling in Sheffield (Crook et al, 1990) has shown this to be significant in terms of the costs and benefits implied for the occupants of different areas, although the

121

distributional equity of such an arrangement depends on the nature of the households in those different areas, their resources and the net rents paid.

Even if genuine historic cost pricing were desirable, on practical grounds it is probably infeasible since local authorities do not in general record outstanding debt on individual properties and therefore would not be able to calculate rents on this basis. More importantly, it can be argued that historic cost pricing is not, in any event, an efficient form of pricing. This brings us to our third issue: under the GVM there is no necessary relation between the rent set for a dwelling and its current value. The use of some form of current value criterion for setting rents runs counter not only to local authority accounting conventions, but also to what many, until the 1989 Act at least, have deemed to be the role of public housing - namely, increasing or maintaining the material welfare of tenants by charging affordable rents; this, in turn, has traditionally meant that rents are not explicitly related to the current value of the dwellings.

Differences in the debt profile of the housing stock and variation in local housing policy across authorities suggest that identical households in identical dwellings in very similar - even contiguous - local authority areas could face very different rents for their dwellings by virtue of their location within a particular authority's boundary, even though they are residing in the same broad market area, such as the TTWA. As Maclennan et al (1991) have suggested, given tenants entitlement to HB, the cost to national taxpayers of supporting the housing expenditure of individual tenants through the HB system will vary between identical tenants in similar areas.

For many authorities at the time of our study the sum generated from gross rental income was less than that needed to meet expenditure, and the GVM did not necessarily distribute this sum efficiently in relation to dwelling values nor equitably between tenants within a local authority area. Thus the alternative methods of rent-setting that might be employed to price local authority housing services and the implications of such alternatives are clearly important subjects for study.

Some alternative rent-setting regimes

We examine two possible alternative rent-setting regimes that might be implemented. The first is the regime suggested by Hills (1988a) concerning the setting of 'target' rents and the second is a regime that bases rents on the capital values of public sector dwellings.

Briefly, the target rent approach suggests that, first, rents in the social housing sector should be related to ability to pay; second, that they need to incorporate an element of management and maintenance; and third that they should represent a rate of return on housing capital reflecting both the first consideration (affordability) and the need to replace (or substantially renovate) the dwelling at the end of (or during) its life; this is allowed for through a depreciation element. The target rent-setting regime would be augmented by an Exchequer subsidy where total revenues so generated fail to meet expenditure on the HRA. The advantages and disadvantages of this scheme are discussed in Bramley (1991) but it does have the advantage of attempting to ensure, in a way that contemporary regimes do not,

> 'that the overall level of rents (is) in line with the means of tenants, while relativities between individual tenants (bear) a defined relationship to the economic cost of providing different dwellings' (Hills, 1988a, p.10).

Thus, in principle at least, both efficiency and a measure of affordability are an integral part of the system.

The principle underlying our second alternative regime - capital value (CV) rents - is that rents should reflect a rate of return on public housing assets competitive with those offered on assets of similar risk. Note that the notion of a rent reflecting capital values needs to be approached with caution. If local authorities were to set rents in relation to capital values and were to act in the manner of private sector investors in rental housing by requiring a 'market' return on dwellings, their significance in the local rented housing market is such that their near monopoly position could lead to monopoly pricing and the attendant allocative and distributional problems. To the extent that a mandatory rate of return was imposed on authorities to obviate such problems, this would represent a loss of local autonomy (as indeed could be the case with a target rent regime) and could engender significant central-local government friction.

While we recognize the possibility of such problems arising, we also recognize that the issue of relating rents to capital values is firmly on the housing policy agenda. They have been recommended by, *inter alia*, Maclennan *et al* (1991) and the reconvened Duke of Edinburgh's *Inquiry into British Housing*. In addition, Central Government, under the 1989 Act, has started the process of defining a particular rate of return to public housing capital for the purposes of subsidy calculation: relating rents to some notion of capital values in the public sector is a political reality.

While ultimately the acceptability and desirability of CV rents depends on the rate of return set, it has to be recognized that current inconsistencies in the pricing of housing capital within and between authorities generate windfall gains and losses for tenants in a manner that a consistent pricing mechanism would not. Moving to CV rents would lead to more consistent pricing.

Moreover, the exercise of examining the relationship between actual rents and those that might be set under a CV regime is of value in itself, even if the latter is rejected as a policy option. The size and distribution of any differences between CV rents and rents actually set can be seen as the sum the society is prepared to forgo in order to generate the benefits for tenants and others that existing pricing mechanisms yield. It may thus assist in the estimation of the value of housing-related externalities noted above.

In respect of both the target and CV rent regimes it is realistic to assume that they would operate in conjunction with a tenant-specific subsidy like HB. However, it can be argued that this weakens the role that target and, particularly, CV rents would play in acting as price signals to consumers, since HB drives a wedge between the rents set and those paid by tenants. We note the traditional argument that the replacement of a price subsidy - which HB effectively is for public sector tenants - with an income transfer to eligible tenants could assist in the restoration of rents as indicators of the cost of resources to consumers. We also recognize that such a change in the nature of HB as received by public sector tenants would almost certainly result in levels of housing consumption below that which they currently experience. We return to the significance of HB in our conclusions.

Clearly in principle the GVM, target rent and CV rent regimes operate in different manners. The preceding discussion implies that a move to an alternative regime would result in rises in rents for at least some tenants. However, the financial benefits which tenants receive as a result of the operation of the existing rent-setting regime and the financial context in which it works, compared to the suggested alternatives, depend on the extent to which the rents set under the GVM (plus adjustments) in our study year actually differ significantly from those that would be set under the alternative regimes. It is quite possible, given the objectives of different authorities and the varying impacts of the subsidy and accounting systems under which they operate, that local authority rents may approximate or even exceed those which might obtain under either target or CV rents. This is an issue central to our empirical work below.

Estimating rents under alternative regimes

Target rent estimates are achieved by following the approach suggested by Hills (1988). This requires setting a rate of return on the market value of a new dwelling equal to 10.5 per cent of national average male earnings, net of national average management and maintenance (M and M) and 1.2 per cent depreciation related to the replacement costs (new construction costs net of a land element) of a dwelling. The 'pure' rate of return calculated for 1988/89 was 1.18 per cent. This rate of return when applied to local dwelling values derived from Right to Buy data gives, when local M and M and depreciation on local new construction costs are included, the target rent. Target rents were calculated as an average for each of the six authorities in the TTWA.

CV rents were calculated by estimating a real rate of return based on an inflation adjusted average of twenty year Treasury Bill rates and building society lending rates, net of the long run annual average real growth in regional house prices. Real growth in house prices was calculated over two regional house price cycles (15 years). On the grounds that investors are likely to take a medium term view of returns from investing in assets such as housing, a seven year average rate of return - 1982/83 to 1988/89 - was also calculated on the same basis. This latter rate was calculated as 4.88 per cent, and this is the rate employed below.

While this 4.88 per cent rate of return is sensitive to the assumptions and time periods employed, it is broadly similar to that suggested in the 1985 Duke of Edinburgh's *Inquiry into British Housing*, which suggested a rate of return of 4 per cent plus an allowance for management and maintenance, and similar to the approximately 4.4 per cent gross rate used by the Government in the calculation of the post-1989 Act subsidy entitlement.

In our analysis of CV rents we employed 4.88 per cent as a gross rate of return and did not allow explicitly for M and M because it is unclear to what extent differences in required maintenance expenditures are already capitalised into the value of the dwelling. The rate of return was also annuitized over a 60 year period to allow for the finite life of dwellings on the assumption that investors would wish to recoup their investment over the life of the dwelling. This approach obviates the need for a depreciation allowance.

To facilitate comparison with target rents, in the first instance the 4.88 per cent rate of return was applied to average RTB values for each authority. Both target and CV rents were compared with actual rents for 1988/89. Further, in order to assess the subsidy or surplus implications for the HRAs of the individual authorities, we compared average rents under the two regimes with 'break-even' rents. Break-even rents are the average rents an authority would need to set if they could rely only on gross rental income to meet that expenditure actually relating to their housing stock. To assess such expenditure certain items, such as expenditure on special services, were excluded (see Walker *et al*, 1991, for the details of calculating break-even rents).

In order to examine the distributional effects of the introduction of a CV rent regime for the households in the JRF survey, individual dwelling values for public sector respondents in Birmingham City were estimated for 1988/89 on the basis of an hedonic regression calculated from building society data for the TTWA, supplied by the Nationwide Anglia Building Society (NABS). This was used to impute dwelling values for the survey respondents in that year. Incorporated in the regression were a set of neighbourhood quality variables, grouped according to their desirability as manifested by their influence on price and ranked

Neighbourhood 1 (least desirable) through Neighbourhood 6 (most desirable). This hedonic explained approximately two- thirds of the variation in prices in the NABS data set. Further details can be found in Walker and Marsh (1991).

Alternative rent-setting regimes - results for 1988/89

Table 8.3 presents the relationship between actual rents and those average rent levels implied under the target and capital value regimes for each of the local authorities in the Birmingham TTWA. A number of points emerge from consideration of these results: the target rent regime implies rent increases on average in all authorities, the maximum being around £7.50 p.w. in Bromsgrove; the range of average rents is broadly the same as under the actual regimes, at around £5.40 p.w. Interestingly, target rents would be sufficient to cover total expenditure as reflected by the break-even rent, in all the authorities except Redditch and Tamworth without requiring any general (as opposed to tenant-specific) subsidies to the Account.

Table 8.3
Average rents under alternative rent-setting regimes, 1988/89, £ p.w.

district	actual average rent	break-even rent	target rent	cv rent @ 4.88%
Birmingham	18.77	20.42	22.59	22.83
Solihull	19.48	20.60	23.27	25.88
Bromsgrove	14.64	17.19	22.21	27.01
Redditch	19.01	32.55	25.37	32.09
Tamworth	19.93	29.54	23.04	26.93
Lichfield	17.03	15.50	19.98	25.37

The CV and target rent regime generate very similar rents in Birmingham. However, under the CV rent regime all tenants would, on average, experience higher rent rises - averaging around £13 p.w. in Bromsgrove and Redditch - than under a target rent regime. Again, only the HRAs of Tamworth and (marginally) Redditch would fail to at least break-even.

Table 8.4 summarizes the gains and losses from the point of view of tenants implied by the potential introduction of the above rent regimes by indicating the average change in rent per dwelling under each regime relative to actual average rents. In addition, we indicate the per dwelling subsidy (+) required or the potential surplus (-) per dwelling generated under each regime by comparing the respective rents with the break-even level.

As the earlier calculations implied, the subsidy required under the target rent regime is concentrated in two authorities in the

126

TTWA (Redditch and Tamworth). This also occurs under the CV rent regime although, overall, the subsidies per dwelling are significantly lower. Four out of the six authorities would generate surpluses and would not require general subsidies to their HRAs.

Both regimes imply rent rises for tenants of an order greater than those incorporated in the annual rent increase guidelines assumed under the Exchequer subsidy calculation in the 1980s: on average rents would rise by 25 per cent across the TTWA under the target rent regime and by 47 per cent (£8.54) under the CV regime. This would suggest, firstly, that in practice careful phasing would be required if either regime were to be introduced and, secondly, that in respect of the CV regime in particular, increasing rents by almost one half in a situation where the majority of tenants already receive assistance would have serious implications for the HB system.

Table 8.4
Gains (+) and losses (-) to tenants and subsidy (+) and surplus (-) implications, £ p.w.

district	break-even rent	target rent regime	req. subs.	cv rent @ 4.88%	req. subs.
Birmingham	-1.65	-3.82	-2.17	-4.06	-2.41
Solihull	-1.12	-3.79	-2.67	-6.40	-5.28
Bromsgrove	-2.55	-7.57	-5.02	-12.37	-9.82
Redditch	-13.54	-6.36	+7.18	-13.08	+0.46
Tamworth	-9.61	-3.11	+6.50	-7.00	+2.61
Lichfield	+1.53	-2.95	-4.48	-8.34	-9.87

It is clear from these results that public sector tenants within the Birmingham TTWA fare less badly under a target than a CV regime. However it is also clear that tenants had not only very different experiences in terms of the recent average rents levied by the constituent authorities, but also would experience different gains and losses on the imposition of different regimes both according to the regimes themselves and the local authority area in which they reside. The contrast between, for example, Birmingham and Redditch under the CV regime and under the target rent regime are instructive in this respect. A key consideration is the manner in which rent rises might be distributed. Since we are dealing with average rents at the level of the local authority itself, the distributional implications cannot be assessed at this level of analysis. To attempt an assessment of this we consider the experience of public sector tenants responding in the JRF survey.

Elsewhere (Walker *et al*, 1991; Walker and Marsh, 1991) we have examined the distributional implications of the CV regime for the local authorities in the TTWA as a whole. Since we have established that the experience of tenants varies according to the local authority in which they reside, we here examine these issues for the largest group of tenants in the TTWA, those in the City of Birmingham. We also limit our examination to the implications of the CV rent regime; the target rent calculation incorporates two elements that are effectively constant across properties - the depreciation element and management and maintenance; in practice the latter would need to be calculated as an average for the stock as a whole. The variable element is the sum generated by applying the rate of return to dwelling values; the target rent will thus vary in the same way as the CV rent, but as Table 8.3 suggests, it will take a lower absolute value.

Consider first the relationship between actual rents set and CV rents by property type presented in Table 8.5. It is clear that the tenants that benefit least from the prevailing rent-setting policy are those that occupy flats and terraced dwellings. Given the rate of return, the difference between CV and actual rents was between £5 and £6 per week for such tenants, compared to £13 and £18 per week for occupants of the other property types.

Table 8.5
Actual rents and CV rents by dwelling type, £ p.a. (rounded)

dwelling type	actual rent as % of cv @ 4.88%	cv rent - actual rent rent
semi-detached house	66	660
terraced house	82	277
bungalow	60	925
flat	80	308
sample mean	76	421
sample size = 111		

The variation in the difference between CV and actual rent across neighbourhood type (Table 8.6) indicates that tenants resident in the lower value neighbourhoods benefit least from the prevailing rent-setting policy. This is particularly so in Neighbourhood 1 in which the mean difference is less than £2 per week. Some 70 per cent of tenants in the Birmingham sample lived in terraced dwellings or flats and 72 per cent were located in Neighbourhoods 1 or 2. While the mean difference is around £8 per week for tenants as a whole, the degree to which CV rents would exceed actual rents for those public tenants in other types of property or in other neighbourhoods is substantially higher than this figure.

Table 8.6
Actual rents and CV rents by neighbourhood, £ p.a. (rounded)

neighbourhood type	actual rent as % of cv rent @ 4.88%	cv rent- actual rent
1	94	97
2	75	384
3	74	491
4	71	554
5	54	950
6	61	1459
sample mean	76	421

sample size = 111

Table 8.7
CV rents and actual rents by income group, £ p.a., Birmingham City

income group (£s)	CV rent (@ 4.88%) - actual rent		actual rent as % of CV rent @ 4.88%
	mean	s.d.	
less than 2,400	450.3	514.7	77.0
2,400 to 5,199	360.2	339.0	77.5
5,200 to 7,799	516.9	308.9	68.5
7,800 to 10,399	416.3	339.6	75.8
10,400 to 12,999	266.6	8.2	83.2
13,000 to 15,599	239.5	380.9	85.9
15,600 to 20,799	361.2	67.4	77.4
20,800 to 25,999[1]	664.2	729.5	69.1
26,000 to 31,199[1]	1924.8	-	43.8
sample mean	411.8	387.1	76.1

sample Size = 106

1. 20,800 to 31,199 contains less than 3% of tenants

The degree to which a tenant benefits from the existing pricing mechanism thus depends on the area and dwelling to which they are allocated. To the extent that household income is not a key consideration in the process of allocating tenants to particular dwellings, we would expect only a tenuous relationship between income and extent to which they benefit. Table 8.7 supports this expectation. While little clear pattern is discernible in the degree to which different income groups benefit from rent-setting policy, middle income groups tend to benefit less than lower income groups.

Table 8.8 brings these considerations together, showing the results of an OLS regression of property type, neighbourhood and income characteristics on the relationship between CV rent and actual rents. Income is not statistically significant while property and neighbourhood characteristics dominate. These factors, however, explain less than half of the variation in the level of benefit received from the existing, compared to the CV, regime; this indicates that actual rents do not consistently reflect the neighbourhood and dwelling characteristics that determine capital values.

Table 8.8
Explaining the CV rent/actual rent relationship

independent variables	dependent variables	
	cv - actual rent	actual as % of cv @ 4.88%
constant	1309.70 **	0.41**
	(148.68)	(0.11)
SEMI-DETACHED	-323.56 *	0.09
	(127.83)	(0.09)
FLAT	-669.11 **	0.24 **
	(121.21)	(0.09)
TERRACED	-568.99 **	0.19*
	(121.34)	(0.09)
NHOOD1	-730.87**	0.35**
	(124.89)	(0.09)
NHOOD2	-477.62 **	0.18 *
	(102.21)	(0.07)
NHOOD3	-390.63 **	0.17
	(134.81)	(0.10)
NHOOD4	-201.48	0.08
	(139.38)	(0.10)
INCOME	0.01	0.001 [1]
	(0.01)	(0.004)
adjusted R^2	0.45	0.25
sample size	106	106

significance level: 0.95 ≥ * < 0.99
** ≥ 0.99
Standard Errors in Brackets

1.   Income in £000s

Since any given rent increase will have most effect on those with lower incomes, a move to rents reflecting a gross return of 4.88 per cent would have a significant impact on the lowest income groups in particular, who would face rent increases of between

£6.75 per week and £10 per week. In practice, since the majority of such tenants are receiving HB the costs of these rent increases would be borne by the taxpayer. National taxpayers are thus those most likely to bear the direct costs of the search for efficiency through the imposition of CV rents.

Some implications of the 1989 Local Government and Housing Act

With effect from April 1990, the 1989 Act introduced a new finance and subsidy system for local authority housing. Its main features include the effective proscription of voluntary transfers from the HRA to the community charge fund and vice versa and severe limitations on the amount of interest from capital receipts which can be credited to the fund - the so- called 'ring-fencing' provisions. The new HRA subsidy incorporates assumptions as to the gross rent and rent increases for each authority. The technical details of this system are discussed elsewhere (DoE, 1990; Hills, 1991a; London Housing Unit, 1990), and here we concentrate on the implications of the gross rent guidelines.

For 1990/91 these guidelines were based on an assumption that £4.677 billion should be raised in public sector rents from a stock valued, on the basis of RTB valuations, at £107.37 billion; this implies a rent level representing around 4.4 per cent of the value of each authority's stock. To the extent that actual rents would need to rise rapidly in some authorities to meet this, a maximum rent increase of £4.50 per week was assumed; to the extent that rents would fall in areas with particularly low valued stock, a minimum rise of 95p was assumed.

A particular feature pertinent to our analysis is that, while the damped and inflation adjusted sum to be raised by an authority is related to the capital value of its stock, the system does not require authorities to set rents on individual properties at a level representing 4.4 per cent of their (estimated) value. Rather, section 162 of the Act requires authorities to have regard to relative rents in the private sector in determining relative rents on different types of property within their stock, but this is not mandatory and is simply one of a number of factors which authorities need to consider. Hence the actual practice of rent-setting is likely to differ from that implied under our CV regime, despite superficial similarities between the two. Indeed there is no requirement that local authorities actually raise the amount in gross rents that the guidelines imply, so that authorities can raise and/or distribute rent increases in the same manner as under the GVM if they so wish.

Analyzing the effects of the 1989 Act on local authorities' rent-setting is a major study in itself. Here we can make only some broad observations on its effects on rents and tenants in the TTWA in comparison with the potential effects of the target and CV regimes.

We can note first that given changes in some of the key parameters in the calculation of both target and CV rents, the

131

rates of return implied for those regimes are lower than in 1988/89 -0.6 per cent for the 'pure' rate of return under the former and 2.75 per cent under the latter. Thus while on average both regimes would imply increases in rents for tenants in the TTWA as a whole in 1990/91, these are lower than those implied for 1988/89 at 17 per cent for the target, and 21 per cent for the CV regime. Moreover in one very significant case - Birmingham - CV rents at £23.73 per week are below both target rents (£28.47) and actual rents (£24.85). This is partly a result of high expenditure on maintenance planned for 1990/91 by the City of Birmingham - an important feature of the practical operation of the 1990 system (see Warburton and Malpass, 1991). It is also significant to note that in the case of both Birmingham and Solihull, the transition from 1989/90 rent levels to those implied by the target and CV regimes for 1990/91 could have been achieved within the maximum increase guideline of £4.50.

The assessment of the distributional implications of the 1989 Act must be approached with great caution, given the available data. However, it would appear that when rents representing a 2.75 per cent rate of return on inflated 1988/89 capital values in Birmingham are compared to rents which tenants would be facing if they experienced the average rent increase for 1988/89 to 1990/91, tenants in lower valued neighbourhoods and in flats and terraced houses would be facing actual rents greater than those that would be levied under a CV regime. This reinforces our belief that tenants in these properties and areas do less well under both the pre- and post-1989 Act regimes, and in practice would lose least - or might even gain - from a move to a rent regime which more adequately reflects capital values.

Conclusions

The results presented above suggest that the rent-setting methods employed in 1988/89, relative to the alternatives examined, generated benefits for tenants which were primarily a function of the type of dwelling, type of neighbourhood and, as expected, local authority area in which those tenants were located. Given the higher rents implied by the alternatives, moving to either a target rent or a CV rent regime in that year would therefore have imposed costs on tenants which would similarly have varied by location. With the change in both the financial regime for local authority housing and in the key parameters of the target and CV rent calculation by 1990/91, tenants in Birmingham City would, on average, have gained from a move to CV rents, particularly those in poorer neighbourhoods and in flats or terraced properties. These results stem from the fact that current rent-setting methods do not appear to adequately reflect the value of housing services consumed by tenants, a consideration which is central to the role and function of rents and one which is a key element in both of the alternative regimes examined.

In general, however, a move to CV rents would have tended, given the exceptions we have noted, to lead to quite significant rent rises across the local authority areas studied. Such rent rises would inevitably have increased both the number and the level of HB claims. This has two implications; first, the role of CV rents in promoting efficient resource use, from the tenants' perspective at least, is seriously weakened; second, the costs of this attempt to ensure such efficiency would largely be met by national taxpayers through the HB system. We would argue that it is likely to be more acceptable to taxpayers for the funding of tenants facing affordability problems to be achieved by incorporating such a consideration into the rate of return required on public housing capital, rather than wholly through the 'explicit' subsidy of HB. Attempts to achieve this result through general subsidies to the HRA or through rent-setting methods which encourage cross-subsidies between tenants are likely to be less efficient than those which allow relative rents to vary with the value of housing consumed, but determine the absolute level of rents with affordability in mind. The appropriate rate of return which should be set to achieve this is a matter for debate and cannot be determined without consideration of the costs and benefits for consumers which pricing mechanisms in other sectors generate. However, to the extent that a target rent regime attempts to achieve both efficiency and affordability in rent-setting, we believe that it is likely to prove a fairer and more acceptable way of determining rents than that implied by a simple CV regime or, indeed, than the methods currently in use in much of the public sector.

Part Four
INHERITANCE, OLDER PEOPLE AND MOBILITY

9 Housing inheritance in Britain: Its scale, value, incidence and uses

Chris Hamnett and Peter Williams

Introduction

The level of owner occupation in Britain has increased rapidly in the last 40 years rising from 3 million dwellings (31 per cent of households) in 1951 to 15.4 million dwellings (67 per cent of households) in 1991. In this period Britain has changed from being a nation of tenants to one where almost two-thirds are owners. The years since 1970 have also seen rapid house price inflation with national average house prices rising from £5,000 to £60,000 - an increase of 1,100 per cent. These two trends - expansion of home ownership and rapid house price inflation - have between them led to major changes in the role of owner occupation in personal wealth holdings and in wealth inheritance. The value of dwellings as a proportion of all net personal wealth increased from 18 per cent in 1960 to 37 per cent in 1975 and 52 per cent in 1989. Not surprisingly, the increase in housing wealth has been reflected in an increase in the value of housing inheritance. Whereas housing inheritance used to be largely confined to the heirs and beneficiaries of private landlords and large wealth owners, the growth of home ownership means that the inheritance of house property many become increasingly common. The implications of this far reaching social change are potentially considerable, but paradoxically very little is known about the scale, incidence or effects of housing inheritance.

Until recently, much academic interest in inheritance related to its role in the distribution of wealth, and focused on inter-generational wealth transmission among the top wealth owners (Atkinson, 1972; Atkinson and Harrison, 1978; Harbury and Hitchens, 1979). This was primarily because wealth has historically been concentrated in the hand of a small minority of large wealth owners.   Little or no attention was paid to housing inheritance until the pioneering early work of Murie and Forrest (1980).   But the late 1980s saw a growing interest in housing inheritance and its implications (Mintel, 1987: Morgan Grenfell, 1987).   The general thrust of such comments was that Britain was witnessing the beginning of a major new phenomenon, which would bring inherited housing wealth to a large proportion of the population.   While some observers pointed to the likely social inequalities in the distribution of inheritance (Hogg, 1987; Forrest and Murie, 1989; Munro, 1988; Hamnett and Williams, 1988), many anticipated a brave new world of widespread housing inheritance in the future.   Thus, Peter Saunders (1986) asserted that:

> 'with 60 per cent of households in the owner occupied sector in Britain and an even higher proportion in other countries such as Australia and the USA, not only is a majority of the population now in a position to accumulate such capital gains as may accrue through the housing market, but *for the first time in human history, we are approaching the point where millions of working people stand at some point in their lives to inherit capital sums far in excess of anything which they could hope to save through earnings from employment...*(1986, p.158 emphases added)

The Chancellor of the Exchequer, Nigel Lawson stated in 1988 that 'Britain is about to become a Nation of inheritors. Inheritance, which used to be the preserve of the few, will become a fact of life for the many.   People will be inheriting houses, and possibly also stocks and shares'.

These are radical statements, but are they correct, or are they no more than hyperbole?   The purpose to this chapter is to explore the available empirical evidence on the present and future scale of housing inheritance, its distribution and uses, and its impact on the housing market in Britain.

Data and methodology

We will use to main data sources.   First the annual information give by Inland Revenue Statistics (IRS) on 'estates passing at death' in Britain from 1968/9 to 1987/88: the last date from which figures are currently available, and second data from a Rowntree Foundation funded national survey of 10,600 individuals carried out for the authors by NOP in Spring 1990 which was designed to find out the number of beneficiaries, their social characteristics, the value and timing of the inheritance and the uses to which it was put.   Such information can only be obtained by survey data.

The Inland Revenue data provides information on the number of estates containing for the purpose of taxation rather than the analysis of inheritance and the figures are based on a *stratified sample* of applications by executors for *grants of representation* or probate for deceased persons estates. In 1987/8, the most recent year for which figures are available, there were 235,000 estates listed out of a total of over 500,000 deaths. The discrepancy is explained by the fact that the sample relates only to those estates which require a 'grant of representation'. Joint property passing to a surviving spouse is excluded, as are certain assets (valued at under £1,500 from 1965-1983, and under £5,000 from 1984 onwards). No details are available of estates where these provisions apply (c.300,000 a year). This is not a major problem however, as property passing between spouses does not constitute inter-generational inheritance, and estates worth less that the minimum threshold are unlikely to contain house property. The advantage of Inland Revenue statistics is that they provide reliable probate based figures on the number of estates passing at death each year which contain house property and its value, as well as data on the overall asset composition of estates, and the value of assets by size bands of estate.

The number of estates containing residential property

The Inland Revenue statistics only provide data on residential property in estates from 1968/9 onwards. Previously, the data was aggregated into a land and property category which was impossible to disaggregate. The categories of residential property employed in the Inland Revenue statistics have frequently been changed but data has been provided on a consistent basis since 1980/81 and, fortunately, this is compatible with data for the years 1969/71.

The number of estates containing residential property has grown only slowly and very erratically from 125, 085 in 1968/9 to 149,265 in 1986/7: an increase of 19 per cent (see Table 9.1). But the 1968/9 figure is abnormally low and may reflect initial unrecording. If 1969/70 is taken as the base year, the number of estates containing house property has not grown at all, but has simply fluctuated between 142,000 and 149,000 estates a year. Even if 1968/69 is taken as a base year and compared to 1986/7, a 19 per cent increase is small compared to the growth of owner occupation over the last few decades, and the 1987/88 figure drops to 125,000. While this figure may be an anomaly, these figures clearly contradict the claims made by the pundits for the rapid growth of housing inheritance. The reality to date is one of stability rather than growth.

There are several possible reasons for this. First, the IRS may be under-recording the growth in the number of estates passing at death containing house property. This seems to be unlikely, as estates containing house property are, almost by definition, going to require probate. A second possibility is that a rise in the number of owner occupier deaths is being offset by a higher proportion of properties passing automatically to spouses under the law of succession which are not recorded by the IRS. This is entirely possible but it should merely delay the final release of property by a few years.

Table 9.1
The number of estates containing UK residential property

	Number of Estates	Total No Estates	% of all Estates	Value of Res Prop (£'s M)	Total Value (£'s M)	% of Total
1968/69	125,085$	271,238	46.1	465	1.923	24.2 GB
1969/70	149,592$	287,239	52.1	501	1.948	25.7 GB
1970/71	142,473$	267,718	53.2	530	1.967	26.9 GB
1971/72	149,052$	288,792	51.2	638	2.275	28.0 GB
1980/81	143,343 @	294,841	48.6	3.057	6.883	44.4 UK
1981/82	147,894 @	295,236	50.1	3.280	7.628	43.0 UK
1982/83	143,980 @	288,199	50.0	3.383	8.211	41.2 UK
1983/84	148,800 @	296,890	50.1	3.683	9.195	40.0 UK
1984/85	147,717 @	273,762	53.9	4.163	10.372	40.1 UK
1985/86	137,486 @	245,071	56.1	4.567	11.482	39.8 UK
1986/87	149,265 @	270,947	55.1	5.398	12.783	42.2 UK

Notes: $ GB Residential Property,
             @ All UK Residential Property on year of death basis

Sources: Annual Inland Revenue Statistics 1970 to 1991 inclusive

The third explanation is that the growth of housing inheritance will lag the growth of home ownership by at least 30, and possibly as much as 40 years. Most of the new generation of post-war owners are still living, and the expansion of ownership from the 1970s will not feed through into inheritance for another 20 years. Our statistical projections (Hamnett, Harmer and Williams, 1991) suggest however that, other things being equal, by the year 2025 the number of estates containing house property could more than double to 340,000 per year as the post war expansion of home ownership works through to housing inheritance.

Other things may not be equal, however, and the final possibility is that the number of inherited houses is not rising because an increasing number of elderly home owners are selling their houses or otherwise disposing of them prior to death, either to fund residential care or to gain access to equity or income from their homes (Hinton, 1986; Leather and Wheeler, 1988, Leather, 1990; Hamnett and Mulling 1992a and b). This is a distinct possibility, but in our view the number of estates containing house property is likely to rise slowly over time.

The figures discussed above all relate to the number of estates passing at death, not the number of potential beneficiaries. But the results of the sample of 10,600 people carried out for the authors by NOP Market Research suggest that the average number of main beneficiaries per estate is almost three. This suggests that a total of 450,000 individuals currently inherit a share of house property each year. This is 1 per cent of the adult population of Britain. On the assumption that each beneficiary lives in a separate household, this suggests that some 2 per cent of households inherit house property each year. This may not seem a very large proportion, but in any 10 year period, 20% of households stand to inherit a share of house property - worth about £20,000 per households on average using 1990 houses prices.

Value of residential property in estates

The number of estates containing UK residential property rose slightly from 46 per cent to 55 per cent from 1968/9 to 1986/7. Taking the early 1970s as a base, the increase has been much less. But the share of residential property as a proportion of the total capital value of estates increased dramatically, from 24 per cent in 1968/9 to 44 per cent in 1981 and it seems to have stabilised at around 40-42 per cent in recent years. This increase reflects rapid inflation in the value of residential assets compared to other assets. The value of residential property in estates rose from £465m in 1968/9 to £5.398bn in 1986/7, an increase of 1060% at current prices. By comparison, the total net capital value of estates (after debts, outstanding mortgages and funeral expenses) grew by 565 per cent and that of non-residential assets by 406 per cent. The value of residential property in estates thus rose 2.5 times faster than the value of non-residential property, and almost all of it is due to house price inflation rather than to an increase in the number of estates containing house property. This suggests that the real future value of housing inheritance will be largely dependent on the future of house price inflation and the state of the housing market.

The proportion of estates containing residential property is now 55 per cent but this is an average figure which ignores the variation in the incidence and value of residential property located in the UK by size of estate. Table 2 shows that only 9 per cent of estates valued at under £10,000 in 1986/7 contained UK residential property. This is not surprising given that the 1986 national average house price was £40,000. The proportion of estates containing house property rose sharply to 49 per cent in the £10-25,000 range before evening out at round 7 per cent of estates worth £25,000 and over.

141

Table 9.2

The proportion of estates containing residential property,
the average value of the property and its proportion of the
net capital value of estates, by size of estate, 1986/7

Net Value of estates	% of estates containing Residential Property	Average value of Property (£,000)	UK Res Prop as % of the total value
£10,000 <	8.6	8.0	7.5
£10-25,000	49.2	15.7	44.5
£25-40,000	75.3	24.9	58.6
£40-50,000	78.7	33.4	58.6
£50-60,000	81.0	38.6	57.9
£60-80,000	78.7	45.5	52.6
£80-100,000	76.0	52.0	46.3
£100-200,000	71.6	66.3	36.8
£200-300,000	71.5	97.8	31.2
£300-500,000	73.7	129.0	26.7
£500,000-1m	71.0	153.0	17.2
£1-2 million	66.9	261.3	14.2
> £2 million	74.0	772.7	19.4
Average	**55.1**	**36.2**	**44.0**

Source: Inland Revenue Statistics, 1990; HMSO (1991)

The value of residential property increases proportionately with the total value of the estate. In estates of under £10,000 (Table 9.2) the average gross value of residential property in estates containing such property was £8,600. In estates valued at £10-25,000 it was £15,700, and in estates of £25-40,000 it was £24,900 rising to £261,000 in estates of £1-2m. In estates worth over £2m the value of residential property increased dramatically to £773,000. This indicates the presence of large country houses, expensive houses in central London or both, and possibly several houses scattered across the country. It is likely that estates under £25,000 containing residential property are concentrated in areas where house prices are lower. The data for earlier years displays a similar pattern although there is a predictable upward distributional creep across categories over time.

The value of UK residential buildings as a proportion of the total capital value of the estates in each size range also varied considerably, from 7.5 per cent of estates valued at under £10,000, rising to an average of 55 per cent of estates worth between £25,000 and £80,000 and 45 per cent of estates valued from £80-100,000. It then falls steadily to 14 per cent of estates worth £1-2m. The figures reveal the considerable importance of residential property in the middle range of estates between £10-80,000 and it

142

can be argued that owner occupation and house price inflation have together created a new class of middle wealth owners. Above this level, residential property is generally less important compared to other, more traditional, sources of wealth such a land and shares. Overall, however, UK residential property constitutes the largest single asset in estates passing at death. The next largest asset category was cash, bank and other interest bearing accounts (27%), followed by UK company securities (15.7%) and UK government and municipal securities (6.6%).

The national figures are revealing but there are considerable regional variations. Unpublished Inland Revenue data shows that the proportion of estates containing residential property in 1981 varied from highs of 55 per cent in Wales and 50 per cent in England, to lows of 38 per cent in Scotland and 36 per cent in Northern Ireland. Even more striking, residential property as a proportion of the total capital value of estates varied from 46 per cent in England and 44 per cent in Wales to 33 per cent in Scotland and 28 per cent in Northern Ireland. These differences reflect historical differences in housing tenure composition and average house prices.

The differential incidence of housing inheritance in Britain

We have shown that the majority of estates include residential property, that it is the largest single component in estates, and that it is of particular importance in middle sized estates worth £25,000-80,000. But who inherits house property or proceeds, and what do they do with it? In order to answer these questions we draw on the results of the NOP survey funded by the Rowntree Foundation.

Of the 10,644 respondents a total of 1,326 (12%) stated that they or members of their immediate households had inherited house property or a share of the proceeds following someone's death. In some cases, two or more inheritances were involved: a total of 1,539 cases. Grossing these figures up suggests that a total of 3.7 million people in Britain (8.5%) or 12.4% of households have inherited house property. But housing inheritance is far from evenly distributed. First, given the generational nature of the phenomenon and the fact that most beneficiaries inherit from there parents, inheritance is primarily a phenomenon of middle age. The survey shows that 6 per cent of inheritances came from husbands and wives, 55 per cent from parents, 12 per cent from grandparents, 17 per cent from uncles and aunts, 3 per cent from brothers and sisters, 3 per cent from other relatives, and just 3 per cent from non-relatives. The average age at inheritance is 50, as we show later this has major implications for the uses to which inheritances are put.

Second, housing inheritance is very unequally distributed by social class and tenure. Although the majority of inheritances 77 per cent were received by those in households headed by social grades

143

B, C^1 and C^2 (managerial, other non-manual and skilled manual workers respectively), this is not surprising as these groups comprise the majority of the sample. But the incidence of inheritance reveals a very different pattern (Table 9.3). Some 26 per cent of A headed households had inherited, followed by 24 per cent of B's, 15 per cent of C^1's, 10 per cent of C^2's, 7 per cent of D's and 5 per cent of E's. The incidence of inheritance among A and B headed households was some 5 times greater than among the E's, and the incidence of multiple inheritance was even more unequal.

Table 9.3
The differential incidence of inheritance by social grade

	A	B	C^1	C^2	D	E	Tot
Inheritors	84	342	356	323	145	76	1326
Total Sample	323	1415	2306	3134	2005	1461	10644
% Incidence	26	24	15	10	7	5	12
Multiple Cases	28	85	49	34	8	6	210
% Incidence	2.3	6.0	2.1	1.1	0.4	0.4	2.0

A similar pattern was revealed where tenure was concerned. The largest number of inheritances (89%) were received by home owners compared to just 6 per cent by council tenants and 5 per cent by private rented and other tenants. though owner occupiers account for 64 per cent of the sample they are clearly over-represented and 17 per cent of home owners has inherited compared to just 3 per cent of council tenants and 6 per cent of private renters. Home owners inherited 6 times more often than council tenants. The differences in the incidence of inheritance by region were less marked than those of tenure of class but they were nonetheless significant: 19 per cent of households in the South West had inherited and 17 per cent in the South East compared to lows of 9 per cent in the North West and Greater London and 7 per cent in Scotland (Table 9.4).

How can we explain these variations? The cause lies in the generational nature of housing inheritance - it is necessary to look to the characteristics of benefactors and their relationship to beneficiaries, to understand inequalities among beneficiaries. The key factor is the housing tenure of benefactors - only home owners or landlords have property to leave, and the fact that ownership is related to social class. This was even more marked a generation ago when home ownership was primarily confined to the middle classes. The home owning middle classes are more likely to inherit

144

today because of the class and tenure of their parents. The regional differences are largely a product of differences in the historical structure of housing tenures. Housing inheritance is more widespread in the South East than in Scotland because home ownership in the region has traditionally been higher than in Scotland. The incidence of housing inheritance is lower in London because inner London had traditionally been dominated by a higher level of private renting and a lower level of home ownership than the national average. It also has higher proportion of young people (who are unlikely to inherit by virtue of their age) than the rest of Britain (Hamnett, 1991).

Table 9.4
The regional incidence of housing inheritance by location of beneficiaries

	Number of cases	% Incidence
South West	160	19
South East	323	17
Wales	94	17
East Anglia	49	13
West Midlands	129	12
East Midlands	94	12
North	69	11
Yorks/Humber	103	10
North West	121	9
Greater London	114	9
Scotland	70	7
Great Britain	1326	12

Source: NOP Survey carried out for the authors

These regional differences in the incidence of inheritance are parallelled by variations in the flows of inheritances within and between regions and in the value of inheritances by region. Table 9.5 shows that in the Midlands and the North the majority (65-85%) of inheritances relate to properties located in the same region as the beneficiary. This suggests that beneficiaries lived in the same region as their parents or other benefactors. The proportion is smaller in the South East (60%), South West (60%), London (35%) and East Anglia (47%) however, which indicates that in these regions, the majority of beneficiaries inherit property located outside the region. This indicates that there is a net flow of inheritances towards the southern regions which probably reflects the tendency of elements of the educated middle classes (who are more likely to receive housing inheritances) it migrate to the region for educational and employment reasons (Fielding, 1989).

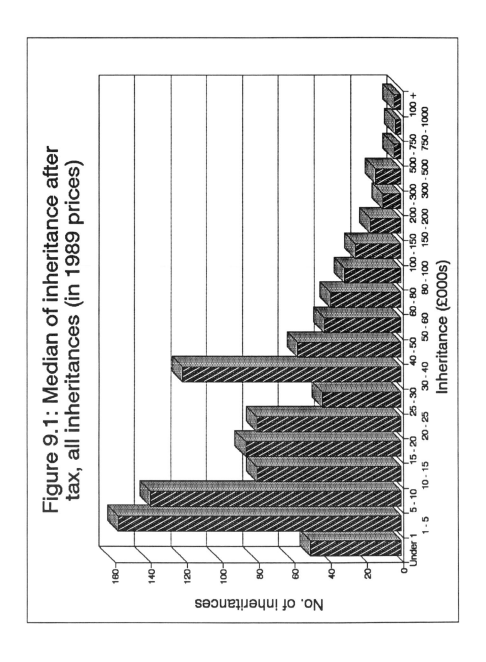

Figure 9.1: Median of inheritance after tax, all inheritances (in 1989 prices)

Table 9.5
The proportion of beneficiaries in a region inheriting property located in the same region

%

Wales	84
Scotland	84
North	75
York Humber	73
North West	73
West Midlands	68
East Midlands	64
South East	60
South West	60
East Anglia	47
Greater London	35

Table 9.6
The ratio of property inheritances from a given region to the number of beneficiaries in the region

South West	1.2
South East	1.2
West Midlands	1.13
East Midlands	1.16
Greater London	1.1
North West	1.07
North	1.02
East Anglia	0.98
Yorks/Humber	0.91
Wales	0.86
Scotland	0.78

Another measure is provided in Table 9.6 which shows the ratio of beneficiaries living in a given region to the number of inherited properties coming from that region. A perfect representation gives a value of 1.0. Figures of less than 1 indicate a net outflow of property and figures of more than 1 a net inflow. It can be seen that there is a small net inflow of inheritances into the South East (1.2), the South West (1.2), Greater London, the East and West Midlands and the North West and a net outflow from Scotland, Wales and Yorkshire and Humberside. The differences provide some support to Forrest and Murie's (1989) claim that: "Generally, the expectation would be of inter-generational transfers flowing from low price to high price regions".

The value of inheritances received

The average value of inheritances received was some £22,000 at current prices, but this includes inheritances received in the 1950s and 60s as well as the 1970s and 80s and when the average in constant 1989 prices was £44,500. The average for the period 1985-89 was £29,700 in current prices and £32,700 in constant 1989 prices. Average values are a useful summary measure, but they are very misleading because of distribution of inheritances by value is negatively skewed with many small inheritances and a few large ones. Figure 9.1 shows the median value of inheritances received in 1985-9 was £5-9,999 (16%), with another 15 per cent between £1-4,999 and 16 per cent between £10-20,000. A further 28 per cent of inheritances were between £20-50,000 and only 18 per cent were worth over £50,000 (survey estimates).

Table 9.7
Average post-tax value of inheritances received by region of beneficiary

	Current Prices	Constant 1989 Prices(£'s)
Greater London	48,503	81,264
East Midlands	30,918	66,740
East Anglia	27,310	62,801
South West	24,172	64,601
South East	20,573	41,257
North West	17,960	27,079
West Midlands	16,270	28,715
Scotland	16,179	43,166
North	15,373	25,910
Wales	14,967	35,357
Yorks/Humber	13,409	22,964
Average (n=1025)	21,989	44,488

The regional differences in the value of inheritance received are very considerable (Table 9.7) and largely reflect differences in average regional house prices. The mean sum inherited averaged £22,000 nationally at current prices, but varies regionally from a high of £48,500 in London to a low of £13,400 in Yorkshire and Humberside. This is a difference of 3.6 times between the largest and smallest regional averages.

A similar pattern emerges if the distribution of average value of inheritance is analysed by the location of the property. The ratio between the highest value region (London, £40,885) and the lowest (Yorks and Humberside, £10,794) is almost fourfold and the average inheritance for beneficiaries from properties in the northern regions was under £22,000. It is clear from these figures that the location of parents and other benefactors does influence both the incidence of inheritance and its value. Housing wealth is concentrated in the

148

southern regions and inheritance ensures that most of it stays there.

Use of housing inheritance

We have discussed the scale, incidence and distribution of property inheritance and have outlined the processes involved and the outcomes they generate. Our purpose now is to examine what people do when they inherit house property. Clearly, it is via the use of the inherited property or proceeds that the process of inheritance is turned into material advantage. In turn this begins a process of cumulative advantage for those who have inherited (and ultimately onwards to their own beneficiaries) and disadvantage for those who have not.

As we have already indicated the scale of housing inheritance is now very substantial and it is growing. The survey results suggest that 2.8 million households (13%) in Britain contain someone who had inherited house property or the proceeds from it. This is one household in every eight. How they put this inheritance to use thus becomes a matter of considerable significance with potentially far reaching impacts on the British economy and society.

How people use their inheritance is likely to be influenced by a wide variety of factors. These might include the value and the characteristics of the inheritance itself, the personal circumstances of the beneficiaries, the size of the inheritance and whether it was shared and with whom. Similarly the age, sex, income, class and current tenure of the beneficiary and their relationship to the benefactor may influence the way inheritances are used. Finally when people inherit and where they inherited property is located are likely to be important since there are considerable temporal and spatial variations in house prices and the choices available to the beneficiaries. The possible combinations of factors are considerable making any precise predictions as to likely use rather problematic.

From our previous research (Hamnett et al 1990) we know that the typical beneficiary was late middle aged (50 plus), and existing owner and middle class. Where inheritances were shared there was a strong likelihood of the property being sold but overall most people followed this course and made use of the proceeds. The present survey supported our earlier findings but the larger sample allows closer examination of a variety of important dimensions including location and gender. Unfortunately, race is not a dimension we can explore as the question is not asked in the Omnibus Survey.

Forms of property inheritance

Discussion of the use of inheritance must be situated within an understanding of the different forms of property inheritance. There were 1539 cases of inheritance of property and/or proceeds from

149

the sale of property. Excluding cases where respondents did not give the type of inheritance or their own current tenure these were broken down as follows.

Table 9.8
Types of property inheritance by sex and tenure of beneficiary

			Sex		Tenure		
	No	%	M %	F %	OO %	LA %	PR %
House property	542	37	37	43	38	21	37
Proceeds from House Property	841	58	57	51	56	78	55
Both Property and Proceeds	82	5	6	6	6	1	8
Total^1–Percent		100	100	100	100	100	100
Number	1465		422	471	1344	79	40

1. Respondents only

A majority of people inherited proceeds rather than property while a small minority of cases involved both (Table 9.8). Earlier we noted that sole beneficiaries are more likely to inherit property than joint beneficaries and that the likelihood of receiving proceeds increased as the number of beneficiaries grew and that the likelihood or receiving proceeds increased as the number of beneficiaries increased (Table 9.8). There is also a gender dimension to the inheritance process with women being slightly more likely to inherit property than men. But as Table 9.9 show this largely reflects the impact of spouse beneficiaries. Local authority tenants are more likely to receive proceeds, not least because most are joint beneficiaries. The evidence suggests that inheritance of property is most likely in cases where the spouse is the benefactor and it diminishes outside of the core family groups benefactions (parents/siblings).

There is an important cautionary note to sound here regarding the forms of inheritance. It is possible that some people have described their property related inheritance as proceeds when in fact as the executors to the will they had instructed the solicitor to sell the property. We cannot assess the impact of this possibility but it may effect the balance between property and proceeds and our assessment of what people do when they inherit property. One clue as to this is that Table 9.8 shows 944 cases where property was inherited (862 plus 82) whilst Table 9.11 shows 1006 cases where the property was sold more or less immediately. This suggests that in some cases where inheritance is given as proceeds it should more accurately be described as property.

The pattern of benefactions is highly age specific with younger people more likely to get a share of proceeds and older people a property (Table 10). While 27 per cent of the inheritances received by respondents in the 18-29 age group were in the form of house property this rose to 63 per cent of inheritances received by those aged 70 or over at the date of inheritance. Using estimates of the age of beneficiaries at the date of inheritance the evidence from Table 9.10 would also suggest there has been little change in the balance between property and proceeds over time and that over the period 1950 to 1990 property inheritance was in the ratio of roughly two thirds proceeds and to one third property.

Table 9.9
Types of inheritance by benefactor and beneficiary

| | Inheritance from | | | | | Inheritance to | | | | |
	Spse %	Par %	Sib %	Par %	ORel %	Self %	Spse %	Par %	Child %	ORel %
House Property	89	42	37	23	19	40	27	42	10	35
Proceeds	10	53	59	71	74	54	69	48	85	65
Both	1	5	4	6	7	6	4	10	5	–
Total %	100	100	100	100	100	100	100	100	100	100
No 1455(1)	83	840	46	178	308					
No 1556(2)						893	465	141	20	32

(1) Excludes Don't Know/Not Stated and Other.
(2) Excludes Don't Know/Not Stated and Other Adult.
Spse = Spouse; Par = Parent; G Par = Grand Parent; Sib = Sibling; ORel = Other Relative.

Table 9.10
Types of inheritance by age of respondent at date of inheritance and the date of inheritance [1]

| | Age at Inheritance[1] | | | | Date of Inheritance | | | |
	18-29 %	30-49 %	50-69 %	70+ %	Pre-1960 %	60-69 %	70-79 %	80-89 %
House Property	27	39	46	63	38	39	39	35
Proceeds	68	54	48	37	61	55	56	59
Both	5	7	6	0	1	6	5	6
Total%	100	100	100	100	100	100	100	100
Total (700/1443)	111	310	238	41	99	145	349	850

Excludes Don't Know/Not Stated and 1990.
(1) Respondents only.

151

Table 9.11
Use of property on inheritance

Outcome	All No	All %	Sole No	Sole %	Joint No	Joint %	Resident1 No	Resident1 %
Occupied by Beneficiary	177	13	116	32	61	6	131	74
Sold more or less immed	1006	74	190	53	799	81	147	15
Rented then sold	20	1	7	2	13	2	3	15
Rented out	12	1	2	-	10	1	1	8
Lived in by others	57	4	16	5	42	4	19	33
Other	90	7	30	8	59	6	32	36
Total	1362	100	359	100	983	100	333	24

(1) the percentages given in the final column express resident beneficiaries in each category as a proportion of total beneficiaries in that category.

Excludes 178 don't know and refused.

Outcomes on inheritance

The forms of inheritance vary along specific dimensions primarily related to the familial relationship between the benefactor and the beneficiary and they are further conditioned by the number of beneficiaries. The survey results showed that, of the 1539 cases of property or property related inheritance, a number of different outcomes arose on inheritance.

The outcomes of inheritance are matters of considerable significance at both the level of individuals and households and with respect to the markets they impact on. It is appropriate to highlight the findings;

    a)   The most common outcome was for the property to be sold more or less immediately. This happened in 74% of all the cases. Thus most property inherited is sold rather than retained.

    b)   In 13 per cent of cases the property was retained for living in by the beneficiary and in a further 5 per cent it was kept 'permanently' for letting out or for use by others.

    c)   Of the 1977 properties occupied by the beneficiary, 49 or 29 per cent were cases where the beneficiary was the spouse. In almost all of these, 47 out of the 49 cases, wives were the joint or part owner. In 131 out of the 177 cases (74%) the beneficiary had lived in the property prior to inheritance.

    d)   In 81 per cent of cases where the inheritance was joint, the property was sold. This contrasted with 53 per cent of sole inheritances. Further analysis on non-resident beneficiaries and excluding those currently or previously resident in the property showed this difference persisted in diminished form (78% of sole non-resident beneficiaries sold immediately in contrast to 87% of joint non-resident beneficiaries).

  e) Of the 77 spouse beneficiaries who gave details as to the outcomes of inheritance, 49 or 63% remained in occupation of the property but 19 of these (24%) sold it immediately or rented it out and then sold.

Other factors which might influence the actions taken on inheriting property include the age of the beneficiary, location of the property and the value of the inheritance. Generally, these went not significant. The decisions taken regarding the property varied little with respect to the age of the beneficiary at inheritance. The average age of the respondent beneficiary who sold immediately was 43, compared to 44 when rented out and then sold. There was little systematic difference in the outcomes when considered in relation to the class and tenure of the beneficiary and the region they lived in. The outcome of inheritance did not significantly vary according to the location of the property inherited.

Table 9.12
Outcome by value of inheritance in 1989 prices (000s)

	<10 %	10-19 %	20-39 %	40-49 %	50-79 %	80-99 %	100> %	Total %	Av No	Value £
Occ by Ben	7	11	32	9	20	8	13	100	108	
Sold	40	18	23	6	5	3	5	100	716	
Rent/Sold	10	–	43	–	27	–	20	100	10	
Rent	33	20	30		–	–	17	100	5	
Lived in	36	16	10	2	18	–	18	100	28	
Other	25	5	26	7	11	5	21	100	53	
Total No.	320	151	222	55	75	29	68		920	

Excludes Don't Know/Not Stated.

Outcomes by value

As suggested earlier the value of the inheritance could be a key factor in the outcomes of the process. Table 9.12 shows that there is a relationship between the action taken on inheritance and value (at 1989 prices). The 'occupied by beneficiary' and the 'sold' categories are evidently the most important with the numbers in the other categories being small. Where the value was low the property was more likely to be sold, where it was occupied by the beneficiary it was more likely to be of a higher value. Thus while only 18 per cent of inheritances where the property was occupied by the beneficiary were worth less than £20,000, 58 per cent of those where the property was sold were in this lower value band.

  There were only 30 cases where there was an outstanding mortgage which could effect the action taken. Although the probable age of many benefactors would mean that they were outright owners at the time of their death this also suggests that any outstanding mortgages were covered by insurance thus clearing the debt. We cannot know the true position. Finally we considered whether there were temporal variations in the outcomes. The British housing market has changed considerably over time and house prices have fluctuated substantially. But although the numbers in each time period were quite large there was very little variation in terms of the outcome over time.

The uses of property related inheritance proceeds

It is evident from the data presented already that there are variations in the outcomes on inheritance. However, setting aside the 6 per cent who were spouse beneficiaries, three quarters of beneficiaries (74%) sold the property immediately or after a period of renting it out. As a consequence most beneficiaries are in a position where they have cash proceeds to deploy. The purpose of this section of the analysis is to examine the way this cash is deployed and the factors which are associated with decisions to use cash in particular ways.

It is appropriate to begin by considering the uses to which cash proceeds were put. In Table 9.13 below the initial and subsequent uses of cash proceeds are given. The distinctions between any initial and subsequent main use require comment at the outset. Respondents were asked to give details of all the different initial uses to which they put their cash proceeds. They were then asked which one of these uses was most of the money spent on initially. Having established these initial patterns respondents were asked to give details of any subsequent use and the main subsequent use to which invested money was put. Our purpose here was to gain insights into longer term financial strategies. From our earlier research it was apparent that many beneficiaries initially invested the proceeds. The question was whether this was a short term strategy or whether it represented a long term goal.

Despite much speculative comment about the likelihood of property purchases flowing from inheritance the dominant initial reaction was to put the money into the building society, bank, shares or other financial investment. This pattern was consistent with our earlier findings. Some 46 per cent of the initial choices were investment related with building societies being the most popular choice. In 18 per cent of cases the money defrayed a mortgage (most commonly a first house) and 14 per cent went into home improvement. As the table shows property related spending attracted 32 per cent of initial choices. Starting a business was a choice in only 2 per cent of cases (though we failed to ask about investment in an existing business). Consumption related expenditure on holidays, cars, education and general use formed 19 per cent of initial choices. The purchase of cars was the most common use (10%) within this broad category.

154

Table 9.13
Initial, main initial and main subsequent uses of property related inheritance proceeds by beneficiaries by type of use

Category	Any Initial Use		Main Initial Use		Main Subsequent Use	
	No	%	No	%	No	%
Housing Related						
Pay Mortgage	44	4	38	5	2	1
Buy House	73	7	73	10	9	4
Buy Exp House	46	4	43	6	9	4
Buy 2nd House	11	1	11	1	-	-
Buy Child House	19	2	12	2	18	7
Buy GChild House	1	-	-	-	-	-
Buy Property*	194	18	177	23	38	15
Home Improvement	148	14	96	13	51	20
All Housing	342	32	273	36	89	35
Start Business	17	2	12	2	1	-
Investment Related						
B. Soc	302	28	231	30	na	
Bank	92	8	66	9	na	
Shares	60	5	31	4	na	
Other	57	5	40	5	na	
All Investment	511	46	368	48	na	
Consumption Related						
Holidays	56	5	20	3	15	6
Car	112	10	53	7	19	8
Education	20	2	11	1	10	4
General Use	24	2	22	3	118	47
All Consumption	212	20	106	14	162	65
Total No/%	1082	100	759	100	252	100

Excludes Don't Know and not stated; Any initial use allows more than 1 answer
* includes paying off mortgage loans

There were 772 positive responses to this questions (and 254 don't knows). Between them there were 1082 initial uses suggesting that considerably less than half the respondents had actually spent the proceeds on more than one use.

As a consequence the pattern of behaviour did not change markedly with initial main uses. Financial investment rose slightly as a proportion of the total to 48 per cent of the cases and building societies strengthened their position from 28 per cent on any initial uses to 30 per cent of main initial uses. Property expenditure also increased to 36 per cent of choices with first consumption related choices fell to 14 per cent.

This modest reshaping would seem entirely predictable given the categories which are likely to attract the bulk of expenditure. Clearly financial investment is the most common single use when property related inheritance is disposed of. The question then is whether this is a short or long term strategy? Respondents were asked about any main subsequent uses to which money invested in the finance market was put. As the table 30 shows there were 454 cases where any identifiable financial investment was made (511 - 57 = 454). Of these 202 or 45 per cent subsequently did nothing more with the money or did not know what had been done. Where there was a change the most common practice was to draw on those investments for general use (47%) but property purchase (15%), home improvement (20%) and the purchase of a car (8%) or holidays (6%) were also identified.

Overall it is apparent that financial investment remained the dominant use but the use of inheritance for property purchase or improvement did increase over time. In the longer term close to 50 per cent of households used most of their inheritance for property related expenditure (273 plus 89 subsequently assuming the two figures represent different households). Assistance to children was noticeably higher in subsequent use suggesting a tendency to set the inheritance aside for use by following generations. Relating subsequent activity to the precise form of investment initially undertaken provided no conclusive evidence except that those with building society investments seemed more likely to take property related decisions (notably by helping children buy and via home improvement).

Other factors

There are a range of other factors which might influence the ways beneficiaries use their inheritance. Space constraints prevent us doing more than briefly mentioning some of our findings. These are as follows;

    a) Examining use by year suggests there has been an overall fall in the proportion of respondents deciding to invest in property by one means or another. There has been a decline in the tendency to pay off mortgages and in the use of proceeds to buy a first home. Building societies have become more attractive as places to invest.

    b) In terms of tenure the results are inconclusive though the pattern of use suggests outright owners were more likely to invest their inheritance than spend it on consumption. This could be age related. It is also probable that a number of the outright owners had acquired that status by using the proceeds to pay off their mortgage with respect to subsequent use of proceeds to pay off their mortgage. With respect to subsequent use of proceeds mortgaged owners were most likely to 'move' their money with improvement, general use, property purchase and holidays dominating.

c) Analysis of use by social class suggested that A/B class beneficiaries were most likely to invest and least likely to spend on consumption. The tendency for C/D/E beneficiaries to spend on property and consumption related uses may be partly explained by the lower value of the inheritance involved.

d) A small but possibly insignificant difference was observable in terms of patterns of use by gender. Women were more likely to spend on property while men were more active in terms of financial investment. This distinction could reflect the difficulties women have faced in entering the property market. Like gender, age can only be discussed with respect to respondent beneficiaries. The evidence suggests quite distinct patterns of use in relation to the different age groupings. Property purchase was most common amongst the younger age groups (up to 39) while improvement was a feature of the uses made by middle aged groups (40-64). Investment was spread across the age spectrum in a series of peaks and troughs but in general terms the propensity to invest increased with age.

e) There were no great differences between sole and joint beneficiaries in terms of use.

f) There was some evidence of regional variations in patterns of use but the cell sizes are small and must be treated with caution.

g) Finally there is the key issue of how use is related to value. Clearly the value of the proceeds once a property has been disposed of (and the mortgage cleared) can be a critical factor in people's decisions as to what to do. The data reveal a complex pattern of use in relation to the value of the proceeds. Although there is some evidence of a fall in consumption based expenditure and a rise in property related expenditure as the value of proceeds increases there is considerable variation. This suggests there is no simple relation between value of proceeds and patterns of use. Second home purchase and moving uptake were clearly related to the higher value inheritances.

The uses of inherited property and proceeds

The analysis has revealed complex and varied patterns of response by beneficiaries to the inheritance of property and proceeds and to their subsequent use. It is quite clear that certain factors would appear to be more important than others although we have not as yet subjected them all to tests of statistical significance.

In terms of forms of inheritance it was apparent that sole beneficiaries (and therefore many spouse beneficiaries and women

157

beneficiaries) were more likely to inherit property than joint beneficiaries. This also had an age dimension in that older people were more likely than younger people to inherit property.

On inheriting a property most beneficiaries sold it more or less immediately. This was particularly true where the inheritance was joint. The most obvious exceptions to this 'rule' were spouse beneficiaries. The decisions taken with regard to the property varied little with respect to age, class, tenure or location of the property. However there did appear to be a relationship between the value of the inheritance and the action taken. Lower value properties were most likely to be sold while higher value properties were more likely to be retained.

It was apparent that most beneficiaries had cash proceeds to deploy. The most common use of these proceeds (about half) was as investments, primarily in building societies but also in banks and into shares. About a third of choices related to property whether in terms of purchase or improvement. Over the longer term some of the proceeds set aside for financial investment were redeployed into property.

The pattern of uses was examined in relation to a number of factors. Over time, it was evident that property now attracted a lower proportion of choices than previously while building societies in particular had strengthened their position as deposit takers. Tenure had no strong impact on use except it seemed likely that existing owners used the proceeds to pay off their mortgages. This was particularly true of beneficiaries in the D/E social class categories. A/B social class category beneficiaries were notably more likely to invest their proceeds but overall the use variations by class were not very great. Sole and joint beneficiaries varied little in the way they used their proceeds but age proved to be an important discriminator. Predictably perhaps, property purchase and improvement was more common amongst younger beneficiaries and investment more likely amongst older beneficiaries. Equally there did appear to be a gender dimension to patterns of use with women being more likely than men to invest in property. Finally, with respect to value, use varied considerably with no discernible pattern.

The outcomes of property inheritance and the uses to which the proceeds are put are for the most part rather predictable. Most property inheritance involves proceeds rather than property and where the latter arises it is normally sold. The most common use of proceeds is in terms of investment in financial products. The deviations from these generalised paths are themselves fairly unsurprising. Spouse beneficiaries tend to retain their property, older people tend to invest while younger people tend to put the proceeds back into property. From what we might surmise about the housing situation of the different groups involved these patterns of use seem to suggest that once a beneficiary's housing position is secured other options are considered.

158

The research has demonstrated an underlying stability about the inheritance process. We cannot assume this will continue forever but it does imply we can begin to make short to medium term predictions which have some likelihood of being borne out in reality.

Conclusions

Housing inheritance has emerged as an important factor in the social and economic structuring of Britain. The scale of inheritance and the uses to which property and proceeds are put suggest it does have specific impacts on the housing market and the financial market. Moreover, it is evidence that, potentially at least, its significance will grow as the number of estates including home increases reflecting the age profile of home owners and home ownership.

As is suggested housing inheritance has the potential to become a very significant feature. However it is apparent that this potential is conditional on a range of factors including the state of the housing market, changing attitudes to ownership and the emergence of alternative routes for channelling the cash value of housing. In this conclusion we will briefly explore each of these.

The state of the housing market

The sharp decline in house prices which has taken place over the last two to three years in many parts of the UK has a range of impacts upon the inheritance process. First there is the impact upon the cash value of housing inheritance. It is difficult to be precise because of the inadequacies of statistics but in areas such as East Anglia, the South East and the South West the price of housing fell in absolute terms in 1990 (Housing Finance, February, 1992) a pattern which was repeated in 1991 (first three quarters) and also included the East and West Midlands, Wales and Greater London.

The fall in house prices reduces the value of property inherited and thus the amount of cash to be redistributed. Clearly in a falling market beneficiaries who then seek to use that cash to enhance their own housing market position may be able to do so at an advantageous price. They may therefore be able to achieve the position they might have expected before prices fell. In addition it is apparent that the market has not been falling consistently across the UK and in some areas, notably Scotland and Northern Ireland the market has remained relatively buoyant. The regional dimensions of housing inheritance have shown there is a general tendency for the flow of proceeds to favour the South East and thus it is entirely possible that a double benefit might arise - the sale of a property in a rising market and the release of cash proceeds for use in a falling market.

The release of cash in predicated on a market where property can be sold. In most parts of the UK the market has been very depressed with the number of transactions falling in almost every quarter since the third quarter of 1988. The large number of unsold new properties and the release of property repossessed by lenders plus all the properties vendors have been holding off the market until prices pick up means there is substantial 'backlog' to clear before a 'normal' market returns. Beneficiaries are normally in the fortunate position of have a home already so most can choose to rent out the property and wait for better conditions. Equally because it is a 'windfall' gain many may choose to sell in depressed conditions and accept a lower price. In that sense beneficiaries could help sustain lower prices and the depressed market.

Attitudes to ownership

The decline in the housing market has resulted in a reappraisal of the merits of home ownership. Over the last few decades there has been an indication that people were increasingly viewing home ownership as an investment good rather than a consumption good. This influenced decisions to buy and sell and added to the instability of the market. With the downturn the investment value of housing has been put into question. There are suggestions that the 1980s were the 'golden era' of home ownership and that the financial gains achieved then are unlikely to be repeated. This then leads to the view that home ownership will be viewed increasingly as a consumption good and that those seeking a good return on their capital will invest elsewhere.

This view of the market is partly based on assessment of the likely demand for property in the next few decades. Household formation rates are predicted to fall sharply thus reducing the demand from new households. At the same time the rate of release of property as a consequence of the death of the owner will increase reflecting the fact that more of those dying will be owners. In these terms demand will fall and supply will increase. This may be balanced to a small degree by increased longevity and by a rise in the demand for second homes but the evidence would suggest a stable market at best rather than boom conditions.

Alternative routes

All this suggests that there will be a dampening of the inheritance potential of home ownership. Indeed as we can see from the collapse of home income plan schemes the fall in house prices (and the rise in interest rates) have had a disastrous impact upon the income existing elderly home owners could draw down from their property. Prior to the collapse in the market it had been suggested that income plans would result in home owners extracting the equity value of their property in their own life time rather than allowing a subsequent generation to do this. This prospect has diminished at present although as the position stabilises (and interest rates fall/stabilise) demand may return for these schemes.

At the same time as home income plans were being promoted so there was a growing debate about other uses for the 'locked up' capital value of housing. Private health care was seem as an obvious route and the government had begun to think in that direction. There have been no further developments in this.

The future

It is apparent that there are many unknowns about the future of housing inheritance. Current circumstances cloud the issue in terms of the significance of its likely impact. Quite clearly people will die and beneficiaries will inherit and we are clear the numbers involved will increase sharply. What we cannot know at this stage is the circumstances in which that property release will take place and the options which may be available. We speculate that market conditions will be less attractive than in the 1980s. Indeed it is possible that like the repossessed properties today, inherited property could create an overhang on the market leaving it in permanent oversupply.

10 Housing and older people: Issues of housing finance

Robin Means, Philip Leather and Sheila Mackintosh

Introduction

As part of the overall Housing Finance Programme, the Joseph Rowntree Foundation funded a number of short research projects which were separate to the main case study teams. One of these projects was a five month 'think piece' and literature review on 'the housing finance implications of an ageing society', which was undertaken by Sheila Mackintosh, Philip Leather and Robin Means at the School for Advanced Urban Studies, University of Bristol.

The resultant report, Housing in Later Life (Mackintosh et al, 1990), reviewed the housing experiences of older people in the main tenures, and also the relationship of housing to care issues; the report concludes by identifying the key housing finance issues raised by an ageing society. It should be stressed that the research was carried out well before any survey findings were available. Also, the authors decided to provide a broad housing overview rather than enmesh themselves in detailed debates about affordability or about what is and what is not a housing subsidy.

This paper looks at the three key issues identified in Housing in Later Life, namely:

1) The affordability of rents and older people.
2) The repair, maintenance, improvement and adaptation problems of elderly owner-occupiers.
3) The increasingly complex interface between housing policies and community care policies.

First, however, it is necessary to say something about ageist assumptions about housing in later life and then go on to profile the likely future demographic and resources profile of older people.

Ageist assumptions about housing in later life

It is probably no longer accurate to claim that the majority of housing debates about older people end up in the never-ending argument about the pros and cons of sheltered housing. At the very least, low income elderly owner-occupiers are seen as representing an important source of house disrepair, while deceased elderly people are seen by numerous researchers as an interesting source of wealth and inheritance for others. However, there is still a tendency to perceive elderly people as either a homogeneous group defined by their biological age or as a group worthy of study because they disrupt mainstream provision. The subtitle of Housing in Later Life is an interesting example of such ageism since it refers to 'the housing finance implications of an ageing society'. This seems to define older people as a problem for housing finance systems, rather than the need to understand the impact of housing finance on older people.

This brings us to the continued tendency of housing researchers to talk in terms of 'housing for the elderly'. This expression manages to include both the classic assumptions. First it talks of "the elderly" when few of us would offer a paper on housing and the young rather than housing and young people.

As Fennell et al (1988, pp.7-8) explain:

> 'We try, wherever possible, not to talk of 'the elderly', 'geriatrics' (as applied to people), 'the elderly mentally infirm', 'the old' or 'the confused'; but, when we do have to generalize, we refer to 'elderly people', 'older people', 'ill people', 'people in old age' or 'confused elderly people'. This is not to deny the physical realities of ageing, disability or dementia, but to try, linguistically, to remind ourselves constantly of human variety in the groups we are categorizing and to underline the 'people-status' (people like us, in other words) of elderly people as opposed to the 'thing-status' (objects inferior to us) of 'the elderly''.

The second problem with the expression 'housing for the elderly' is that it uses the preposition 'for', thus further confirming the assumed passive state of most elderly people. Housing is seen as something provided for elderly people rather than seeing all elderly people as playing an active role in their own housing outcomes, irrespective of tenure and income (Means, 1990). And yet accumulating research evidence on how later life is experienced stresses that it is not a period of retreat, withdrawal, passivity and dependence but rather "a time of active challenge: a time when perhaps more than ever they need to be able to respond imaginatively to change" (Thompson et al, 1990). Changes in later life may be about coping with the impact of housing benefit changes, how to fund repairs or whether to move into sheltered housing, just as much as it might be about coping with illness or bereavement or the marital problems of the children.

Future demographic trends

John Ermisch (1990) in Fewer Babies, Longer Lives has carried out a detailed review of likely future demographic patterns. As can be seen from the table there is going to be no explosion in the overall size of the population nor any explosion in the percentage of the population who are over 65. The two different projections are based on different assumptions about future fertility rates amongst women with the principal projection assuming a higher rate than the variant projection. As Ermisch concludes:

> 'While the elderly's share of the population is forecast to increase, in both projections, the major shift toward an elderly population does not begin until the second decade of the 21st century. It is not until the third decade of the next century that the total dependency ratio - the numbers of children and elderly to workers - increases much above today's. These developments in the next century reflect the ageing of the baby boom generation born in the 1960s'.

It is often argued that the most significant trend will be the ageing of the elderly population itself. Again, the figures supplied by Ermisch suggests that this will not become a major phenomenon until well into the 21st century.

Ermisch goes on to consider the implications of these projections for the future demand for both large and small properties. He concludes that the 1990s will be characterised by a household composition shift towards larger households. However, the situation is reversed after the turn of the century, when age changes will see a shift back in favour of smaller dwellings, perhaps moderated by the growing affluence of the population. Overall, he feels that:

> 'In the housing market, these developments first favouring and then shifting against larger dwellings will be reflected in the relative prices of dwellings of different size. In the council and housing association sector, these developments in the size distribution of households would need to be taken into account more directly in planning housing provision' (Ermisch, 1990, p.40).

Table 10.1

Size and age structure of the projected population of Great Britain

Lower variant projection	1987	1997	2007	2017	2027
Size ('000s)	55355	56198	56251	56093	55353
Per cent aged:					
65-74	8.9	8.6	8.3	10.5	11.1
75 and over	6.7	7.4	7.8	7.9	9.6
Dependency ratios:					
(per cent)					
*Child (aged 0-15)	31.3	31.4	28.4	27.8	28.6
**Elderly (aged 65+)	24.2	25.0	24.7	28.8	33.6
Total	55.6	56.4	53.0	56.6	62.2
Principal projection					
Size ('000s)	55355	57062	58110	58869	59616
Per cent aged:					
65-74	8.9	8.4	8.1	10.0	10.3
75 and over	6.7	7.3	7.5	7.5	8.9
Dependency ratios: (%)					
*Child (aged 0-15)	31.3	33.8	32.8	30.7	32.7
**Elderly (aged 65+)	24.2	25.0	24.6	27.8	31.6
Total	55.6	58.8	57.4	58.5	64.3

*Persons aged 0-15 as per cent of persons aged 16-64
**Persons aged 65 and over as per cent of persons aged 16-64.

Source: Ermisch (1990) Fewer Babies, Longer Lives, Joseph Rowntree Foundation, p.26.

Elderly households and their resources

The ability of elderly people to pay for their housing will depend largely upon their resources. The initial report from the Programme Core Team of the Housing Finance Initiative (Maclennan et al, 1990) supports previous research that elderly people have low incomes relative to the rest of the population. For most people retirement marks a significant drop in income levels. Estimates of the level of income reduction vary, with some commentators suggesting that it is as high as 50 per cent on average, but others giving figures of 24 per cent for one-earner households and 32 per cent for two-earner households (Walker and Hutton, 1988). For most people post-retirement income comes mainly from social security benefits. Sixty per cent of pensioners depend on state benefit for 80 per cent or more of their income, and for 20 per cent of these it is their sole source of income (Age Concern, 1989).

The state pension has increased in value over the last 20 years but most of this increase occurred in the 1970s when pensions were linked to increases in earnings. Since 1980 pensions have been linked to rises in the retail price index. The net result has been to depress the value of pensions relative to earnings as wages have risen faster than prices through the 1980s. Bull and Poole (1989) estimate that whereas 58 per cent of elderly people are on or below 140 per cent of income support level (the normally accepted indicator of poverty) only 2 per cent of people over retirement age are in the wealthiest fifth of the population. This gloomy picture is only modified slightly when savings and debts are considered. The core team report suggests savings are higher and debts are lower for the 60+ group compared to other age cohorts (Maclennan et al, op cit, pp.46- 47).

The income situation of elderly people is not expected to improve markedly in the foreseeable future. Bosenquet and Propper (1991) have looked at income prospects for elderly people in the 1990s. They concluded that "the outlook for the next decade for the elderly consumer does not look positive". The real value of the basic state pension fell in the 1980s and this trend is likely to continue in the 1990s. There is no sign that occupational pensions are about to transform the incomes of any but a small minority of elderly people. The latest coverage figures suggest 52 per cent of employees have access to such schemes but many are not indexed to inflation, while many employees have had disrupted work careers and so fail to accrue full entitlement. Finally, "the interaction between state benefits and the private market means that for some, occupational pensions act only to replace income that would otherwise be provided by the state". Bosenquet and Propper, also, look at wealth distribution amongst elderly people. They conclude that the 1990s will see a 20:30:50 segmentation of income and wealth distribution amongst elderly households:

'The highest income group will be made up of those who are either just entering retirement or who will retire during the decade and who have the advantages of long unbroken years of labour participation, home ownership and index-linked pensions. The 30 per cent in the middle will probably be housing rich, but have low incomes, the result of lower occupational and state pensions. The ability of this middle group to release their housing wealth will depend crucially on the rate of the housing market and so the economy as a whole. The bottom group will remain dependent on state pensions, and so their income will depend crucially on social security policy in general and pension policy change in particular'
(Bosenquet and Propper, op.cit, p.278).

The paper will now look at the implications of this income segmentation in terms of the three key issues defined in the final chapter of Housing in Later Life (Mackintosh et al, 1990), namely:
1) The affordability of rents and older people.
2) The repair, maintenance, improvement and adaptation problems of elderly owner-occupiers.
3) The increasingly complex interface between housing policies and community care policies.

Affordability of rents

The 1988 Housing Act and the 1989 Local Government and Housing Act creates a new rent framework and a framework that is leading to major rent rises. However, at the time of writing Housing in Later Life, we felt it was not possible to assess the likely detailed impact on older people. However, we did point out:-

'The majority of older people who are renting have low incomes and are already heavily dependent on the housing benefit system for help with rent costs. Significant rent rises will therefore only be sustained if the housing benefit system is adapted to meet the additional costs, unless older people are to be expected to devote much higher proportions of their incomes to rent'
(Mackintosh et al, op cit., p.135)

The importance of this issue has been confirmed by the main survey teams, even though their interviews were carried out too early to capture the main impact of rent changes. In Paying for Britain's Housing, Maclennan et al (1990, p.24) show from the survey teams' data that "in all regions except London, the council sector's share of the elderly, at around a quarter of all residents, was double that of the owner-occupied share". They then go on to draw out the full implications of this:

'It is apparent that almost half of households in social housing in Britain do not now have access to employment income, and this stands in contrast to the sector two decades ago. This yawning gap in the sources of income has to be at the forefront of any discussion of the housing subsidy system.'
(Maclennan et al, 1990, p.36).

These are views which we share and since non employment income associated with retirement dominates the situation, there is a need to focus upon housing subsidy and older people in socially rented housing. We hope that all those involved in housing finance debates will take note, but hopefully in a way which does not stigmatise these elderly renters.

Maintaining owner-occupied properties in later life

Paying for Britain's Housing (Maclennan et al, op cit) has far less to say about elderly owner-occupiers since the focus is upon mortgage payments rather than the repair, maintenance, improvement and adaptation of the home. Yet this is the crucial issue for many elderly owner-occupiers since the vast majority have paid off their mortgage. Their difficulty is how to maintain their properties when on low incomes. The 1986 English House Condition Survey (DOE, 1988b) confirmed previous surveys that older people are disproportionately likely to experience poor housing conditions. For example, although making up only 10 per cent of households in the 1986 survey, those with a head aged 75 or more occupied almost one third of dwellings lacking basic amenities. Forty three per cent of owner-occupied households with a head over retirement age in 1986 had repair costs of £1000 or more (at 1986 prices) with 10 per cent having costs greater than £5000.

As one would expect, the vast majority of these elderly people are on very low incomes. However, they do have sizeable amounts of equity tied up in their houses. The 1986 English House Condition Survey found that more than 80 per cent of households headed by a person aged between 65 and 74, and nearly 70 per cent of those headed by a person of 75 or older, had equity of at least £25,000 in 1986 (see Figure 10.1). An equivalent figure in Spring 1991 might be about £50,000. As might be expected, the regional breakdown shows that older households in the South East have higher amounts of equity than those elsewhere (see Figure 10.2).

However, the majority of older people possess considerably more equity than the current cost of repairing their homes (see Figure 10.3). The key question is whether such equity is likely to be used more and more by elderly owner-occupiers to meet their repair costs. We are doubtful about whether this will happen. First, many of the main mechanisms (e.g. home income plans) for releasing large amounts of equity are complex and offputting to potential consumers. Second, there is no overall policy relating home equity to entitlement to state benefits. For the majority of benefits, home equity is not taken into account at all and government policies towards the expansion of home ownership have stressed the importance of inheritance. There are potentially many other calls on home equity which should be taken into account before it can be assumed that this source could be used on a major scale to finance building works, although it could be argued that investment in the protection of home equity might be considered a priority. Third, it is also clear from the EHCS that there are wide variations in the amount of wealth which elderly households have available. It is those households living in properties in the poorest condition and requiring the most expensive works, who are likely to have the least resources. Finally, to borrow against home equity in practice requires that a household has adequate income to meet

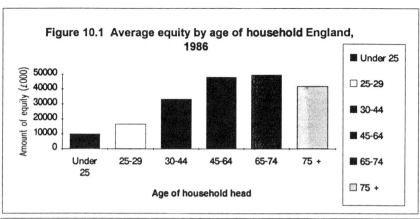

Figure 10.1 Average equity by age of household England, 1986

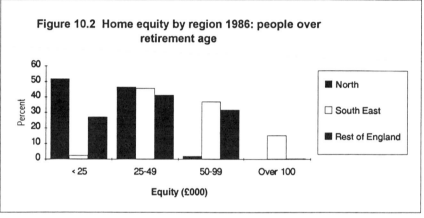

Figure 10.2 Home equity by region 1986: people over retirement age

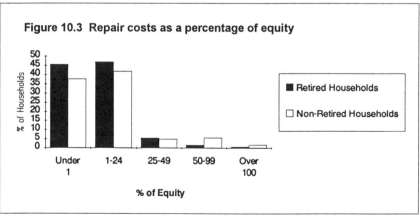

Figure 10.3 Repair costs as a percentage of equity

interest charges, or is eligible for DSS help, or has a sufficient margin of equity to permit some or all of any interest charges to be rolled-up. Many households will fall outside this group.

The new renovation grant system might be expected to help those low income elderly people in poorly repaired, and perhaps low equity property. The new system includes a minor works grant for the first time for works costing under £1000 which may be welcomed by many older people on low incomes who wish to undertake work but do not want the disruption of a full renovation grant. However, these small grants are discretionary and are only being offered by approximately 75 per cent of local authorities. For larger grants under the new system applicants have to undergo a test of resources (Leather and Mackintosh, 1989) and it is not yet known if the introduction of means testing has discouraged large numbers of potential applicants. Certainly, many elderly people are only able to fund their repairs if they are able to put together a complex funding package which might include an improvement grant, an interest only maturity loan (with the interest paid by the DSS) and perhaps a one off grant from the community care element of the social fund. Many elderly people will lack the knowledge, expertise or confidence to put together such packages. The likelihood of these emerging will depend often on the availability or non-availability of specialist advice from organisations such as Anchor Staying Put projects and Care and Repair projects (Leather and Mackintosh, 1990; Harrison and Means, 1990).

Owner-occupation in later life will be a boon to many. With the mortgage paid off, housing costs will drop at a time when weekly income is reduced, thus avoiding a major decline in living standards. For many, there is the prospect of a move from a family home to a smaller property, thus releasing equity to be used in a variety of ways. But others will be trapped in poorly repaired property of limited value with few assets around which to develop a maintenance and repair strategy in their later years.

Meeting care needs

This paper does not offer the space to take a detailed look at all aspects of the growing inter-relationship between paying for housing and paying for care. This relationship exists irrespective of whether payment is made from individual resources or from public subsidy. Here are just a few of the issues:-

1) The White Paper on community care (Department of Health, 1989) stresses the importance of Care and Repair and Staying Put projects because of their potential to stop elderly people drifting into residential care because of housing problems. This statement is made in the chapter on 'the roles and responsibilities of social services authorities' and yet it is unlikely that many social services departments will provide significant funds for such projects which are seen as a housing responsibility. However, if housing agencies

remain the dominant funder, the main performance indicator is likely to be the amount of money spent on property repair whereas community care cases may need a limited patch repair strategy because of frailty and low life expectancy (Harrison and Means, 1990).

2) There is a lack of policy co-ordination between the Department of the Environment, the Department of Health and the Department of Social Security over such issues as the capital and revenue funding of sheltered housing schemes. This is leading housing associations to set rents which exclude elderly people who are neither well off nor who have access to full housing benefit protection. This is another example of the traps faced by those who are 'not rich, not poor' (Bull and Poole, 1989). Part of the underlying difficulty may be a lack of agreement about who should fund the care element of all 'special need' housing schemes. Is the DOE showing an increased reluctance to see this as their responsibility or will a more 'liberal' regime be ushered in with the arrival of Sir George Young as the Housing Minister?

3) Many commentators have charted the 1980s explosion in private residential and nursing home care (Challis and Bartlett, 1987; Firth Report, 1987; Laing and Buisson, 1988) but the focus has usually been upon how this growth was funded through the liberalisation of social security regulations in the mid 1980s. And yet estimates suggest that just under 50 per cent of residents have their fees paid fully or partly from DSS payments (Laing and Buisson, 1988 p 44). Little is known about how the rest fund their care but there is little doubt that a major funding element will be from house sale receipts. One of the major changes to be implemented in the community care system is that from April 1993 access to public subsidy to fund institutional care should only be made available after a social worker or care manager has assessed the client as requiring residential or nursing home care (Department of Health, 1989). However, it is clear that many elderly people have the resources to buy such care if they or their relatives consider this to be the best option, and the private home care market will increasingly facilitate this to happen by developing specialist financial advisory services.

The impact of the present 'mishmash' of housing and care policies upon elderly people will not be uniform. It is clear that 'better off' elderly people will have increasingly not only the resources to buy care services, but that private sector suppliers will be increasingly in a position to respond to this market in a flexible way. This could be through offering nursing homes, residential homes, continuing care communities, sheltered housing for sale, home equity release schemes or private home care schemes. The situation for the majority, however, is far less certain. Above all, there is the continued failure of central government to recognise that the availability of good quality, easy-to-maintain and affordable housing has to be the cornerstone of community care policies (Means, 1991).

172

Conclusion

Housing in Later Life (Mackintosh et al, op cit) has helped to identify the major housing finance issues faced by older people and the information generated by the housing finance survey teams will further add to our knowledge about the importance of factors such as tenure and location. Such snapshot information needs to be backed up by a detailed investigation of the long term housing strategies of older people:

As yet we know very little about how older people come to decisions about whether to stay put, trade down, relocate in a more attractive area, or move to a different tenure. How do they come to a decision to do repair work, and are strategies devised to get the house in good condition to last the rest of their lives? These and other questions are largely unexplored (Mackintosh et al, 1990, p.141).

These types of individual housing management decisions can only be addressed by considering older people's life histories. Much of the variation and inequality in later life is due to life course experiences in the housing and labour markets rather than being the result of old age itself. Any examination of housing decisions in old age needs to take account of housing histories and how these intersect with employment careers and domestic/household changes. Important choices that have major repercussions and implications for later life may well be made in middle age. A life-history approach that considers the past and present decision-making of people in a range of different housing types would give a new perspective on housing outcomes in later life.

11 Housing and long-distance mobility in Britain

Moira Munro and Peter Symon

Introduction

In academic and popular debate on labour mobility, housing tenure has often been identified as an important element in a worker's decision as to whether or not to relocate (Champion et al, 1987; Forrest et al, 1991). In particular, council housing has long been criticised as representing a barrier to mobility, particularly for manual workers (Robertson, 1978). In the local authority sector, subsidy is 'tied' to dwellings and this is widely argued to have been a key negative influence on labour mobility. Although council housing subsidy is now less locationally tied than in the past, being increasingly replaced by housing benefit which is a personal subsidy (Gordon, 1990), there remain significant administrative barriers which would be expected to obstruct desired mobility in the council sector. In a free market view of the world, it is asserted that such housing 'barriers' to labour mobility continue to reduce labour market 'flexibility' and that, as a consequence, even in periods of buoyant demand for manual labour, unemployment remains higher than it otherwise would be in the absence of such 'rigidities' (Minford et al, 1987). Housing policies are thereby seen to contribute to regional imbalances in the economy and to stifle national economic growth.

While we believe that this view is an over-simplification, it is not our purpose here to provide a detailed critique of these arguments (for a fuller critique see MacGregor et al, 1992). Rather, our intention is to present evidence of the decision to move from the point of view of the labour migrant him or herself, focusing on the wide range of factors that can be expected to impinge upon that decision. Most work analysing the links between housing and labour mobility has been based upon studies using aggregated data, which do not permit the detailed examination of behaviour by individuals and households which we believe to be essential in disentangling the effect of tenure from other variables. Examples of this approach are the multivariate analyses of housing and labour market circumstances by Hughes and McCormick (1981) and McCormick (1983). They found that private renting exerted the greatest independent increase in the propensity to move. Mortgaged owner-occupation recorded a weaker positive association with mobility while local authority tenancy and outright owner-occupation significantly discouraged mobility. In such an approach, tenure may appear to be a powerful explanator but it may simply be acting as a proxy for a range of variables that are more directly responsible for mobility. This problem was addressed in a later paper by Hughes and McCormick (1985) exploring the possibility that the low mobility of council tenants was due to a reduced desire for mobility. Although their research led them to reject that hypothesis, we would argue that there is considerable scope for examining factors which have so far remained unmeasured.

Labour market influences upon mobility

It is useful to turn the question of mobility around: not to ask why are people prevented from moving, but rather to ask, in what circumstances would we expect an individual to wish to undertake a long-distance move. Such a starting point immediately acknowledges the normality of immobility. Many people can be expected to have strong ties with their local area and such ties may become stronger the longer the period of residence (so-called cumulative inertia). There is a considerable locally-tied investment in the formation of social and labour market linkages that needs to be set against the possible benefits of mobility. Casual observation would suggest that most people do not continuously and actively evaluate their utility maximising options in the labour and housing market, constantly alert for better opportunities elsewhere.

The labour market would be expected to provide unequal opportunities for mobility, depending on starting point and possible trajectory over the working lifetime. These are determined in large part by the types of work that people do, but are also influenced by the individuals own preferences and personal characteristics. In order to understand the way in which housing markets impinge on labour market mobility, it is important not to neglect the labour market context in which labour moves take place. A simple typology might be based on two main dimensions: first, whether the move is career-progressive or horizontal, and second, how the individual is recruited into the job. Three main alternatives are considered, first, internal-contracted, where the worker moves within the same firm; second, contracted external moves where the worker finds and then moves to a job with another firm, and finally where the move precedes the finding of a job, a speculative move. (Fig 11.1).

176

Figure 11.1
A simple typology of long-distance labour market moves

	move	
recruitment	progressive	horizontal
contracted: external	1	2
contracted: internal	3	4
speculative	5	6

While this framework is not suggested as a rigid or complete characterisation, the cells are illustrative of the different range of opportunities in career terms that may face a long-distance mover. They vary in the risks associated (internal moves are likely to have the most predictable conditions, in contracted external moves it will be possible to ascertain some of the key conditions, while the speculative move is a leap into the unknown). The cells also vary in relation to the costs of the move. Internally contracted moves may attract considerable support from the employer, especially if the move has been instituted at their behest, and similarly those recruiting workers over a long-distance may cover some part of the costs of moving. The speculative move is least likely to have associated financial support. The gains available from such moves are also differentiated, where progressive career moves would bring greater immediate rewards than horizontal moves in general.

To the extent that different occupations have opportunities concentrated in different cells of the matrix, the costs and benefits from mobility are likely to be different for different parts of the labour force. Our key concern in this paper is to contrast the labour market characteristics of those who move long-distance with those who do not. In particular the hypothesis that manual workers, who have been the main focus of policy concern (Gordon, 1990), are concentrated in the relatively more risky and less advantageous cells in the matrix of possible mobility will be explored. Manual workers do not typically enjoy a career hierarchy in the sense that many professional or managerial occupations do, so it would be expected that long- distance moves would typically be horizontal in the sense that the same work would be done, although there might be a difference in pay. It might also be expected that the labour markets for manual jobs are considerably more localized than those of professionals and consequently it may be harder for a worker to contract a long-distance move. Without the opportunity for significant upward mobility, it would be expected that the gains from moving long-distance would be less. Indeed, the loss of local contacts through which many less-skilled jobs are filled might be a definite disadvantage.

Non-manual workers will also face differential opportunities for moving. Some jobs will provide relatively few opportunities, either because local reputation and contacts are important (for example those in professional practices such as dentists or lawyers) or because the job-skills are not readily transferable to another location (an example here would be those associated with employment in capital city operations, such as the civil service or the stock exchange). For some types of profession a nationally operating labour market may make changing employers an important route to promotion (some public sector workers might be an example), while others may be expected to advance within the firm's hierarchy, between branches in different localities (managers in retail or banking are examples). The significant and substantial differences between the labour market opportunities for long-distance mobility are generally ignored in work that examines simple relationships between SEG, tenure and mobility.

As well as the nature of the jobs that people do, their own characteristics would be expected to influence the level of mobility. Perhaps the clearest-cut example of where mobility may directly reduce the level of unemployment is when workers who become unemployed leave an area in order to seek work elsewhere. The propensity to get 'on your bike' (after the infamous remark by Norman Tebbit) has been related to housing through the social security system: whereas renters will have their rent fully paid during bouts of unemployment, home owners have only interest payments made and even those not immediately. The growth of mortgage payment protection insurance plans may have slightly blurred the distinction between renting and owning in this respect. However, while it is possible, with difficulty, for mortgaged owner-occupiers to maintain owner-occupation in the short run in the face of unemployment, it is almost certainly unsustainable to maintain owner-occupation in the long run under such circumstances. Thus, owner-occupiers are faced with the probability of losing their home when they become unemployed and the great cost and distress of this outcome is argued to increase the incentive for owners to take up work: even if it is not ideal and even if it requires moving away from a preferred area (Hughes and McCormick, 1981). Conversely, it has been argued that the majority of the unemployed simply have too few resources to pursue job opportunities further afield or that, relative to incomes, the cost of searching for employment or actually moving is highest amongst the lowest income groups (Hey and McKenna, 1979; Maclennan and O'Sullivan, 1986). The labour analyst's orthodox view of a speculative mover, attracted by lower unemployment rates and/or higher wages, requires that the unemployed worker has sufficient resources to sustain both the expense of moving and the cost of living in the new location while work is sought. There would also be psychic costs associated with bearing the risk of failure: the mover might prefer to return to unemployment in the origin area rather than face unemployment in a new area. We would argue that the recognition of such costs of and constraints on mobility begins to redress the imbalance in discussions of mobility prevalent during the 1980s which tended to blame the immobile unemployed for their plight. Rather, we would place emphasis upon the difficulties and disadvantages of mobility to the unemployed, including the loss of local networks and contacts which we have already mentioned as being crucial in recruitment into many lower skilled jobs.

Two further labour market characteristics which may impinge on the propensity to move are also examined in our work. The first is the 'dual career' issue. Essentially, this issue brings gender into the centre of the debate about long-distance mobility. As the number of working women has increased, a growing literature has focused attention on the particular issues facing households where both spouses or partners (hereafter described simply as 'spouses') are pursuing independent careers (Bonney and Love, 1991). It would be expected that otherwise similar individuals would face different incentives to move depending on the employment situation of their spouses. Where their spouse is following a career, there is the problem of identifying a second suitable job in the new area. The losses to the household may well outweigh the advantages, if finding another job proves difficult. There is a distinction between two-career and two-earner households here: in both there are similar financial issues, but difficulties are compounded where both are on a career track which has its own imperatives for mobility and advancement. The final labour market issue explored here is whether long-distance movers are, in a sense, 'chronic' movers. We know that immobility is the norm, reflecting attachment to place, home, family and friends. The rate of long-distance mobility is low and could equally well result from a few people moving long-distance often or from a larger number of people moving long-distance infrequently. In this paper we analyse the balance between these two types of mover.

In the remaining part of this chapter we shall consider the role of employment-related factors in the decision whether or not to move long-distance. After discussing the data which we collected to examine the mobility of British households we first discuss the familiar relationship between housing tenure and long- distance mobility which, in effect, defines the problem with which most research has been concerned. The labour market characteristics of long-distance movers are then considered in four sections and their characteristics are compared with those of short distance movers and with non-movers. Finally, the consequences of the decision whether or not to move, are considered.

The study

The research is based on samples of movers and non-movers matched with respect to age and socio-economic group. These samples were drawn from a large household survey conducted in early 1989 for a study of housing economics supported by the Joseph Rowntree Foundation (Maclennan et al, 1990). We identified the geographical origin and destination of the household's last move, where the move was completed during the five year period up to the time of the survey. For our follow-up sample we took 100 per cent of those labour market movers who had moved 50 kilometres (approximately 30 miles) or further in the last five years (the 30 mile threshold is often used to determine entitlement to employers' assistance with relocation expenses). Only 199 households had moved long-distance to their current address in the previous five years (2.1 per cent of the entire housing finance study sample; excluding retirement moves and moves to study, which accounted for a further 0.6 per cent).

We then selected similar sized samples of stayers (who hadn't moved in the five years up to 1989) and short-distance movers (who had moved less than 30 miles in their last move). These groups matched long-distance movers with respect to age and socio-economic group. (The sampling methodology is reported more fully in McGregor et al, 1992.) The selection of the variables on which to match the three groups reflects the strong relationships identified between these variables and the propensity to move: more professional and managerial occupations are strongly associated with mobility and younger people tend to be more mobile than older people (Champion and Fielding, 1992). That is, apart from housing variables and the more detailed labour market information that remained to be collected, the intention was to have three groups who were largely similar in the sense that they would be expected to be a mobile sector of the population.

Table 11.1
Housing tenure and mobility (row percentages)

| | movers | | stayers | sample |
	long-distance	short-distance		size
owner-occupier	35	27	38	243
public tenant	12	34	54	68
private tenant & other	44	48	8	64
average	33	32	36	375

As Table 11.1 shows, despite controlling for age and SEG the housing tenure apparently retains the well-established effect on mobility propensities. Long-distance movers are over-represented amongst both private tenants and owner-occupiers. Short-distance movers are over-represented in both the private and the public rented sectors. Stayers are over-represented in public renting and in owner-occupation. This pattern reflects the long term decline of the private rented sector (Gordon, 1990) indicating that the sector provides little long-term accommodation, serving both long- distance and short-distance movers who require short-term accommodation. Confirming the earlier studies, public rented housing is associated with some short-distance mobility but appears to discourage long-distance mobility.

180

The characteristics of long-distance movers

Career paths

Our evidence confirms that opportunities for 'career' movement and progress are associated broadly with the kind of business that the individual is employed in. Those employed in the service sectors were considerably more mobile than those in the manufacturing sectors, as table 11.2 shows. Conversely, a greater proportion of stayers and short-distance movers worked in manufacturing or construction. Long-distance movers were particularly over-represented in SIC 8 (banking and financial services) and SIC 9 (other services including public services).

Table 11.2
Household head's industry sector and mobility (row percentages)

| | movers | | stayers | base |
	long-distance	short-distance		(=100%)
manufact.& constr.	23	29	47	133
services	38	32	30	219
average	32	31	36	352

Long-distance movers were educated to a significantly higher level than either short-distance movers or stayers (see Table 3). Fully 42 per cent of long-distance movers were graduates and in addition a substantial proportion of graduates possessed higher degrees. The high educational qualifications of many long-distance movers tends to support the notion that long-distance movers are competing in national rather than local labour markets, in which educational 'credentialism' is more important. On the other hand, only 19 per cent of short- distance movers were graduates. Employers are faced with competition on a national basis for qualified labour, but tend to recruit locally for lower grade jobs.

Another indication of the existence of different career types can be found in the expressed estimation of the importance of mobility to the career of movers and non-movers. While there may be an element of post-hoc justification in this (movers would not wish to admit that their own mobility had been pointless nor would stayers necessarily be reconciled to any slowing in their career progression) the differences are striking. Over half of the long-distance movers say that being mobile is either very or fairly important in their careers compared to 37 per cent of short-distance movers and just 29 per cent of stayers (Table 11.4).

Table 11.3
Household head's educational attainment and mobility (column percentages)

| | movers | | stayers | average |
	long-distance	short-distance		
has degree	42	19	33	31.5
no degree	58	81	67	68.5
base (=100%)	118	115	110	343

Table 11.4
Importance of mobility for career advancement (column percentages)

| | movers | | stayers | average |
	long-distance	short-distance		
very/fairly important	55	37	29	40
not important/applicable	45	63	71	60
base (= 100 %)	97	97	99	293

We have already noted that long-distance mobility is more prevalent amongst managerial and professional groups than amongst manual workers. As Forrest and Murie remark (1991:67), long-distance mobility 'is more likely to be in BMWs rather than on bikes and it can be heavily subsidized by employers'. The role that employers play in encouraging and assisting mobility has become increasingly important, as indicated in studies by Forrest and Murie (1987; 1991), Salt (1991), Munro and Symon (1990) and the Institute of Manpower Studies (1987). We have reported elsewhere in fuller detail the results of our research into in-company moves (McGregor et al, 1992). In the household survey (of both internal labour market movers and people not moving within companies) we found that nearly two-thirds (63 per cent) of the long-distance movers received employers assistance with their move. Of these, about one half said that they would not have moved without it. As hypothesized, employers assistance is particularly associated with those contracting moves in internal or external labour markets. Assistance might be expected to be associated with situations in which the mobility of employees is important to the employer as much as to the employee. Such assistance significantly reduces the costs of moving and will often greatly reduce the anxiety surrounding the process (guaranteed house sales, mortgage subsidy, temporary accommodation and so on).

Differences in the importance of career imperatives are apparent in the respondents' expressed reasons for moving. The survey asked movers to select their main reason for moving from a list of twelve. Nine of these were 'job' related reasons and were aggregated into a single category. The results are presented in Table 11.5: not surprisingly, labour market reasons are much more important for long-distance movers than short distance movers, but there is not a simple association between long-distance mobility and labour market factors. Neither are short distance moves prompted only by housing factors. 'Family' or 'personal' reasons are significant in prompting mobility in both groups. For long- distance movers these tended to be moves back to home areas or to be closer to family. In contrast short distance moves were more often a result of marital separation, to leave the family of origin or to get married. This complexity was evident in the earlier work by Johnson et al (1974) who first identified the importance of non-labour market factors in prompting long-distance mobility.

Table 11.5
Main reasons for moving (column percentages)

	movers		average
	long-distance	short-distance	
labour market	4	72	39
housing or area	58	8	33
family or personal	38	18	28
other	-	2	1
base (= 100 %)	117	122	239

Unemployment

Our research confirms that movers and non-movers are differentiated by their experience of unemployment. Stayers and long-distance movers are more likely than short distance movers to have had a recent spell of unemployment. Compared to short distance movers, long-distance movers are most likely to have been unemployed immediately before the move. Duration of unemployment is very different for the longer distance mover and the stayer: long-distance movers had very much shorter periods of unemployment while stayers are much more likely to have been unemployed for over a year. This is consistent with long-distance mobility as a possible response to unemployment, but only for a limited period of time. As the duration of unemployment lengthens, and the resources of the household diminish, there is progressively less and less possibility of bearing the costs of a move. Longer term unemployment is also, of course, associated with increased difficulty in re-entering the labour market.

The majority of households were headed by married couples (74 per cent were married or living as married at the time of the interview). For a small minority, the move was associated with marital separation or relationship breakdown and/or the formation of a new partnership. In this section, we shall consider the labour market experiences of married (or co-habiting) couples who constituted intact households before and after the move or, in the case of stayers, whose household composition remained the same during the period under discussion.

The evidence of this survey seems to support the hypothesized effect of dual-careers on mobility. Table 11.6 shows that the majority of long-distance movers are drawn from households typifying the traditional nuclear family model in which the husband worked in full-time paid employment and the wife was not in paid employment. Most stayers also exhibited this pattern of joint economic activity, whereas most short-distance movers were both in full time work before the move. This confirms the expectation that when both spouses are in full time employment there are likely to be more resources to support a move for housing or investment reasons. Considering *all* households, the great majority had either both adults or just the head of household in full-time work, just 16 per cent of the sample exhibited other patterns of economic activity. Long-distance movers and stayers were over-represented within the 'less conventional' group: in each case about the same number fell into this category as into the two full time workers group.

Table 11.6
Economic activity and mobility in married couple households
(column percentages)

	movers		stayers	average
	long-distance	short-distance		
both in paid employment	37	56	54	49
only husband in paid employment	49	37	37	41
only wife in paid employment	5	4	4	4
neither in paid employment	9	4	5	6
base (= 100 per cent)	87	79	95	261

Previous moves

Our evidence suggests that long-distance movers were more likely than short-distance movers to have previous experience of moving long-distance. Over 70 per cent of short-distance movers had made no long-distance move in the last ten years and only 9 per cent had made two or more (see table 11.7). Conversely, just under half of the long-distance movers had made at least one long-distance move in addition to their latest move. When earlier job-related long-distance mobility was examined, the distinction between long-distance and short-distance movers became even clearer: 86 per cent of long-distance movers said that they had already moved long-distance for work reasons at some time in their past, compared with only 14 per cent of short-distance movers.

Table 11.7
Number of long–distance moves in the previous ten years (column percentages)

	movers		stayers
	long-distance	short-distance	
none	-	73	37
one	52	18	34
two	23	4	14
three or more	25	5	15
base (= 100 per cent)	122	119	241

The apparently higher propensity to move among long-distance movers was also indicated by recent experience of applying for jobs and plans for the future. Although such questions are inevitably hypothetical and consequently not to be interpreted too literally, the comparison between the responses of long-distance movers and the rest is stark. Respondents were asked whether they or their partner had seriously considered starting or applying for any job that was 30 or more miles away (not including any that had actually been taken). Half of those who had seriously considered such a job were long-distance movers. When asked about prospects in the next year or so, over half of those who thought they might take up a distant job were long-distance movers (16.7 per cent of all long-distance movers fell into the category of possible movers).

When asked, more generally, how likely it was that they would move long-distance in the next five years, long-distance movers were most over-represented among those who thought it was very or fairly likely. Forty four per cent of long-distance movers considered it to be very or fairly likely that they would move 30 miles or more over the next five years, compared to 20 per cent of short-distance movers and 14 per cent of stayers (table 11.8).

In summary, it appears that the long-distance movers identified here are different from the other groups in that they have generally experienced more long-distance mobility. This may be an independent factor but is more likely to result from the different career paths identified above.

Table 11.8
Likelihood of moving long-distance in the next five years (column percentages)

	movers		stayers
	long-distance	short-distance	
likely	44	20	14
unlikely	56	80	86
base (=100%)	118	115	130

Mobility and careers

An important part of the research project was to compare and contrast circumstances before and after the move. The median date of moves by both long-distance and short distance movers was mid-1987. Stayers were asked parallel questions to the movers about their situation before and after that date. We shall briefly discuss the housing and labour market outcomes and also the perceived standard of living of movers and non-movers.

Only two public sector tenants in our sample remained public tenants after the move (although other long-distance movers entered the tenure). 26 per cent of long-distance movers changed tenure as they moved compared to 31 per cent of short distance movers. The greatest inter-tenure flow for both types of move was between renting and owning (17 per cent of long-distance movers and 25 per cent of short distance movers). Long-distance movers rely disproportionately on private rented housing both before and after the move. As a result of these changes, as is consistent with the socio-economic group breakdown of the sample, owner-occupation remains by far the most dominant tenure (77 per cent of all sample). The public rented sector houses 17 per cent of the sample: mainly stayers, while the private rented sector accounts for 5 per cent in total.

Income distributions before the move were broadly similar (as would be expected given that the sample controlled for age and socio- economic group) but stayers were under-represented at the top of the income distribution, while long-distance movers were under-represented at the lower end of the income distribution. This difference was broadly maintained following the move, so that the long-distance movers appear to be richer on average than the short- distance movers or stayers.

Following the move, the distribution of economic activities appears remarkably stable. However, this belies a considerable amount of adjustment at the individual level. For all categories of move the most common outcome was for joint economic activity to stay the same, but while for short-distance movers nearly three-quarters maintained the same pattern of activity, among long-distance movers under half did so. In under 10 per cent of short distance mover couples did the woman's participation in the labour market change, compared to 18 per cent of long distance movers where the woman's participation increased and 14 per cent where it reduced. Our evidence then lends support to the hypothesis that couples who both work are more likely to have to make labour market adjustments in undertaking a long-distance move: certainly in this survey having two full time earners is most commonly associated with short distance mobility.

It is clear that both possible consequences of moving are demonstrated here: in some cases participation in the labour market increases (this may be associated with higher costs forcing increased work, or better opportunities encouraging or enabling increased participation) and in some cases participation decreased. These changes must be placed in the context of the underlying (and locally differentiated) changes in the labour market. Among the stayers, while two-thirds of couples maintained the same pattern of labour market participation over the time period, there appeared to be a tendency for women to increase their participation amongst the movers. Our investigation suggests that, not only are dual earners less likely to undertake a long-distance move, but also it is harder for both spouses to remain in employment after moving long-distance.

Table 11.9
Perceived change in standard of living since January 1984 or since move (column percentages)

	movers		stayers
	long-distance	short-distance	
better	75	63	55
same	17	20	26
worse	8	17	19
base (=100%)	122	119	133

Table 11.9 shows that long-distance movers were more likely than short-distance movers or stayers to perceive that their standard of living had improved since 1984. Nearly 27 per cent of long- and short- distance movers thought their standard of living was much better than it had been, compared to 8 per cent of stayers. Conversely, 19 per cent of stayers thought that their standard of

living was now worse or much worse compared to 17 per cent of short- distance movers and just 8 per cent of long-distance movers.

Conclusions

In this chapter we presented evidence, confirming the evidence from previous studies, that tenure bears a strong relationship to the propensity to move: private tenants are the most mobile over long-distances and public tenants are least mobile, with owner-occupiers somewhere in between these two groups of tenants. This relationship persisted despite our sample control for age and SEG.

However, the main point of this chapter has been to explore some key labour market characteristics that have generally remained unmeasured in previous research but which would be expected to be associated with mobility. Labour market characteristics are strongly differentiated in many respects between the different categories of migrant, even though differences between long-distance movers, short-distance movers and non-movers with respect to age and socio-economic group have been controlled for. In particular, the notion of a career path seems particularly important in distinguishing the mobile from the less mobile and is likely to underpin the finding that long-distance mobility is concentrated to some degree amongst a group which moves relatively frequently. Subjectively and objectively, the long-distance move appears to have improved the economic position of the household, confirming that mobility is indeed associated with career progression.

These results suggest caution in placing too much emphasis on the housing system as an influence on labour mobility patterns. The importance of the labour market and the differences in the available career paths suggest that we cannot reject the hypothesis that people are pre-selected by their labour market imperatives into different tenure groups to some degree - that is housing may be selected in the light of the expected demands of the labour market. Research should concentrate on detailed behavioural analyses of a wider range of factors, including labour market and personal characteristics, when examining the interaction between housing and labour mobility.

Acknowledgements

The authors wish to thank Alex Marsh for useful comments on the draft manuscript.

Part Five
FUTURE PROSPECTS

12 Housing and the UK economy: The boom, the bust and beyond

Duncan Maclennan and Kenneth Gibb

12.1 The boom, the bust and beyond

Until the 1990s there was, in Britain, relatively little detailed interest in the connections between the housing market and the national economy. Income growth was, correctly, viewed as an important influence on housing quality improvements and tenure shift and, especially in periods of recession, the employment effects of housing orders were recognised to be important. With regionally divergent house prices in the 1980s some economists had begun to consider feedback effects from price rises on labour mobility and wage determination. However, it was only really with John Muellbauer's work on the consumption, supply side and inflation consequences of rising house and land prices, reinforced subsequently by Ermisch's edited volume, that more than passing attention was given to the national economic role of the housing system (Muellbauer and Murphy, 1989; Muellbauer, 1990; Ermisch, 1990).

As academic findings on the role of housing in the economic "boom" of 1986-89 were being disseminated the national economy and the housing market had already moved into a deep, interrelated recession. Within two years from 1988 to 1990, pundits had begun to recognise that the housing market was apparently capable of deepening and prolonging a recession as well as accelerating and heightening a boom. Taking boom and bust together, and indeed looking as far back as the early 1970s, there is now a case for examining how the housing sector has influenced national economic instability and whether damaging effects of fluctuations can be mitigated in the future. There is, undoubtedly, much merit in examining how the housing sector can facilitate and reinforce short term economic recovery. Even more important is the necessity of establishing a flexible and fair housing system which will enhance national growth in the longer term. It is essential that short term recovery oriented "solutions" do not compromise desired longer term changes in the structure of housing policies. This paper emphasises the longer term view.

The paper is not such a review, nor a theory, nor a model. Rather it is a "connected" mapping of the key issues, written with a view to arousing comment on how best to structure a review of current developments and future prospects for housing and the economy. The paper first indicates the extent of tenure change in Britain in recent years, considering the role of housing policy in this process. The impacts of financial deregulation and developments in the housing market are considered in the next section, as part of a discussion of the main features of the boom and bust periods. The question at the heart of the paper is whether the instability observed was due to specific, "one-off" effects or rather that they reflect some basic characteristics of the UK housing system. The final section outlines policy measures which could be used to reduce the destabilising role of housing in the national economy and relates then to the suite of policies which would also secure fairer, and better, housing policy outcomes.

12.2 Tenure change in Britain

Compared with other developed countries, Britain has one of the highest levels of owner occupation at more than two-thirds of all housing. Interestingly, Britain also has one of the lowest levels of private renting (7 per cent) with the remainder consisting of a substantial proportion of public sector housing. These tenure shares, described in table one since 1970, set Britain apart from other OECD countries.

There are important regional differences in owner occupation. Wales and England have levels of owner occupation greater than the national average while Scotland has a level of ownership at just over 50 per cent. These differences are explicable in terms of regional incomes, the greater extent and growth of municipal housing and a resistance to the speculative demand for owner occupation (Scotland has always had lower house prices than Southern England, although this varies during the house price cycle).

In this section we will consider the major housing policy reasons for the growth of home ownership. Housing market, income growth and financial developments are considered in section III. Two, related aspects of housing policy are important in this discussion: the role of discounted council sales made possible through the Right to buy legislation initially enacted in 1980; and, the continuing imbalance in the provision of subsidy to different housing tenures.

192

Table 12.1
Housing tenure in the UK, 1970-90

year	owner occupied	public rent	private rent	other	total dwellings
1970	50.0	30.4	19.6		18.7M
1971	50.6	30.6	18.9		19.0M
1972	51.6	30.5	17.9		19.2M
1973	52.5	30.4	17.1		19.4M
1974	53.0	30.7	16.3		19.6M
1975	53.4	31.1	15.5		19.9M
1976	53.7	31.4	14.8		20.1M
1977	54.1	31.7	14.2		20.3M
1978	54.7	31.7	13.7		20.6M
1979	55.3	31.5	13.1		20.8M
1980	55.5	31.1	12.7		20.9M
1981	56.6	30.3	10.8	2.2	21.0M
1982	58.2	29.2	10.4	2.3	21.2M
1983	59.5	28.3	9.9	2.3	21.4M
1984	60.6	27.6	9.4	2.4	21.6M
1985	61.6	26.9	9.0	2.5	21.8M
1986	62.7	26.2	8.6	2.5	22.0M
1987	63.8	25.4	8.2	2.6	22.2M
1988	65.1	24.4	7.7	2.7	22.4M
1989	66.6	23.3	7.4	2.8	22.6M
1990	67.5	22.6	7.1	2.9	22.7M

Source: Council of Mortgage Lenders, Housing Finance No.11, p.31.

Note: 'Other' mainly consists of housing associations.

Between 1980 and 1991 more than 1.3 million dwellings were sold at discount to sitting tenants. Survey data estimates that the average discount (based on years of tenancy) is around 40-45 per cent of the estimated value of the property (Maclennan, Gibb and More, 1991). Discounts on flats may be as high as 70 per cent. Sales have not been uniform, regionally or temporally but rather have come in fits and starts and are more concentrated in areas with higher levels of owner occupation. Right to buy households tend to be older, with incomes of around 60 to 75 per cent of owner occupiers as a whole (Nationwide Anglia, 1989; Forrest, Murie and Williams, 1990). The effect of the discount is to reduce the price to income ratios of former council tenants to a level below that of all other first time buyers or borrowers as a whole (respectively 1.91, 3.03, 3.81 in 1989). This is also true of the ratio of mortgage advances to household income (respectively 1.67, 2.27, 2.06 in 1989) and allows former tenants to borrow a greater proportion of the property value than other first time buyers or all other borrowers (respectively 87.1%, 75.1%, 54.2% - all figures from Nationwide Anglia, 1989, p.3).

In addition to the Right to Buy, there has been a long list of policies aimed at further widening home ownership in Britain, particularly down-market and for more marginal households through policies grouped together under the heading low cost home ownership. These policies, accurately described as niche products, include tenants buying equity in their properties in tranches (shared ownership) and calculating a mortgage on the basis of current gross rents after the same discount as the Right to Buy (Rent to Mortgage). These policies have had more symbolic than numerical impact.

The tax and subsidy system in Britain discriminates markedly between housing tenures. The owner occupier mortgagor receives 25% tax relief on interest payments on the first £30,000 of their mortgage. As an asset-holder, they are exempt from capital gains and income tax, As a consumer, owner occupiers do not pay VAT and will in 1993 begin to pay a banded property tax (although the council tax will be paid by all households). Low income owner occupiers, borrowers and outright owners, have no recourse to income-related housing benefit which is restricted to tenants. Mortgagors who qualify for income support (the British form of social security) can, however, get help with their interest payments. Tenants on low income are eligible for housing benefit, although this is restricted in the private rented sector where a rent officer can determine whether a rent is reasonable and therefore eligible for benefit expenditure. Social sector tenants may also receive some form of price subsidy through subventions from central government and also implicitly through historic cost accounting and rent pooling.

This is not the place to discuss the impacts of the tax expenditures received by home owners except to say that evidence (Maclennan, Gibb and More, 1991) suggests that formal subsidy to owners outweighs that received by tenants at relatively low household incomes (£5,000 per annum) and that tax expenditures are regressive - the top third of owners receive two thirds of mortgage interest tax relief. Furthermore, tax expenditures, in the face of inelastic housing supply, are probably capitalised into higher house prices with implications for the cyclical nature of the housing market.

12.3 The boom

The period 1981-1989 witnessed (though at different rates in different regions of the country) a rapid growth in the number of home owners from 11.9 million to 15 million. Mortgage holders in the same period grew from 6.2 to 9.1 million households. The home-ownership share rose from 55 to 67 per cent and real house prices increased by more than a half. Table 2 shows the long term pattern in real house prices and nominal house prices in the U.K.,

Greater London and Scotland. There was no simple, single "cause" of these important developments but rather a range of different influences operating. Specifically these related developments in the financial sector, the housing market and in economic policy. Each of these areas of influence is examined below.

Table 12.2
Real house prices 1970–92 (%) [1]

Year	U.K.	Greater London	Scotland	R.P.I.
1970	0.8	4.7	2.1	6.4
1971	3.8	8.9	0.0	9.4
1972	23.8	32.9	6.9	7.1
1973	25.6	20.8	28.8	9.2
1974	-5.6	-13.2	-2.4	16.1
1975	-17.0	-23.8	-10.3	24.2
1976	-8.7	-12.2	0.0	16.5
1977	-8.4	-8.2	-6.0	15.8
1978	5.9	6.13	5.1	8.3
1979	14.4	21.2	6.6	13.4
1980	0.4	2.0	-5.7	18.0
1981	-9.4	-12.5	-6.2	11.9
1982	-7.0	-8.6	-10.6	8.6
1983	3.1	8.22	1.1	4.6
1984	5.0	8.6	3.6	5.0
1985	0.8	6.45	-2.0	6.1
1986	13.2	20.4	1.5	3.4
1987	7.1	16.2	0.6	4.2
1988	17.3	12.7	1.5	4.9
1989	1.8	-1.2	0.2	7.8
1990	1.0	-8.2	16.1	9.5
1991	-1.8	-3.6	7.8	5.9
1992(Q2)	-1.7	-9.9	-5.2	4.0

Source: Housing and Construction Statistics
Note: 1992 Figures are the first two quarters

Deregulation and housing finance

Integration of global capital flows and deregulation of domestic capital markets have been a predominant feature of the advanced economies over the last 15 years. In the UK the housing finance circuit was historically less segmented from the national capital market than in many other advanced economies but deregulation has still had major effects on the price and availability of mortgage credit.

The removal of exchange controls and then, by 1981, the removal of the "corset" on bank lending encouraged banks to expand mortgage lending and compete with building societies. Building societies countered the growth in the banks share (to a fifth of new lending by 1985) developing new savings and loan products and, by offering higher return deposit rates. The mortgage rate shifted up relative to bank base rates as societies terminated their rate-setting cartel and shifted to new approaches to rationing funds. Further legislative change in 1986 facilitated further structural changes in the lending industry and created new links between lending, insurance and estate agency activities. Societies diversified both their sources of funding (increasingly relying on wholesale money market funds up to a Treasury imposed limit of 20 then 40 percent of lending - a limit which major societies are now approaching) and their sources of earning income (though additional sources were still tied to the level of housing market activity).

The switch, after the early 1980s, from a traditional "queueing" form of rationing, i.e. "non-equilibrium" rationing, to "equilibrium" rationing (see: Stiglitz and Weiss, 1981; Llewellyn and Holmes, 1991) has had potentially major impacts on the housing system. Equilibrium rationing for societies involves not only mortgage rate setting but the manipulation or selection of lending criteria such as loan to price ratios, loan to income ratios and so on. Both of these ratios appeared to increase sharply in the 1980s. Loan income multiples rose from 1.67 to 2.13, second income multiples increased and average loan to value ratios rose from 74 per cent to 81 per cent.

These changes in society behaviour are likely to have had three major effects. In the first place rationing of a disequilibrium nature ended in the market, and though this may be generally welcomed on efficiency grounds it also removes a critical brake on lending towards the peak of housing market activity. A second implication was that the changes led to higher loan default rates because of larger loan to income and price ratio probabilities, and this is important in a context where societies were persuaded downmarket by government to finance low income owner occupation initiatives (thus raising the concern that the "bust" has disproportionately impacted on the "new" owners of the 1980s). A third point was that the changes also facilitated equity withdrawal through the development of equity release products (though more important in banks) or looser scrutiny of the purposes of second mortgages.

The personal sector

In the personal sector as a whole, debt grew rapidly throughout the 1980s, at an average annual rate of 19 per cent. The bulk of this increase was housing loans. At the same time assets in the personal sector also increased sharply, and in the housing sector the gap between housing values and outstanding loans grew from £271bn to £742bn between 1980 and 1988. Conventional measures of equity withdrawal suggest that after running at around £4-£5 billion in the early 1980s, withdrawal peaked at £17bn in 1988 (see table 3). Research carried out for the Joseph Rowntree Foundation (not a national sample) suggests that "mis-used" second or additional loans backed by housing asset values added a further £3bn - £5bn to withdrawal (Maclennan, Gibb and More, 1991). Miles (1992) estimates that the marginal propensity to consume out of equity withdrawal is somewhere between 0.5 and 0.75 and may even be as high as 0.78. And, of course, there were likely to have been major but still unverified direct effects of wealth increases (the "feel good factor") on consumption. There are few analysts who now doubt that the housing price bubble, fuelled by real economic policy and housing market factors and facilitated (but not caused) by deregulation, accelerated the 1988 boom.

Table 12.3
Housing equity withdrawal 1980-90 (£ million)

year	net new loans for house purchase	private fixed residential investment	home improve- ments	others	equity withdrawal nominal	real 1985 prices
1980	7368	6115	1594	-163	-177	-252
1981	9483	6174	1800	177	1331	1684
1982	14128	6850	1927	756	4954	5348
1983	14520	7757	2230	-456	4998	5566
1984	17031	8979	2451	-1123	6724	7131
1985	19033	9323	2814	-623	7519	7520
1986	26985	10993	3364	-370	12998	12571
1987	29256	12724	3626	-256	13162	12221
1988	40050	15943	4210	588	19308	17087
1989	33658	16230	4422	1022	11984	9839
1990	32067	14205	4743	-298	13417	10066

Source: Miles (1992), Table 5, p.70.
Note: equity withdrawal is equal to the first column (net new loans) minus the sum of PFRI, home improvements and 'others' (mainly sales to public tenants)

However the period 1981-1988 also put in place a personal sector exposed to mortgage interest rate rises, and particularly where these rate rises were aimed at cooling the housing market. Llewellyn and Holmes (1991) identify several examples of this happening. First, there was a sharp rise in capital gearing (the ratio of outstanding mortgages to the value of the housing stock) in the housing market in the 1980s (although it took to 1985 to reach the 1970 level of 23 per cent, so perhaps this was a readjustment to a desired level of debt made possible by deregulation). Second, total personal debt to income ratios rose from 57 percent to 115 percent from 1979-89. Third, the average mortgage debt to income ratio rose from 33 to 68 percent over the same period. Fourth, the total assets to income ratio of the personal sector rose, largely due to house price increases, from 4.9 to 7.2 between 1979 and 1988. Finally, the proportion of disposable income absorbed in servicing debt had risen from 5.4 to 13 percent between 1982 and 1989, and for first-time buyers the proportion for mortgage only payments rose from 19 to 33 percent.

Real factors and the housing sector

Financial deregulation did not, of course, operate in a vacuum. The liberalisation of housing finance, particularly after 1985, occurred in a context where the real economy was growing and confidence increasing, real interest rates were low and the stock of money increasing rapidly (a policy scenario introduced after Black Monday in 1987). In this period the increase in general inflation was relatively low but real asset values were accelerating and a well formed house price bubble was already inflating.

In the housing market the demand for credit was fuelled by several real factors. There were demographic factors in the form of a growing number of new households reflecting the 60's baby boom cohort. Also, rising incomes, reduced income taxes and falling unemployment all contributed to increasing housing demand, backed up by a strong aspiration/preference for home-ownership. There were also specific tax changes (the poll-tax replacing rates and the "advance" announcement of the ending of dual MIRAS) which created one-off or finite increases in housing demand. At the same time, there was a continued shortage of quality rental housing, in both private and public sectors and a housing subsidy system in which all employed households with moderate or above incomes received higher subsidies in owning rather than renting. Finally, all of these elements have to be placed in a disorderly context of housing supply where land and construction costs rose in real terms throughout the 1980s (Bramley et al, 1990; Bramley, 1992) point to the low price elasticity of supply in the British housing system at a level for new build of around 1.0).

It is clear from these points that the general macroeconomic policy arrangements were inflationary for the housing sector and that "one-off" as well as enduring housing policy arrangements were, given British consumer preferences and housing "psychology", likely to generate a severe increase in housing prices. It would seem odd to lay any "blame" for events at the feet of a near "first-best" housing finance market. A recent study, for Fannie Mae, of major economy housing finance systems placed the UK as "best" on 5 out of 6 efficiency criteria (Diamond and Lea, 1992). The difficulties arose, rather, from macro-policies which failed to recognise the nature of UK housing markets and their associated policy distortions. Support for credit controls as a 'second-best' policy response to a given distortion in the housing sector (such as the impact of tax expenditures) would have to be carefully articulated and its impacts fully evaluated before it could acquire credibility.

It is also questionable (given the debt/lending scenario outlined above for 1988), whether policy that sharply increased interest rates which was espoused to control and end the boom was well designed. It is all too apparent that such a policy selection would be likely to have adverse impacts on all recent buyers (either new first-time buyers or those trading up) and would penalise the high proportion of 95 percent plus loans (56 per cent of first time buyers had loan to value ratios in excess of 90 per cent, and were extremely exposed by international standards (Lomax, 1991) to the prospect of loan default). Higher interest rates would also, of course, ultimately adversely affect *all* housing asset values, thus sharply reducing household wealth.

Two questions regarding policy at that time are worth considering. First, there is a major difference between "cooling" and "killing" the housing market and this raises the question whether mortgage rate increases were too sudden and too steep. Should policy have aimed for stable house prices - and not just by interest rate means but by innovative fiscal policies? Secondly, it is apparent from the JRF work and official statistics that not all regions of the UK had "enjoyed" the price-boom/equity withdrawal effects experienced in southern Britain. The question arises as to whether general interest rate rises to cool the southern housing boom were equitable in their effects on northern Britain, let alone on corporate and small business borrowers? Obviously they were not; non-southern home-owners and the economic base of the economy were undoubtedly greatly damaged by efforts to control the boom. The answer does not lie in re-regulating the mortgage finance sector. Rather, there is a need to scrutinise more carefully the housing market and related factors which produced such damaging regional and sectoral imbalances. This issue is pursued further in the concluding section but before such consideration it is pertinent to focus on the post 1988 "bust" in more detail.

12.4 The bust

At the end of 1988, and well prior to ERM entry, the government sharply increased interest rates to cool the boom, reduce consumption and raise savings rates. The net savings rate had fallen sharply in the period 1984-88 from 0.11 to 0.05 as the gross savings rate remained nearly constant at 0.24 but increased borrowing reduced the net rate.

Increased mortgage rates for new borrowers (see table 4 which contrasts mortgage rates with society deposit rates to savers and with bank base rates) rose quickly (existing borrowers face lags in increases and decreases as a reported half of them have annual revision agreements). By mid-1989 they had risen from 9 to 15 per cent and remained there before beginning to fall in late 1990 (at the time of UK entry into the ERM). Higher rates also confronted the construction sector and business investors, with subsequent unemployment consequences.

The immediate reaction, and disproportionately in the previously over-heated southern markets, was a reduction in sales of new and existing units but with new construction only reducing with a lag. The Inland Revenue have estimated that the volume of residential sales fell from 2.2 million in 1988 to around 1 million in 1991. Such a predictable reaction had typified earlier downturns in previous UK house price cycles, but in this instance the sharp increases in interest rates had a proportionately greater impact on the consumption and spending of recent, existing borrowers. From the Joseph Rowntree Foundation household survey (Maclennan, Gibb and More, 1990; 1991) it was estimated that the proportion of income devoted to housing by first time buyers in 1987 and 1988 exceeded a half in 1989 and into 1990. For the wider sample of all owners captured in the Department of the Environment 5 per cent (of mortgage transactions) sample survey, the average repayment (after MIRAS) to income ratio, which had drifted up from 15 per cent in the early 1980s to 17 per cent by 1987, peaked at 26.3 per cent in 1990.

Table 12.4
Interest rates 1975–91(%) [1]

Year	Building Society Gross Deposits	Mortgages	London Clearing Bank Base Rate
1975	11.00	11.08	10.47
1976	10.80	11.06	11.11
1977	10.58	11.05	8.94
1978	9.64	9.55	9.04
1979	12.07	11.94	13.68
1980	14.77	14.92	13.32
1981	13.13	14.01	13.27
1982	12.57	13.30	11.93
1983	10.39	11.03	9.83
1984	11.06	11.84	9.68
1985	12.41	13.47	12.25
1986	10.92	12.07	10.70
1987	10.16	11.61	9.74
1988	9.16	11.05	10.09
1989	12.04	13.70	13.85
1990	14.03	14.98	14.75
1991	12.81	14.19	12.25

Source: Housing Finance (1991) Table 23.
Note: 1989-91 are averaged from monthly data.

House prices began to weaken, in southern Britain throughout 1989, in real terms though nominal price increases were nationally greater than zero in 1990. In previous house price cycles, nominal house prices had not fallen over the previous quarter century. The typical adjustment pattern in the downswing was that prices fell in real terms as general inflation rates outstripped small positive nominal house price gains. The withdrawal of transactors/sellers in previous downswings has created an effective house price ratchet for non-first time buyers. It is important to recognise that three-fifths of transactions in the market are partly driven by the state of the market - most moves involve existing owners usually moving small distances and such moves are postponable when market activity is slack and sales chains more difficult to effectuate.

The post-1989 bust has been different - although inflation rates were increasing into 1990 there were sharp falls in nominal prices (with large regional fluctuations). According to the Nationwide Anglia building society, house prices in the UK were roughly flat in nominal terms between 1989 and 1990 (first quarter to first quarter). In 1990-91 the same figure produced an annual fall of 8.2 per cent and in 1991-92 prices fell another 4.0 per cent. Comparable figures for Greater London were falls of 4.9 per cent, 5.6 per cent and 7.5 per cent. In all three years, Scottish house prices have, however, risen by between 5 and 12 per cent. In the 1989 context the upward shift in interest rates was significant in scale and had a marked effect on first time buyer demand. However, what was truly distinctive in the most recent bust was the rapid increase in repossessions. The number of borrowers with 6-12 months arrears rose sharply from 42,800 in 1988 (the lowest figure since 1983) to 66,800 in 1989, 123,100 in 1990 and 290,000 by 1992 (mid-year). Repossessions rose with a lag from 15,800 to 43,900 (1988) to 75,600 (1991) but, largely due to society rescheduling of mortgage debt rather than mortgage rescue schemes, these have fallen back to an estimated 69,000 for 1992. There is a concern, however, that with business failure rates still increasing and 60,000 bankruptcies expected in 1993, that have repossessions related to business failure are likely to increase.

These repossessions were geographically concentrated in southern Britain (the Scottish rate was, in 1990, a tenth of southern England). It has been widely reported that in order to guarantee a quick sale selling agents were prepared to accept offers which covered outstanding debt. The volume of repossessions, methods of selling, and the growing unsold stock of newly completed homes meant that there was, in some regions, a stock of unsold units approximating to (at least) a year's supply. In consequence nominal and real house prices continued to fall. Since 1989 it is estimated that they have fallen furthest in London and the South East, though later and smaller (if any reductions) occurred the further one moved from the capital. It is important to recognise this regional dimension - not least as it can be construed as a confirmation of Muellbauer's central argument (Muellbauer, 1990). The Scottish economy, with a larger rental sector and historically more stable house price evolution easily outperformed other regions in the 1989-1991 period. Over the period 1988-1992, the North, North-West,

Scotland and Yorks-Humberside have incurred nominal price increases of at least 25 per cent. In Greater-London, the South-East, East Anglia and the South-West, nominal falls have exceeded a quarter. These regional differences require further analysis (Meen, 1990, argues that models of regional house price determination are required before we can fully address these questions).

It is clear that once real house prices (and nominal prices) began to fall they sparked a cumulative deflation of the previous bubble. Higher interest rates initially reduced consumption and construction, dented transactions volumes (which halved between 1988 and 1992) and this had a major knock-on effect on the demand for related items such as white goods, and for estate agency and legal services. Microeconomic studies indicate that movers spend 5-7 per cent of the value of new homes on the frictional and furniture (etc) costs of relocation. There is no precise estimates of the extent to which reduced transaction volumes and new sales curtailed employment in the "white goods" and related sectors - the web of spending connections from housing into the economy needs to be probed. Transactions related spending, which the Bank of England have noted as significant, may be an important addition to housing equity withdrawal in stimulating consumer demand.

Construction starts had increased by 50 per cent between 1985 and 1989, but by 1992 were almost a quarter lower than the 1985 total. Job losses in the construction industry, since the peak of the boom, have now reached close on quarter of a million. And there have been negative effects on the building materials industry. For instance, stockpiles of bricks now exceed a year's supply - in contrast to a four week stockpile in 1988. Employment in brick production has fallen by a quarter since 1987, a quarter of the capacity of the cement industry is now un-used and the production of roof tiles has fallen by a third. Against this dismal trading background, profits and share prices for building and materials firms have slumped. All of these cutbacks have a negative, multiplied effect thus further reducing incomes, housing demand and confidence.

By 1990 rising unemployment levels (with unemployment now having risen for the last 29 months) whether from the general recession effect or driven by housing sector slump further fuelled repossessions. As interest rates began to fall, not least after joining the ERM, the housing market did not "pick-up" as in previous cycles but continued to be problematic as existing owners repaid debt rather than move and as more owners faced repossession with rising unemployment rates. It is noteworthy that in 1991 and 1992 mortgage rates were at around their broad average for the 1980s, though of course sharply reduced inflation rates implied higher real interest rates.

12.5 Beyond 1992

Sluggish recovery

Throughout the spring and summer of 1992 there has been a growing concern that the national economy would not recover without increased housing market activity. And as interest rate reductions were, until Black Wednesday, not a policy option, a number of "schemes" to stimulate the market were advocated - usually focused around some *ad hoc* expansion in the value of mortgage interest tax exemptions or, in one case, providing compensating tax relief for transactions which left the seller making a loss (Woolwich building society). With sterling now floating it is unlikely that interest rates much below the German level can prevail for any lengthy period, otherwise further downward pressure on sterling will occur. Thus in or out of the ERM there still needs to be an active search for policies to assist market recovery.

It is not at all clear, however, that the wide range of measures featured in the press would be effective. Consumer surveys indicate that the vast majority of Britons still aspire to own their homes. And since the end of 1991 reducing interest rates and rising incomes for those in employment indicate an "affordability" ratio, or price to income ratio, which is now below the 1980s average. But the market remains sluggish.

Fear, or more positively confidence, is the key to the present position. House prices have continued to fall and potential purchasers aware of the new "affordability" ratios have held off from buying as they are concerned that purchase deposits (often the entire "life-savings" of first time buyers) will be eroded, quickly leaving them with no or negative equity. And, of course, reductions in unemployment generally lag increases in output and incomes. There was also the possibility, prior to Black Wednesday, that mortgage rates would rise if interest rate increases were required to support sterling. The continuing downward trajectory of sterling is already raising concern that interest rates may have to rise again.

First time buyers cannot hold-off purchasing forever, and the supply of quality rental alternatives is also sticky. Reduced nominal interest rates (though real mortgage rates remain high in comparison with the 1980s) and the prospect of some inflationary impact of devaluation, following departure from the ERM, have created a scenario more familiar to UK home buyers. It is likely that the first time buyer market will recover next year, with the Halifax predicting a small increase in real prices.

It has to be recognised, however, that rising first time buyer demands and purchases may be slow to generate a more widespread increase in transactions. For still falling house prices, in the worst affected markets, have contributed to a widespread phenomenon of negative equity. The exact figures are unknown, disputed figures of 1 million to 2 million (of 9.7 million mortgage holders) have been produced, indicating that substantial price increases may be required before market transaction volume recovers. This issue, however, requires some investigation. The heaviest net equity losers are likely to be those who purchased in 1987-1989. Arguably, however, if the average household moves every 10 years or so those who purchased in 1980-1984 have still made equity gains and they are likely to trade in the medium term. This issue needs to be understood more clearly if any firm connections are to be made between first time buyer resurgence and wider economic recovery.

There must also be some medium term concern that in the northern regions where price falls have been modest, and equity losses slight, any general policy to stimulate the market does not trigger off more sustained price increases. Government has to keep a keener eye on the regional impacts of policies with general impacts on the housing market. Further, the devastated state of the construction industry is such that any sharp increase in housing demand may meet an initially sticky response as the industry reorganises itself. The reduced asset value base of firms, through falling banked land prices and lower share prices, may also mean higher risk premia and a higher cost of development funds.

It is not just consumers and developers who are likely to emerge from the record period of instability from Black Monday to Black Wednesday with assets and expectations dented. Building societies have had margins trimmed and there is a serious issue as to how many remained in the black because of insurance commission income (and commission on endowment-linked mortgages) rather than net returns on mortgage lending. It is likely that internal "equilibrium" rationing criteria may have altered and become more prudent. This may well reduce cyclical instability in the market but at the same time reduce the proportion of very high loan to price mortgages. If purchasers are not only more risk sensitive but also required to provide more equity for purchase then there is likely to be a less rapid growth in low income home ownership and an increase in the stock demand for rental housing. This may create quite serious problems for younger households as rental providers, with few subsidies, have to compete with the subsidised home-ownership sector for land and property. Unless this imbalance is addressed there will always be pressures on households to become owners before they are ready to do so - the fiscal system will encourage them to take the risk of ownership at all costs.

The societies were, of course, insured against all but 20 per cent or repossession losses. The mortgage insurance sector carried most of the financial losses associated with repossessions, at a time of more general industry difficulties, and solvency ratios were more that halved. Premium rates have risen and may well do so again, and this is also likely to discourage marginal purchasers. Some consideration will also have to be given to the development of financial instruments more suited to low income borrowers confronted with volatile interest rates and house prices. Already one major insurer is investigating insuring first-time buyers against equity loss. Undoubtedly more varied forms of mortgage instrument can be developed.

The longer term

There is now little doubt that sustained real house price appreciation, and associated land cost increases, have had a damaging effect on the national economy. A relatively stable sterling outside of the ERM will be facilitated by a more stable housing market, and upon any return to an ERM-type mechanism or European convergence plans it is essential that housing prices and housing debt are somehow kept in check. Otherwise the national economy will be damaged by the housing sector consequences of internationally determined mortgage rate fluctuations.

Undoubtedly there were elements of Black Monday to Black Wednesday which were unique. However, strongly cyclical and rising real house prices have been the feature of the last twenty years - we have had three housing booms, not one. There are "fundamentals" of British housing policy, which are different from our European partners, and which appear to contribute to housing market instability. The key housing policy changes which could either prevent instability or cushion its impacts include: developing the private rented sector, reforming the planning system, modifying mortgage contracts to support mortgagors, and re-structuring the range of benefits and subsidies received by owner occupiers.

Expanding the supply of private or near private rental housing would help to forestall unduly early entry into owner occupation and will require more equal subsidies to like households in different tenures as well as looking at the tax treatment of landlords vis a vis other businesses. Reform of the planning system is necessary to provide a planning process which is sensitive, and quick to react to market pressures. This is arguably the most serious source of supply inelasticity in the British housing system. It is also important to protect mortgagors in the deregulated financial climate. Indexed-linking of mortgages is an important innovation but lenders must be persuaded (by legislation if necessary) to require owners to have a tranche of equity in their homes so that temporary or small price falls are sustainable. The most direct way to do this is to enforce maximum loan to value ratios which are also the maximum recoverable proportion of any default (in proposing this in another context, LLewellyn and Holmes, 1991, do point out that this may lead to further borrowing to make up the difference from other lenders but if this could be overcome lenders would be aware of the moral hazard position of the borrower who had a loan to value ratio above the maximum permitted).

More fundamentally, there have to be changes to the relative subsidy position of owner occupiers, both in terms of the tax

205

advantages they currently enjoy, and, because of the lack of a benefit scheme to protect vulnerable owner occupiers from default and repossession (both sets of proposals have recently been made by the Joseph Rowntree Foundation and the Duke of Edinburgh Inquiry into British Housing, 1991). It is important in the context not just to focus on MIRAS. Although landlords can set interest payments and other expenses against income such relief is limited by the maturity of most landlords portfolios and, unlike home owners, they pay tax on rental income and capital gains tax on disposal. Restructuring assistance to the home-owner sector to introduce a mortgage benefit scheme, which would slow repossessions and reduce "cumulative" downward pressures, give confidence to lenders and borrowers and would insulate low income owners from rate increases generated by international rather than domestic pressures. This will be essential if the UK re-enters the ERM. It seems economically and politically absurd to retain the present MIRAS system within which two-thirds of tax reliefs accrue to the richest third of owners. It is unlikely that such owners have serious negative equity problems or that reducing their MIRAS would shift either their tenure or voting loyalty.

These policies, in the past, have been argued for on the basis of efficiency and fairness. Now there is a keener imperative that the structure of housing policies should be designed to support macroeconomic growth and stability objectives. There is a prima facie case that the measures outlined above, albeit crudely, would have such an impact. But a more rigourous and informed testing of these ideas, and those advocated by such as the Nationwide Building Society (who proposed an initial doubling of MIRAS to be followed by the medium term phasing out of tax relief to be replaced by a lump sum subsidy to first time buyers only), is required. This will require housing-economy models and debates to be examined in relation to their technical and empirical validity. For instance, do any of the existing models include allowances for the economic effects of changing volumes of transactions, negative equity or shifts from rented to owned housing? If not, then amendments will have to be made if policy changes are to be simulated at the national level.

12.6 Conclusion

British housing policy has, for several decades, been fixated with the growth of home ownership. If these high levels are to be sustained or even increased, cognizance must be taken of the important linkages that exist between housing and the economy. In this paper we have charted and attempted to explain informally the most recent boom and bust in the UK housing market, pointing to factors unique to the period (macroeconomic policy, financial deregulation, demographics) and factors inherent to the housing sector (taxation, supply inelasticity etc). In turn, we reviewed some of the tentative connections made between the housing sector and the macroeconomy, notably in the form of equity withdrawal and its effects on consumer spending, and on the supply side, the inflationary effects of rising house and land prices.

Our knowledge of the interactions between housing and the economy has grown markedly over the last 5 years. But there are still important gaps in how such connections are made and modelled, in identifying regional patterns and so on. These gaps need to be remedied not for academic nicety but to have clearer understanding of how policy, in the housing sphere, can be restructured to assist the national economy. Present arrangements appear to generate cyclical instabilities which are problematic now but will become even more damaging if the UK re-enters the ERM. It is time for Britain to put its house in order and for government to recognise that to sustain stable, high rates of home-ownership in the long term that a fresh approach to subsidy policy for that sector is required.

Notes

1.   Acknowledgements are due to the Economic and Social Research Council and the Joseph Rowntree Foundation for their long term support of this work. Thanks to Margaret McConnachie for research assistance in the preparation of this paper. A version of this paper was presented at the 1992 AREUEA/USC conference on Housing Markets in an International Setting, Los Angeles, California, October 1992.

References

Age Concern (1989) *Older People in the United Kingdom - Some Basic Facts.* London: Age Concern.

Association of District Councils (1991) *Survey on Council House Rents, Housing Subsidy and Capital Expenditure 1991/92.* London: Association of District Councils.

Association of Metropolitan Authorities (1991) *New Financial Regime Survey Report 1991.* London: Association of Metropolitan Authorities.

Atkinson, A (1972) *Unequal Shares: Wealth in Britain.* London: Penguin.

Atkinson, A and Harrison, A (1978) *Distribution of Personal Wealth in Britain.* Cambridge: University of Cambridge Press.

Atkinson, A and King, M (1980) 'Housing Policy, Taxation and Reform', *Midland Bank Review*, Spring.

Barrett, S and Fudge, C (1981) 'Examining the Policy-Action Relationship', in Barrett, S and Fudge, C (eds) *Policy and Action.* London: Methuen.

Berthoud, R (1988) 'Social Security and the Economics of Housing', *PSI Bulletin*, August.

Bonney, N and Love, J (1991) 'Gender and Migration: Geographical Mobility and the Wife's Sacrifice', *Sociological Review*, Vol.39, pp.335- 48.

Bosenquet, N and Propper, C (1991) 'Charting the Grey Economy in the 1990s', *Policy and Politics*, Vol.19, No.4, pp.269-282.

Boviard, A, Harloe, M and Whitehead, C (1985) 'Private Rented Housing: Its Current Role', *Journal of Social Policy*, Vol.14.

Bramley, G (1989) 'The Demand for Social Housing in England in the 1980s', *Housing Studies*, Vol.4 No.1.

Bramley, G (1991) *Public Sector Housing Rents and Subsidies.* SAUS Working Paper No.92, School for Advanced Urban Studies, University of Bristol.

Bramley, G, Bartlett, W, Franklin, A and Lambert, C (1990) *Housing Finance and the Housing Market in Bristol.* York: Joseph Rowntree Foundation.

Bramley, G (1992) *The Impact of Land Use Planning and Tax Subsidies in the Supply and Price of Housing in Britain,* paper presented at an International Housing Finance Systems Workshop, Vienna, January.

Bromwich, M, Napier, C and Whitehead, C (1991) *Housing Association Accounting.* London: Institute of Chartered Accountants in England and Wales.

Brownhill, S, Sharp, C, Jones, C and Merrett, S (1990) *Housing London: Issues of Finance and Supply.* York: Joseph Rowntree Foundation.

Bull, J and Poole, L (1989) *Not Rich, Not Poor: Housing Options for Elderly People on Middle Incomes.* London: SHAC and Anchor Housing Trust.

Cameron, S. J, Nicholson, M and Willis, K. G (1991) *Housing Finance in Newcastle.* York: Joseph Rowntree Foundation; and London: National Federation of Housing Associations.

Case, F. E (1968) 'Code Enforcement in Urban Renewal', *Urban Studies.* Vol.5, pp.277-289.

Central Statistical Office (1991) *Monthly Digest of Statistics.* February. London: HMSO.

Challis, L and Bartlett, H (1987) *Old and Ill: Private Nursing Homes for Elderly People.* Research Paper No.1. London: Age Concern Institute of Gerontology.

Champion, A and Fielding, A (eds) (1992) *Migration Processes and Patterns, Volume 1.* London: Belhaven Press.

Champion, A, Green, A and Owen, D (1987) 'Housing, Labour Mobility and Unemployment', *The Planner,* Vol.73, pp.11-17.

Coleman, D (1989) 'The New Housing Policy - A Critique', *Housing Studies,* Vol.4 No.1.

Coombes, M and Raybould, S (1991) *Housing Research Findings No.30.* York: Joseph Rowntree Foundation.

Counsell, G (1990) 'Clinging to the Wreckage', *Roof,* May/June.

Crook, A. D. H, Eastall, R, Hughes, J, Sugden, J and Wilkinson, R (1990) *Housing Finance in Sheffield: The Impact and Incidence of Housing Subsidies.* York: Joseph Rowntree Foundation.

Crook, A. D. H, Kemp, P, Anderson, I and Bowman, S (1991) *The Business Expansion Scheme and Rented Housing.* York: Joseph Rowntree Foundation.

Crook, A. D. H (1986) 'Privatisation of Housing and the Impact of the Conservative Government's Initiatives on Low Cost Home Ownership and Private Renting between 1979 and 1984 in England and Wales: 4', *Environment and Planning A* Vol.18, pp.1029-37.

Crook, A. D. H and Martin, G (1988) 'Property Speculation, Local Authority Policy and the Decline of Privately Rented Housing in the 1980s: A Case Study of Sheffield', in Kemp, P (ed) op.cit.

DeBorger, B. L (1985) 'Benefits and Consumption Effects of Public Housing Programs in Belgium: Some Aggregate Results', Urban Studies, Vol.22, pp.409-419.

Department of the Environment (1987) Housing: The Government's Proposals. (Cm 214) London: HMSO.

Department of the Environment (1988a) English House Condition Survey. London: HMSO.

Department of the Environment (1988b) The New Financial Regime for Local Authority Housing in England and Wales. London: Department of the Environment.

Department of the Environment (1990) Housing Subsidy and Accounting Manual 1990. London: Department of the Environment.

Department of the Environment (1991) Annual Report 1991. London: Department of the Environment.

Department of Health (1989) Caring for People: Community Care in the Next Decade and Beyond. London: HMSO.

DeSalvo, J. S (1971) 'A Methodology of Evaluating Housing Programs', Journal of Regional Science, Vol.11, pp.173-185.

DeSalvo, J. S (1975) 'Benefits and Costs of New York's Middle Income Housing Progam', Journal of Political Economy, Vol.83, pp.791-807.

Diamond, D and Lea, M (1992) The Efficiency of Housing Finance: A Comparative Analysis - Research Findings, paper presented at Housing Finance conference on European Cities, the Hague, April.

Eastall, R and Kleinman, M (1989) 'A Behavioural Model of the Supply of Re-Lets of Council Housing in England', Urban Studies, Vol.26.

Ermisch, J (1990) Fewer Babies: Longer Lives. York: Joseph Rowntree Foundation.

Ermisch, J (ed) (1990) Housing and the National Economy. London: NIESR.

European Capital Co Ltd (1991) Housing Associations Improved Access to the Capital Markets. York: Joseph Rowntree Foundation.

Frazer, R and Platt, S (1988) 'Breaking the Link without Breaking the Bank', Roof, Sept/Oct.

Fennell, G, Phillipson, C and Evers, H The Sociology of Old Age. Milton Keynes: Open University Press.

Firth Report (1987) Public Support for Residential Care: Report for a Joint Central and Local Government Working Party. London: DHSS.

Forrest, R and Murie, A (1987) 'The Affluent Home Owner: Labour Market Position and the Shaping of Housing Histories', Sociological Review, Vol.35, pp.370-403.

Forrest, R and Murie, A (1989) 'Differential Accumulation: Wealth, Inheritance and Housing Policy Reconsidered', Policy and Politics, Vol.17, pp.25-39.

211

Forrest, R and Murie, A (1990) *Selling the Welfare State*. London: Routledge, 2nd edition.

Forrest, A and Murie, A (1991) 'Housing Markets, Labour Markets and Housing Histories, in J. Allen and C. Hamnett (eds) *Housing and Labour Markets: Building the Connections*. London: Unwin-Hyman.

Forrest, A, Murie, A, Doogan, K and Burton, P (1991) 'Labour Mobility and Housing Provision: A Review of the Literature'. School of Advanced Urban Studies, Working Paper No.98. Bristol: SAUS.

Forrest, R, Murie, A and Williams, P (1990) *Home Ownership: Differentiation and Fragmentation*. Unwin Hyman: London.

Gardiner, K, Hills, J and Kleinman, M (1991) *Putting A Price on Council Housing: Valuing Voluntary Transfers*. WSP/62, London: STICERD, LSE.

Gibb, K (1992) 'The Council Tax: The Distributional Implications of Returning to a Tax on Property', *Scottish Journal of Political Economy*, Vol.39, pp.302-18.

Gordon, I (1990) 'Housing and Labour Market Constraints on Migration across the North-South Divide' in J. Ermisch (ed) - op.cit.

Greve, J and Currie, E (1990) *Homelessness in Britain*. York: Joseph Rowntree Foundation.

Hamnett, C (1984) 'Housing the Two Nations: Socio-Tenurial Polarisation in England and Wales, 1961-81', *Urban Studies*, Vol.21, pp.389-405.

Hamnett, C (1991) 'A Nation of Inheritors? Housing Inheritance, Wealth and Inequality', *Journal of Social Policy*, Vol.20, pp.509-36.

Hamnett, C, Harmer,M and Williams, P (1991) *As Safe as Houses: Housing Inheritance in Britain*. London: Paul Chapman.

Hamnett, C and Mullings, B (1992) 'A New Consumption Cleavage? The Case of Residential Care for the Elderly', *Environment and Planning A* - forthcoming.

Hancock, K and Munro, M (1992) 'Housing Subsidies, Inequality and Affordability: Evidence from Glasgow', *Fiscal Studies*, Vol.13, pp.71-97.

Harbury, C (1962) 'Inheritance and the Distribution of Personal Wealth in Britain', *Economic Journal*, Vol.72, pp.854-868.

Harbury, C and Hitchens, D (1979) *Inheritance and Wealth Inequality in Britain*. London: George, Allen and Unwin.

Harloe, M (1985) *Private Rented Housing in the United States and Europe*. Beckenham, Kent: Croom Helm.

Harloe, M (1987) 'Manifestos for Change? A Critique of Recent Proposals for Housing Reform', in Brenton, M and Vingerson, C (eds) *The Year Book of Social policy 1986-7*. London: Longmans.

Harmer, M and Hamnett, C (1990) 'Regional Variations in Housing Inheritance in Britain, *Area*, Vol.22.

Harrison, L and Means, R (1990) *Housing: the Essential Element in Community Care*. London: SHAC and Anchor Housing Trust.

Hancock, K (1991) *Can't Pay, Won't Pay: Economic Principles of "Affordability"'*, Centre for Housing Research, University of Glasgow, mimeo.

Hey, J and McKenna, C (1979) 'To Move or Not to Move?' *Economica*, Vol.46, pp.175-85.

Hills, J (1987) *Subsidies to English Local Authority Housing since 1981*, Welfare State Programme Research Note No.6. London: STICERD/LSE.

Hills, J (1988a) *Twenty First Century Housing Subsidies: Durable Rent Fixing and Subsidy Arrangements for Social Housing.* Discussion paper WSP/33, London: STICERD/LSE.

Hills, J (1988b) 'Hitting the Target', *Roof* Sep/Oct.

Hills, J (1989) *Distributional Effects of Housing Subsidies in the United Kingdom.* Discussion Paper WSP/44, London: STICERD/ LSE.

Hills, J (1991a) *Unravelling Housing Finance.* Oxford: Claredon Press.

Hills, J (1991b) *Thirty Nine Steps to Housing Finance Reform.* York: Joseph Rowntree Foundation.

Hills, J and Mullings, B (1990) 'A Decent Home for All at a Price Within Their Means', in J. Hills (ed) *The State of Welfare.* Oxford: Clarendon Press.

Hills, J, Hubert, F, Tormann, H and Whitehead, C (1990) 'Shifting Subsidy from Bricks and Mortar to People: Experiences in Britain and West Germany', *Housing Studies.* Vol.5 No.3.

Hinton, C (1986) *Using Your Home as Capital.* London: Age Concern.

Horseman, E (1978) Inheritance in England and Wales, Evidence provided by Wills', *Oxford Economic Papers*, Vol.30, pp.409-22.

Houlihan, B (1988) *Housing Policy and Central-Local Government Relations.* Aldershot: Avebury.

HCEC (1982) *The Private Rented Housing Sector Volume 1.* London: HMSO.

Hughes, G and McCormick, B (1981) 'Do Council Housing Policies reduce Migration between Regions?' *Economic Journal*, Vol.91, pp.919-37.

Hughes, G and McCormick, B (1985) 'Migration Intentions in the UK: Which Households want to Migrate and which Succeed?' *Economic Journal*, Vol.95 Supplement, pp.113-23.

Inquiry into British Housing (1985) *Report.* London: NFHA.

Inquiry into British Housing (1991) *Second Report.* York: Joseph Rowntree Foundation.

Institute of Manpower Studies (1987) *Relocating Managers and Professional Staff.* IMS Report No.139. Brighton: IMS, University of Sussex.

Johnson, J, Salt, J and Wood, P (1974) *Housing and the Migration of Labour in England and Wales.* Farnborough: Saxon House.

Kemp, P (1988a) *The Future of Private Renting.* Salford: University of Salford.

Kemp, P (1988b) 'The Impact of the Assured Tenancy Scheme, 1980-1986', in P. Kemp (ed) *The Private Provision of Rented Housing*. Avebury: Aldershot.

Kemp, P (1990) 'Shifting the Balance between State and Market: the Reprivatisation of Rental Housing in Britain', *Environment and Planning A*, Vol.22.

Kleinman, M (1991) *A Decade of Change: Providing Social Housing 1980-90*. York: Joseph Rowntree Foundation.

Laing and Buisson (1988) *Care for Elderly People: The Developing Market for Nursing and Residential Homes and Related Services in Britain*. London: Laing and Buisson Publications Ltd.

Leather, P (1990) The Potential Implications of Home Equity release in Old Age', *Housing Studies*, Vol.5, pp.3-13.

Leather, P and Mackintosh, S (1989) 'Means-testing Improvement Grants', *Housing Review*, Vol.38, No.3, pp.77-80.

Leather, P and Mackintosh, S (1990) *Monitoring Assisted Agency Services: Part 1, Home Improvement Agencies - An Evaluation of Performance*. London: HMSO.

Leather, P and Wheeler, R (1988) *Making Use of Home Equity in Old Age*. London: Building Societies Association.

Llewellyn, D and Holmes, M (1991) *Competition or Credit Controls?* Hobart Paper Institute of Economic Affairs: London.

Lomax, J (1991) 'Housing Finance: An International Perspective', *Bank of England Quarterly Bulletin*, February 1991.

London Housing Unit (1990) *Local Government and Housing Act (Housing)*. Local Government Information Unit Special Briefing No.33.

Lowe, S and Watson, S (1990) *From First Time Buyers to Last Time Sellers: An Appraisal of the Social and Economic Consequences of Equity Withdrawal from the Housing Market*. Mimeo, University of York.

Lumby, S (1984) *Investment Appraisal*. Wokingham: Van Norstrand.

Mackintosh, S, Means, R and Leather, P (1990) *Housing in Later Life*. SAUS Study No.4, School for Advanced Urban Studies, University of Bristol.

Maclennan, D (1982) *Housing Economics: An Applied Approach*. London: Longmans.

Maclennan, D (1986) 'The Pricing of Public Housing in the United Kingdom', *Inquiry into British Housing: Supplement*. London: National Federation of Housing Associations.

Maclennan, D (1988) 'Private Rental Housing: Britain Viewed from Abroad', in P.Kemp (ed) - op.cit.

Maclennan, D and O'Sullivan, A (1986) *The Housing Market Costs of Long Distance Migration*. Centre for Housing Research Discussion paper No. 10. University of Glasgow.

Maclennan, D and Gibb, K (1990) 'Housing finance and Subsidies in Britain after a Decade of Thatcherism', *Urban Studies*, Vol.27, No.6, pp.905-918.

Maclennan, D, Gibb, K and More, A (1990) *Paying for Britain's Housing*. York: Joseph Rowntree Foundation.

Maclennan, D, Gibb, K and More, A (1991) *Fairer Subsidies, Faster Growth: Housing, Government and the Economy.* York: Joseph Rowntree Foundation.

Maclennan, D and Williams, R (1991a) *Affordable Housing in Europe.* York: Joseph Rowntree Foundation.

Maclennan, D and Williams, R (1991b) *Affordable Housing in Britain and America.* York: Joseph Rowntree Foundation.

Maclennan, D and Williams, R (1991c) *Housing Subsidies and the Market: An International Perspective.* York: Joseph Rowntree Foundation.

McCormick, B (1983) 'Housing and Unemployment in Great Britain', *Oxford Economic Papers*, Vol.35, pp.283-305.

McGregor, A, Munro, M, Heafey, M and Symon, P (1992) *Moving Job, Moving House: The Impact of Housing on Long-distance Labour Mobility.* Centre for Housing Research and Training and Employment Research Unit. University of Glasgow.

Malpass, P (1990) *Reshaping Housing Policy: Subsidies, Rents and Residualisation.* London: Routledge.

Malpass, P and Murie, A (1990) *Housing Policy and Practice.* Basingstoke: Macmillan, 3rd edition.

Malpezzi, S, Tipple, A. G and Willis, K. G (1990) *Costs and Benefits of Rent Control: A Case Study in Kumasi, Ghana.* World Bank Discussion Papers No.74. Washington D.C.: The World Bank.

Mason, C, Harrison, J and Harrison, R (1988) *Closing the Equity Gap?* Small Business Research Trust.

Means, R (1990) 'Allocating Council Housing to Older People', *Social Policy and Administration*, Vol.24, No.1, pp.52-64.

Means, R (1991) 'Community Care, Housing and Older People: Continuity or Change', *Housing Studies*, Vol.6, No.4, pp.273-284.

Meen, G (1989) 'The Ending of Mortgage Rationing and its Effects on the Housing Market: A Simulation Study', *Urban Studies*, Vol.26

Meen, G (1990) 'The Macroeconomic Effects of Housing Market Policies under Alternative Mortgage Conditions', in Ermisch, J (ed), *Housing and the National Economy*, op.cit.

Milner Holland Committee (1964) *Report of the Committee on Housing in Greater London.* London: HMSO.

Minford, P, Ashton, P and Peel, M (1987) *The Housing Morass.* London: Institute of Economic Affairs.

Mintel (1987) *New Wealth and the Individual.* London: Mintel.

Morgan Grenfell (1987) 'Housing Inheritance and Wealth', *Morgan Grenfell Economic Review*, No.45, November.

Muellbauer, J (1990) 'The Housing Market and the UK Economy: Problems and Opportunities', in Ermisch, J (ed) - op.cit.

Muellbauer, J and Murphy, A (1989) *Why has UK Personal Savings Collapsed?* Credit Suisse First Boston, July.

Munro, M (1988) 'Housing Wealth and Inheritance', *Journal of Social Policy*, Vol.17, pp.417-36.

Munro, M and Symon, P (1990) 'Planning for Strathclyde's Regeneration', *Town Planning Review*, Vol.61, pp.41-57.

Murie, A and Forrest, R (1980) 'Wealth, Inheritance and Housing Policy', Policy and Politics, Vol.8, pp.1-19.

National Federation of Housing Associations (1989) *Review of Policy on Rents.* London: NFHA.

Nationwide Anglia Building Society (1989) *Lending to Former Council Tenants.* Nationwide Anglia: London.

Neary, J. P and Roberts, K. W. S (1980) 'The Theory of Household Behaviour under Rationing', *European Economic Review*, Vol.13, pp.25-42.

Nevitt, A (1966) *Housing, Taxation and Subsidies.* London: Nelson.

Nicholson, M and Willis, K. G (1991a) 'Costs and Benefits of Housing Subsidies to Tenants from Voluntary and Involuntary Rent Control: A Comparison between Tenures and Income Groups', *Applied Economics*, pp.1103-1115.

Nicholson, M and Willis, K. G (1991b) *Benefits of Subsidised Housing Programmes.* Housing Finance Discussion Paper No.6. York: Joseph Rowntree Foundation.

Nueberger, H (1990) 'The Quality Link', *Roof*, May/June.

Olsen, E. O (1972) 'An Econometric Analysis of Rent Control', *Journal of Political Economy*, Vol.80, pp.1081-1100.

Olsen, E. O and Barton, D. M (1983) 'The Benefits and Costs of Public Housing in New York City', *Journal of Public Economics*, Vol.20 pp.299- 332.

O'Sullivan, A (1984) 'Misconceptions in the Current Housing Subsidies Debate', *Policy and Politics*, Vol.12, pp.119-144.

Pryke, M and Whitehead, C (1990) 'Private Finance for Social Housing: Enabling or Transforming', *Findings No.24*, York: Joseph Rowntree Foundation.

Pryke, M and Whitehead, C (1991a) *An Overview of Recent Changes in the Provision of Private Finance for Social Housing.* Discussion paper No.28, University of Cambridge: Department of Land Economy.

Pryke, M and Whitehead, C (1991b) *Mortgage Backed Securitisation in the UK: A Wholesale Transformation of Housing Finance?* Monograph No.22 University of Cambridge: Department of Land Economy.

Pryke, M and Whitehead, C (1992) *The Securitisation of Mortgage Finance: Transformation or Minor Change?* Discussion Paper (forthcoming) York: Joseph Rowntree Foundation.

Pryke, M and Whitehead. C (forthcoming) *Private Finance for Social Housing: Enabling or Transforming.* Monograph No.23, University of Cambridge: Department of Land Economy.

Ricketts, M (1981) 'Housing Policy: Towards a Public Choice Perspective', *Journal of Public Policy.* Vol.1, pp.501-522.

Robertson, G (1978) *Housing Tenure and Labour Mobility in Scotland.* Scottish Development Department Economics and Statistics Unit, Discussion Paper No.4.

Rosenthal, C (1989) 'Income and Price Elasticity of Demand for Owner Occupied Housing in the U.K.: Evidence from Pooled

Cross-sectional and Time-series Data', *Applied Economics*, Vol.21, pp.761-777.

Royal Commission on the Distribution of Income and Wealth (1977) *Third Report on the Standing Reference* (Cmnd 6999). London: HMSO.

Salt, J (1991) Labour Migration and Housing in the UK: An Overview', in J. Allen and C. Hamnett (eds) - op.cit.

Saunders, P (1986) 'Comment on Dunleavy and Preteceille', *Society and Space*, Vol.4, pp.155-164.

Schwab, R (1985) 'The Estimation of the Benefits of In-Kind Government Programmes', *Journal of Public Economics*, Vol.27, pp.195-210.

Sheffield City Council (1989) *City of Sheffield Housing: Annual Statistical Report 1988/9*. Sheffield City Council.

Stiglitz, J and Weiss, A (1981) 'Credit Rationing in Markets with Imperfect Information', *American Economic Review*, June.

Thompson, P, Itzin, C and Abendstern, M (1990) *I Don't Feel Out: The Experience of Later Life*. Oxford: Oxford University Press.

Walker, A (1986) *Housing Policy, Taxation and Reform*. London: CHAS.

Walker, B and Marsh, A (1991) *Housing Subsidies in an Urban Area: A Comparison of Owner Occupiers and Local Authority Tenants*. paper given to the ESRC Urban and Regional Economics Conference, July 4-5 1991.

Walker, B, Marsh, A and Dixon, A (1991) *Housing Finance and Subsidy in Birmingham*. York: Joseph Rowntree Foundation.

Walker, R and Hutton, S (1988) 'The Costs of Ageing and Retirement', in R. Walker and G. Parker (eds) *Money Matters*. London: Sage.

Warburton, M (1990) 'Bite the Bullet', *Roof*, May/June.

Warburton, M and Malpass, P (1991) 'Riding the Rent Rocket', *Roof*, July/August, pp.27-29.

Whitehead, C (1991) 'Innovative Financing Strategies for Affordable Owner-Occupied and Rented Housing', Paper given to Urban Affairs Group, Environment Directorate, Paris: OECD, October.

Whitehead, C (1991) 'Discussion of 'The Business Expansion scheme and Rented Housing', seminar on *The BES and Rented Housing: What Next?*, London, July 1991.

Whitehead, C and Kleinman, M (1986) *Private Rented Housing in the 1980s and 1990s*. Cambridge: Granta Publications.

Whitehead, C and Kleinman, M (1988) 'Capital Value Rents' in P. Kemp (ed).

Wilcox, S (1991) 'Shuffling the Pack', *Roof*, September and October, pp.28-9.

Wilkinson, M and Wilkinson, R (1982) 'The Withdrawal of Mortgage Tax Relief: A Survey and Evaluation of the Debate', *Policy and Politics*. Vol.10, No.1.

Willis, K. G (1980) *The Economics of Town and Country Planning*. London: Collins (Granada).

217

Wood, G (1988) 'Housing Tax Expenditures in OECD Countries: Economic Impacts and Prospects for Reform', *Policy and Politics.* Vol.16 No.4.